Dr Rafiq Zakaria has had a distinguished career in fields as varied as law, education, journalism, politics and Islamic studies. He is a chancellor's gold medallist of the Bombay University, having come first in the M.A. examination. He obtained a Ph.D. with distinction from London University and was called to the Bar from the Lincoln's Inn. After a successful legal career he was elected to the State Legislature of Maharashtra, India, in 1960; he served as a minister in the government for fifteen years. He was then elected to Parliament and became deputy leader of the ruling Congress party when Indira Gandhi was Prime Minister. She appointed him Prime Minister's Special Envoy to the Muslim world in 1984. He has twice represented India at the United Nations, in 1965 and in 1990.

Dr Zakaria is an eminent Islamic scholar and is the author of several books, including *A Study of Nehru*; *Razia, Queen of India*; *The Rise of Muslims in Indian Politics*; *The Trial of Benazir: An Insight into the Status of Woman in Islam*; and *The Struggle within Islam*. He has been associated with various social and educational organizations and has founded a dozen educational institutions of higher learning in Bombay and Aurangabad. He is the Chancellor of the Urdu University in Aligarh. He lives in Bombay with his wife, Fatma, who was Senior Assistant Editor at *The Times of India* for several years and is now Executive Editor of *The Daily* in Bombay.

MUHAMMAD AND THE QURAN

RAFIQ ZAKARIA

PENGUIN BOOKS

PENGUIN BOOKS

Penguin Books India (P) Ltd, B4/246 Safdarjung Enclave, New Delhi 110 029 India
Penguin Books Ltd, 27 Wrights Lane, London W8 5TZ, England
Penguin Books USA Inc. 375 Hudson Street, New York, New York 10014, USA
Penguin Books Australia Ltd, Ringwood, Victoria, Australia
Penguin Books Canada Ltd, 10 Alcorn Avenue, Ontario, Canada M4V 3B2
Penguin Books (NZ) Ltd, 182–190 Wairau Road, Auckland 10, New Zealand

First published 1991

Copyright © Rafiq Zakaria, 1991
All rights reserved

The moral right of the author has been asserted

Printed in England by Clays Ltd, Bungay, Suffolk
Filmset in Lasercomp Bembo

To

My Sons
Arshad and Fareed,

who wanted to have
a correct perception of
the religion
into which they have been born,
so that they could
share the knowledge with
their friends of Harvard and Yale,
where misconceptions about Islam still persist.
In the words of Benjamin Disraeli,
they may have to 'learn to unlearn'.

To

My Sons

Arbad and Fareed,

who wanted to have

a correct perception of

the religion

into which they have been born,

so that they could

share the knowledge with

their friends of Harvard and Yale,

where misconceptions about Islam still persist.

In the works of Benjamin Disraeli,

they may have to learn to unlearn."

CONTENTS

CONTENTS

PREFACE

The idea of writing this book came to me after reading Salman Rushdie's *Satanic Verses*. Its acclaim by a large number of non-Muslim intellectuals and its popularity, especially after the *fatwa* by the late Ayatollah Khomeini, convinced me that a fair picture of Islam needed to be presented once again in order to remove much of the distortion that has crept into its perception. A great many books have, no doubt, been written to remove, in particular, the prejudices against the Prophet Muhammad and the nature of his mission. But somehow, the same old distortions that had remained dormant for a while have once again surfaced in recent times. The personal character of Muhammad is assailed and the divine nature of the Quran denied. There has, in effect, been a renewed attempt, to use a cliché, to put new wine in an old bottle.

I need not go into a detailed comparison of what was written in the past with what is being written now. For even a cursory glance at the mass of literature on the subject will help establish the fact that, in reality though not in appearance, there has not been much change in the attitude of the West towards Islam. The old prejudices and misunderstandings persist. Apparently, the billions of dollars that some of the oil-rich Muslim rulers have spent on propagating the cause of Islam in Europe and America have not helped, nor have popular demonstrations and protests by Muslims. On the contrary, these seem to have only hardened prejudices and helped spread the impression among non-Muslims that Islam has in fact no answer to its critics. But then, the record cannot be set right by angry outbursts. Abuse is no answer and vehement diatribe no substitute for argument.

Mine is a modest effort to meet prejudice by reason, distortion by fact, and calumny by a sober analysis of events as adduced from unimpeachable historical records. The book is not the life story of Muhammad, nor does it give a translation of the whole text of the Quran. It is an attempt to bring out the essentials of what Allah has pronounced and what his Messenger preached and practised. The reader can get a glimpse of the main events in Muhammad's life from the Chronological Survey (pp. 401–16). I have tried in Part I to deal, as exhaustively as possible, with those aspects of the Prophet's life wherein he has been attacked by his detractors.

Was Muhammad an imposter? Was his mission a fraud? Is the Quran a fabrication? Is it merely the rantings of a deranged mind? Was the Prophet a man of no character – a voluptuary, who married one wife after another? A schemer who had no hesitation in compromising even the basic tenets of his faith to obtain some worldly gain? A warmonger, who spread his religion by the sword? These are charges which have been hurled against him over the centuries. I have tried to answer them rationally. I have let facts speak for themselves.

Instead of giving my personal views I have quoted the studied observations of highly respected persons, both Muslims and non-Muslims; their testimony lends authority to the assessment of the various issues under dispute. Unfortunately, Muslim theologians have, by and large, closed the door of *ijtihad*, or independent thinking, for the past several centuries; what has come down to them from the past has been accepted by them as if it has divine sanction. Juristic activity, which was the hallmark of Islam, has more or less ceased; what is continued is the quibbling of commentators and interpreters over non-essential things. These people are to a large extent responsible for vitiating the attitude of the world towards Islam, indulging as they do in ignorance of realities, distortion of history and prejudicial judgements born out of vested interest and factional strife. They cannot claim to have served Islam. On the contrary, they have allowed themselves to play into the hands of others – more often than not, unwittingly – but on that account they cannot be absolved of the blame for the distortions and misrepresentation from which Islam has suffered.

The book also contains a selection of Quranic verses, freely translated by me in contemporary, spoken language. Of the 6,666 verses, I have selected 1,111. It is not possible even for Muslims, much less non-Muslims, to understand the Quran without an acquaintance with the circumstances in which each revelation descended on Muhammad. I have culled from each chapter, as best I could, the essential principles as contained in the picturesque passages. These reveal the nature and spirit of Islam and bring out clearly its message of monotheism and the consequences of good or bad deeds for this life and the life hereafter. Some of the verses also throw light on the role of the Prophet as he propagated his faith. In order to have a clearer understanding of the verses selected, I have given a brief summary of each chapter of the Quran. Thus, I have attempted to integrate the life and mission of Muhammad with the commandments of Allah. I have consulted several translations of the Quran in English. But I have relied heavily on the translation of the eminent commentator Allama Abdullah Yusuf Ali; he has been my unfailing guide.

The stories of the prophets from Adam to Jesus, as narrated in the Quran, are included in a separate part in this book (pp. 347-94). They give an illustrative insight into the values that the faithful are asked to emulate. I have greatly benefited in understanding their thrust and that of the teachings of the Quran from the commentaries of Maulana Abul 'ala Maududi. His creative ability and analytical mind have ably cleared much of the mysterious coverings and confusing connotations that have gathered round the Book. His magnum opus, the voluminous *Tafheemul Quran*, remains unrivalled as a work of highest scholarship in the field of *Tafsi* literature of modern times.

My task in presenting Muhammad and the Quran has not been easy; I am neither a scholar of Arabic nor do I claim to be an authority on Islam. But I have been a life-long student of my religion, which has always fascinated me; I have worked a great deal on it, and written at length on different aspects of it, both religious and historical. The response has been encouraging. That is, in fact, one reason why I have felt emboldened to undertake the present work. I was moved, primarily, by the urge within me to set the record straight; to present Muhammad and the Quran in the right perspective and help remove the misunderstanding and the misrepresentation that have gathered round them. I am not so foolish as to think that my book is an antidote to all that has been said and written against Islam. Many great minds have attempted to produce such a work in the past. Their contributions have, indeed, been immensely valuable. I have drawn a great deal on them. But, despite the efforts by these Muslim scholars and the sympathetic expositions of the well-meaning orientalists, Muhammad continues to be maligned and the teachings of the Quran misunderstood. It is painful that this remains the case, even in the free and liberal environment of today. No one has described this better than a well-known Jewish writer, who became a Muslim and took the name of Muhammad Asad.

The Western attitude is not one of indifferent dislike as in the case of all other 'foreign' religions and cultures; it is one of deep-rooted and almost fanatical aversion; and it is not only intellectual but bears an intensely emotional tint. Europe may not accept the doctrines of Buddhist or Hindu philosophy, but it will always preserve a balanced, reflective attitude of mind with regard to those systems. As soon, however, as it turns towards Islam, the balance is disturbed and an emotional bias creeps in. With very few exceptions, even the most eminent of European orientalists are guilty of an unscientific partiality in their writings on Islam. In their investigations, it almost appears as if Islam could not be treated as a mere object of scientific research but as an accused standing before his judges. Some of these orientalists play the part of the public prosecutor bent on securing a conviction; others are like a counsel for defence who, being personally convinced that his client is guilty, can only half-heartedly plead for 'mitigating circumstances'. All in all, the technique of the deductions and conclusions adopted by most of the European orientalists reminds us of the proceedings of those notorious Courts of Inquisition set up by the Catholic Church against its opponents in the Middle Ages: that is to say, they hardly ever investigate historical facts with an open mind, but start, almost in every case, from a foregone conclusion dictated by prejudice.

I am conscious of my limitations; I embarked on this arduous venture because, as a Muslim, I felt it my duty to present the essence of my religion to all those who have not either properly understood it or have failed to appreciate it. My shortcomings may, therefore, be overlooked in the spirit that has motivated me, namely to share my understanding of Muhammad and the Quran with both those who admire the Prophet and those who revile him.

I shall feel amply rewarded if my book will help dispel at least some misgivings about Islam and bring a little light into the dark corners that exist in the thinking world, so that the faith which has moved millions of people for more than fifteen centuries is somewhat better understood.

Several friends have helped me in this endeavour; I cannot mention them all. But I must acknowledge my debt, first, to Dr F. M. Kulay, whose knowledge of Arabic and Islamic theology is profound. He has helped me, in particular, to capture in modern English the spirit of the Quranic verses. I am also grateful to the two distinguished heads of my institutions, Principal A. A. Munshi of the Maharashtra College of Bombay, and Principal Mazhar Mohiuddin of the Maulana Azad College of Aurangabad, who have assisted me in finding the right references. Savita Chandiramani has painstakingly read the proofs. I am indeed beholden to her.

I owe much to Mr Girilal Jain, scholar-editor and doyen of Indian journalism, for painstakingly going through the manuscript and making some critical suggestions. Lastly, I have no words to express my debt to my wife, Fatma, whose editorial competence resulting from her long experience in journalism has always been a great asset to me. I was often impatient and irritated with her unceasing and tireless editing, but the end result has been gratifying. And more than rewarding.

RAFIQ ZAKARIA

PART I
INTRODUCTION

There is no god but God, and
Muhammad is His Prophet

THE PROPHET'S MISSION

The Quran is the basis of Islam; its verses, at once stirring and soothing, forceful and gentle, tender and terrifying, breathtaking and awe-inspiring, have moved millions of Muslims through the ages. They continue to do so today. Muhammad was, indeed, the medium of the divine will as expressed in the Quran. And as the eminent Orientalist Professor H. A. R. Gibb has said, 'No man in fifteen hundred years has ever played on that deep-toned instrument [the Arabic language] with such power, such boldness and such range of emotional effect as Mohammed did.'[1]

To Muslims, the Quran is the creation of God. However, it is equally important to remember that there could have been no Quran without Muhammad. He is not only its transmitter but also the embodiment of its teachings. Hence, it is as much a history of his life; there are references in it to his work and mission, his struggles and even his personal affairs. These are regarded universally as factually accurate. Even his critics accept them as much more reliable than any other record, traditional or critical.

George Sale was the first to translate the Quran into the English language. He wrote a long critical essay on the Prophet's life that formed the introduction to his translation. He called it 'The Preliminary Discourse'; this was in consonance with the approach of many a classic commentator, for Muhammad and the Quran are inextricably intertwined.

The Quran was revealed to Muhammad in the seventh century, a time of instability all around. Judaism and Christianity were in decline and plagued by internal conflicts. They had yet to envelop Europe. The great empires of Iran and Byzantine were interlocked in bloody wars. In Asia, paganism was rampant in many parts, though Buddhism and Confucianism had made some inroads here and there. In such troubled times, in the desert lands of Central Arabia, far away from centres of civilization, Muhammad proclaimed the oneness of God and brought the Quran to his people, who lived by primitive practices which glorified superstition and witchcraft and who spent all their energies in endless tribal warfare.

Muslims believe that God gave the Quran to Muhammad; he himself had no hand in its creation. That is why they resent the slightest suggestion of alteration or modification in it, whatever the compulsions. Even Muhammad could not change a word in it: that, as the Quran says, would have brought the wrath of Allah on him. How then can any man now, or ever, engage in such an exercise!

The Quran is, therefore, regarded by Muslims as immutable and unchangeable, not metaphorically or symbolically but literally. This is a matter of faith for them, and reason can never deflect them from it. Just as there are people who argue that God is the creation of man, there are those who insist that Muhammad authored the Quran. It is pointless to argue with them. Muslims go by what Imam Ghazzali, one of the greatest thinkers in the annals of Islam, has said: 'Where reason departs, faith enters.'

What is divine and what is mundane? What is spiritual revelation and what is personal creation? Such questions have troubled enquiring minds for ages. But they are not germane here. Nor is this the place to go into a discussion of various philosophical theories about the supernatural. We are concerned with the believers for whom the invisible supernatural is more real than the visible material. The Quran emphasizes this again and again; it is the pivot of the faith of Muslims. There is no human partnership in the Quran; it is all of God. And what is of God, cannot be changed by man.

Like Jews and Christians, Muslims believe that God is the Creator of all that exists on this earth as in the heavens, and that nothing moves except by His will. But while the Torah and the Bible are not regarded by most Jews and Christians as the actual Word of God, as uttered by Him, Muslims regard every word of the Quran as His Word. They revere other prophets and accept their scriptures as these were originally revealed; but to them, Muhammad is the culmination of the prophetic order. He is God's last messenger – 'the seal of the prophets'. Why the last and the seal? The poet-philosopher Iqbal has given the answer:

In Islam, prophecy reaches its perfection in discovering the need of its own abolition. This involves the keen perception that life cannot forever be kept in leading strings; that in order to achieve full self-consciousness man must finally be thrown back on his own resources.[2]

Prophecy, however, does not create divinity; prophets were not divine. They were only God's instruments, sent by Him to transmit His message. That is why the Quran insists on making clear that Muhammad was human and so were all other prophets. They emphasize His supremacy and make it clear that only to God is man accountable for his deeds and misdeeds. He is the final arbiter of man's destiny, and on the Day of Judgement He will reward the virtuous and punish the wrongdoer. His message, therefore, is final. No one can sit in judgement on it. Muslims believe that it has come verbatim to them through Muhammad. He had no other power; he asked for none, and was given none. He was told by his detractors to establish his claim of prophethood by performing some miracle; he told them unhesitatingly that his only miracle was the message revealed to him by God. His mission was to transmit it to his fellow beings, and in this he never wavered. He had to struggle hard and suffer a great deal, but ultimately he succeeded; and his success astounded the world. H. G. Wells, despite his critical attitude to him, conceded:

Islam prevailed because it was the best social and political order the times could offer. It prevailed because everywhere it found politically apathetic peoples, robbed, oppressed, bullied, uneducated and unorganised and it found selfish and unsound governments out of touch with any people at all. It was the broadest, freshest and cleanest political idea that had yet come into actual activity in the world and it offered better terms than any other to the mass of mankind.[3]

It was politics in the highest sense of the term: the upliftment of the poor and the care of the downtrodden, which Muhammad believed could only be achieved by following the path shown by God. As he struggled, God guided him. The Quran is the sum total of that guidance. As he gathered followers, they looked up to him with awe and reverence. He was the favoured one of God; he could not be one like them. He admonished them that they were wrong to think so; no man, however great or noble, could be compared with God. Hence He alone was worthy of man's worship.

Muhammad went about his task in all humility; he assumed no airs – spiritual or temporal. Being human, he sometimes faltered, and on occasion God reprimanded him. For instance, when a blind man came to seek his guidance on some religious matter, he was engaged in a serious discussion with an important tribal leader whom he was trying to persuade to accept Islam. He therefore sent the blind man away rather abrasively. Allah immediately cautioned him through a revelation, which forms a part of the Quran. It is entitled 'He [Muhammad] Frowned':

> The Prophet, with a frown
>   on his face,
> Turned the blind man away.
> He had come to him
> To understand the Book
> And perchance
>   to grow spiritually
> Or to receive correct admonition,
> Which might have profited him.
> But one who was full of himself,
> You attended to, O Muhammad!
> However, the blame is not yours
> If he does not respond.
> But the blind man who
> Came earnestly to you
> And with fear in his heart,
> You were unresponsive to him.
> This, by no means, should have happened.
> This is, indeed, Our admonition.

(80:1–10)

On other occasions, Muhammad would be reminded of what he was expected to do or refrain from doing; it was in a way an interaction between God and His messenger. Before God, Muhammad always humbled himself. He warned his followers that he was not to be bracketed in any way with God. He was so careful in this regard that he did not allow any portrait or statue of himself to be made or a shrine to be built on his grave, lest the faithful start worshipping him along with God. There are numerous traditions suggesting that he strongly disapproved of his deification. Indeed the Quran testifies that God can have no partner: *shirk*, or associating others with God, is as grave a sin as *kufr*, or denial of the existence of God.

But despite this, his followers, in their enthusiasm, have tried to deify him; in fact among some sections of Muslims, he is held dearer than God. To quote the renowned Christian scholar of Islam Professor Wilfred Cantwell Smith, 'Muslims will allow attacks on Allah; there are atheists and atheistic publications, and rationalist societies; but to disparage Muhammad will provoke from even the most "liberal" sections of the community, a fanaticism of blazing vehemence.'[4]

Through the centuries that have witnessed the spread of Islam in different parts of the world, colourful legends and fanciful myths have, no doubt, been woven around Muhammad, often as a reaction by the faithful to Muhammad's denunciation by his critics. This has happened despite the Prophet's incessant warnings. A number of traditions disapprove of such adoration; repeatedly Muhammad told his followers that he was like one of them, as human as they are.

For instance, he once saw some palm-growers engaged in a particular kind of grafting, and advised them against it. They followed his advice, but the result was a considerable decline in the yield. When the Prophet learnt about it, he told them, 'I am a mere human being. When I command you to do anything about religion in the name of God, accept it, but when I give my personal opinion about worldly things, bear in mind that I am a human being and no more.'[5]

Some of the Quranic revelations have often been attacked on the grounds that they were conveniently concocted by Muhammad in order to cope with certain problems and situations. But even a cursory reading of the verses will show that the whole scheme of the Quran is based on God's guidance in the day-to-day life of the

Prophet. Verses came down to him as admonitions or directives to show the right path or to correct a wrong. Hence these could not deal with general or moral issues alone; they took into account specific events. Muhammad's critics have charged him with manipulation to suit an exigency, particularly of a personal nature. For example, he received a revelation exonerating his youngest wife, Aisha, of the charge of infidelity; he was allowed to marry his cousin Zainab, who was the wife of his adopted son, Zaid; a revelation told him how to settle his quarrels with his wives. But these were important events in the Prophet's life, and they were bound to have repercussions on the community at large. He sought God's guidance and he received it. Through the revelation in the case of Aisha, the direction about adultery and slandering a chaste woman was given; through the revelation about Zainab, restriction on adoption was promulgated; and through the revelation about the wives of the Prophet, a certain code of conduct between husbands and wives was issued.

In fact, the Quran gives advice on many matters of everyday life, such as how a Muslim should enter a house, how he should greet someone, and how he should dress or talk. One could understand the argument about manipulation if the verses about Aisha, Zainab or Muhammad's wives were solitary instances; but they are not. They form part of a general pattern. The Prophet is presented in the Quran as the best example of its teachings and a perfect model of human behaviour. To have omitted references to incidents which caused worry to him and concern to his Companions would have been incongruous. His life was an open book; it had to be, if the Quranic teachings were to be properly understood and strictly followed by the faithful. Therefore he kept his Companions fully aware of every movement of his; he hid nothing from his followers.

In many respects, the Quran differs from all other scriptures. It is not only a Book of ethics, morality, philosophy and metaphysics: it is also a practical guide. Lessons are to be drawn even from verses that were of local relevance. They may be more historical than religious, more worldly than other-worldly, but their ethical importance cannot be gainsaid. In fact, more often than not, there is a fusion of the material and the spiritual; sometimes one predominates, sometimes the other. Moreover, Muhammad's life is a mirror for his followers; in him they see the fruition of the Quranic values – he is the ideal to be followed. But he was one of them till the last. He talked and laughed like them, wept and grieved, married and produced children just as they did.

Unlike other religious leaders, Muhammad was as much a preacher as an administrator; as much a judge as a law-giver; as much a warrior as a peace-maker. He cannot be put in a strait-jacket. He was chosen to be the conveyor of truth through the Quran; it came piecemeal, with instructions varying from occasion to occasion. From these, principles emerged, almost naturally, though their interpretations have differed through the ages. Again, as the Prophet was a model for the faithful, every action of his had to be open to public scrutiny. In other religions, myths and legends envelop the personalities of their prophets; there is little historical evidence to substantiate their words and deeds. That is not the case with Muhammad, who lived and died in the blaze of his times. Rama was born five thousand years ago, so it is not possible to have a historical record of his life. This is also the case with the Buddha, Moses, Zoroaster and even Christ. In Muhammad's case, we have an extensive record of his life and activities, even if it is somewhat imperfect by today's standards. As the eminent historian Professor Philip K. Hitti has put it, in his *History of the Arabs*, he is 'the only one of the world's prophets to be born within the full light of history'.[6]

In the course of time Muhammad became the object of deification by his followers; even his sayings were corrupted and his actions misrepresented. Muslim historians and commentators failed to view his life in the context of the particular environment in which he functioned; nor did they attach importance to the age in which he lived. They attributed sanctity to what was temporary or transitory, and mixed the spiritual with the temporal. In the process, they fossilized Islam and transformed Muhammad from a democrat to a dictator. He was of course a revolutionary; his commands were all pervasive. But he did not change the modes and habits of his people by turning these upside-down. He retained several old customs and traditions, modifying many but without uprooting them.

The Quran itself directed Muhammad to proceed cautiously, through persuasion not coercion. In the end, he succeeded in establishing a social order which, in less than a hundred years, changed the shape of much of mankind. As Winwood Reade, in his classic *The Martyrdom of Man*, has observed:

Instead of repining that Mahomet did no more, we have reason to be astonished that he did so much. His career is the best example that can be given of the influence of the Individual in human history. That single man created the glory of his nation and spread his language over half the earth.[7]

The Quranic revelations did not come to Muhammad as a whole; they were sent, as I have said, piecemeal. This was a continuing process, starting when Muhammad was forty years old and lasting until his death, twenty-three years later. They have, therefore, to be viewed from the angle of what is known in Islamic theology as 'occasions of revelations'. They are a vital part of the Quran. The tone and tenure of the revelations differ from time to time. They came down sometimes in a few verses, sometimes as a whole chapter. The Quran is repetitive both in its narration and in its commandments; it had to be so as it dealt with different events, which demanded repetition of earlier narration or directive or commandment. However, all through its verses, the central message, namely the oneness and supremacy of God, is continuously dinned into the ears of the faithful; he is repeatedly warned that there can be no compromise on this question. It is in the light of this that the incident known as the 'Satanic Verses', which has recently received worldwide attention through Salman Rushdie's novel of the same name, needs to be scrutinized and analysed.

In *The Satanic Verses*, Rushdie retells the incident in his characteristic style. In order to gain adherents, he says, the Prophet recites the revelation regarding the three goddesses – al-Lat, al-Uzza and Manat – worshipped by the pagans, describing them as 'the exalted birds' whose 'intercession is desired indeed'. The gathering in the Kaaba, consisting of both pagans and Muslims, bursts out in 'shouts, cheers, scandal, cries of devotion to the goddess Al-Lat'. Later, reports Rushdie – after the 'deal' with the pagans falls through – the

Prophet 'stands in front of the statues of the Three and announces the abrogation of the verses which Shaitan [Satan] whispered in his ear. These verses are banished from the true recitation, al-qur'an. New verses are thundered in their place.'

This is the same version that orientalists have circulated, based more or less on the earliest records as put forth by some Muslim historians, with their own distortions. According to them, this incident occurred soon after the Prophet began preaching publicly. It has been given a great deal of prominence by Muhammad's critics, because it is said to expose the hollowness of his mission – in particular the divinity of the Quran, which is the basis of the faith of Islam. Because this incident has been used to cast doubt on the character and integrity of Muhammad, it must be examined thoroughly and understood in its proper historical perspective.

As I have already explained, the cardinal feature of Islam, as propagated by Muhammad, is the doctrine 'There is no god but God. He is the Creator of everything. He sees everyone but no one sees Him. He is omnipotent and omniscient. Between Him and His creatures there are no intermediaries.' This, in essence, is Islam's conception of monotheism, which is absolute, unqualified and un-compromising; no man or god is allowed to mediate between God and his creation, animate or inanimate. Prophets are only the means of communicating His message; they are not endowed with any power to influence His decision or modify His approach to His creatures. Each man will be judged by God according to his deeds or misdeeds on the Day of Judgement. Those who follow the Prophets and act righteously will be rewarded; those who defy them and indulge in wrongdoing will be punished. This is the kernel of the teachings of the Quran.

Let us take a close look at the alleged incident, which is supposed to have taken place in the early years of his prophethood. One day he was reciting the chapter Al-Najm ('The Star') to a congregation in the Kaaba, the House of God, built by Prophet Abraham. He is said to have uttered the verses, 'Have you ever considered about al-Lat, al-Uzza and the third goddess Manat? They are exalted birds, whose intercession is hoped for', and hearing this there was a stir in the gathering, which comprised both pagans and Muslims.

These were the three goddesses most revered by the pagans, and a reference to them from the lips of the Prophet pleased them. They took it as a sign of reconciliation on his part; and, in their excitement, they too prostrated themselves along with the Muslims. Later, the archangel Gabriel, who was the medium for transmitting the divine revelations, is reported to have told Muhammad that the verses were prompted by Satan and had, therefore, to be abrogated. Hence these verses came to be known as the 'Satanic Verses'.

Clearly, the story is not only a negation of the teachings of the Quran, which emphasizes the central message of monotheism, but also a betrayal of Muhammad's mission. Early in his prophetic career when the pagan leaders of Mecca pleaded with him to accept their idols so that they in return would accept his God, Muhammad told them firmly, 'Even if you put the sun in my right hand and the moon in my left, I will not stop preaching that God is one and He alone is worthy of worship.'

Ibn Ishaq (d. 768), the first to make a mention of the incident through a tradition purported to have been transmitted through various narrators, attributed it to the Prophet's uncle, Ibn Abbas (d. 687). Ibn Ishaq included it in his Sirat Rasul Allah, a biography of the Prophet. The pages of this voluminous work remained scattered at many places and were collated only after a lapse of a hundred years by Ibn Hisham (d. 834), who edited it. The book became the source material for all subsequent biographies of the Prophet. But Ibn Hisham did not include the tradition pertaining to the 'Satanic Verses' in his edited version. Presumably, he regarded it as unreliable. It was, however, incorporated by other historians and commentators, like Waqidi (757–822), Ibn Sa'd (764–845) and Tabari (839–923).

Ibn Ishaq's contribution to Islam is most valuable, particularly for the details of the life of the Prophet; but often he tends to be irresponsible. He has been sufficiently meticulous in the collection of facts, but sometimes he does not distinguish between fact and fiction. That is why many of his contemporaries denounced him; they accused him of being emotional, lacking in balance and prone to romanticizing events. Imam Malik, one of the founders of the four principal schools of Muslim theology, who was a contemporary of Ibn Ishaq, called him 'a devil'. Hisham bin Urama, another prominent theologian of the time, said, 'The rascal lies.' Imam Hanbal, one of the greatest jurists of Islam, refused to rely on the traditions collected by him.

There were many other learned men who held similar views about Ibn Ishaq's work. The same is more or less true of his successors, like Waqidi, Ibn Sa'd and Tabari; their works are said to contain 'fabulous material'. Unfortunately, they form the principal sources of historiography of early Islam; hence to my mind these authors are, in respect of incidents like the 'Satanic Verses', the main culprits. Their contributions, otherwise, are no doubt of great value; nor can it be denied that they were motivated by the best of intentions. But the damage they have done to Islam by incorporating unchecked reports in their works here and there is incalculable. Ibn Khaldun (1332–1406), the greatest of Muslim historians, wrote in the foreword to his monumental *Muqaddimah*:

The outstanding Muslim historians made exhaustive collections of historical events and wrote them in book form. But then, persons who had no right to occupy themselves with history introduced into those books untrue gossip which they had thought up or freely invented, as well as false, discredited reports which they had made up or embellished. Many of their successors followed in their steps and passed that information on to us as they had heard it.[8]

He singled out Waqidi in this respect.

Sir William Muir, in his *Life of Mahomet*, has taken full advantage of what Waqidi and Tabari have reported on the 'Satanic Verses' incident to defame the prophet. He writes:

It is hardly possible to conceive how the tale, if not in some shape or other founded in truth, could ever have been invented. The stubborn fact remains, and is by all admitted, that the first refugees did return about this time from Abyssinia; and that they returned in consequence of a rumour that Mecca was converted. To this fact the narrative of Waqidi and Tabari affords the only intelligible clue. At the same time it is by no means necessary that we should literally adopt the exculpatory version of Maho-metan tradition, or seek in a supernatural interposition, the explanation of actions to be equally accounted for by the natural workings of the Prophet's mind. It is obvious that the lapse was no sudden event. It was not a concession won by surprise, or an error of the tongue committed unawares, and immediately withdrawn. The hostility of the people had long pressed upon the spirit of Mahomet; and, in his inward musings, it is admitted even by orthodox tradition that he had been meditating the very expression which, as is alleged, the devil prompted him to utter.[9]

The report of the incident was also used by the German scholar Dr A. Sprenger, in his work *Leben des Muhammad*, to show the weakness in Muhammad's character; he has laboriously and cleverly sifted material, but his approach lacks historical accuracy. Apart from the Muslim traditionists, he also relied on what the Christian monks told him; but Richard Bell remarks that 'the traditions with regard to these are very untrustworthy'. There were many other scholars, like H. Grimme and H. Lammens, who were vociferous in denouncing Muhammad as a false Prophet, though Grimme believed that he was a great social reformer, who rebelled against unequal distribution of wealth. Lammens admitted that most Muslim traditions were unreliable, but used such of them as suited his purpose and interpreted them with the same hostile animus against Muhammad as was exhibited by earlier Christian writers.

Sir Syed Ahmad Khan (1817–98), the foremost Muslim leader of undivided India in the late nineteenth century and the founder of the Aligarh Muslim University, was so upset with these diatribes against the Prophet that he abandoned all his work in India, and left for London to gather material from the archives of the British Museum and the India Office Library. He stayed in London for two years at his own expense, collected all the material he could, and wrote a voluminous book in Urdu called *Khutabat-e-Ahmediya*, which he then had translated into English. He analysed the episode of the 'Satanic Verses' extensively and proved, by quoting several juristic authorities, particularly Imam Fakhruddin Razi and the foremost Quranic commentator, Ahmed al-Baihaqui, that there is not one iota of truth in it.

Sir Syed quoted Hafiz Ibn Hajr, one of the most respected theologians of that time, as saying that in 'most of the traditions relied upon by Tabari there is no basis at all'. After testing the basis of the traditions in question, Maulana Shibli Nu'mani, the noted author of *Seeratun Nabi*, has come to the conclusion that Waqidi 'had no love for truth and thrived on gossips and scandals'. Ibn Sa'd used the relevant tradition from Ibn Ishaq, but hedged it by saying it was 'an interpretive jugglery'. Yet, on the basis of these false and discredited reports, one orientalist after another has accepted the incident of 'Satanic Verses' as true; they have even embellished it in their own characteristic style and painted Muhammad as a small-time operator without any conviction, who was ready to compromise even on the basic issue of monotheism to suit the exigencies of the situation.

Maxime Rodinson writes in his book *Mohammed*: 'There was one incident, in fact, which may reasonably be accepted as true because the makers of Muslim tradition would never have invented a story with such damaging implications.'[10] But that is precisely what they have done; even contemporary evidence, now available in plenty, discounts it. Likewise, despite his sympathetic understanding of the Prophet, Montgomery Watt devotes several pages to this incident in his book *Bell's Introduction to the Qur'an*. He writes, 'In essentials, it would seem that the account is true since no Muslim could have invented such a story about Muhammad and, indeed, there is confirmation of it in the Quran.'[11] Both assumptions are wrong; but they are eagerly put forth by orientalists, with few exceptions. They have done more to damage the integrity of the Prophet than anything else. The matter has lately assumed grave dimensions because of Salman Rushdie's lurid picturization of this incident in his novel *The Satanic Verses*; it has opened old wounds and has once again deeply hurt the religious susceptibilities of Muslims the world over.

That makes it all the more necessary for us to go into detail about this incident, as it attacks the very basis of the Quran. When, how and where were the 'Satanic Verses' uttered by the Prophet? What was their impact on believers and non-believers? Were these verses really abrogated later and was the Prophet 'reproofed' by God for his lapse? Does the incident fit into the pattern of Muhammad's life and character?

Mohammad was an orphan, belonging to the Hashimite family of the leading tribe of Quraish. He led a simple life, working as a shepherd. Then, he got a job as trade agent for a rich widow, Khadijah, who was so impressed by his honesty that she married him. He was then twenty-five, and she more than forty.

Muhammad often went to the hills to meditate; one day, on Mount Hira, he received a revelation through archangel Gabriel that set him on a new path. He abjured idol-worship and began preaching that there is no god but God, and He alone is worthy of worship. He was jeered at and opposed by the idol-worshippers, mainly by his own kith and kin, the Quraishites. They were the guardians of the Kaaba, which then housed hundreds of idols. They tried to bribe Muhammad with wealth and position to give up his opposition to idol-worship, but he refused.

The incident of the 'Satanic Verses' was an attempt by the pagans to discredit Muhammad and to show that his devotion to Allah and dedication to His worship was of a doubtful nature. It strikes at the very root of Islam, for without monotheism, Islam becomes worthless as a religion.

Maulana Abul 'ala Maududi, the founder of Jamaat-i-Islami (the foremost fundamentalist organization in South Asia) and a highly perceptive moden exegetist of the Quran, has delved deep into the matter and analysed the facts and circumstances cogently in his work *Tafheemul Quran* (*The Meaning of the Quran*).

To begin with, he gives the varying versions of different Muslim chroniclers and exegetists and then shows how each of them contradicts the other. Further, none of them has produced any reliable evidence; everyone has indulged in deduction. He then analyses the occasion when the 'Satanic Verses' were said to have been uttered by the Prophet at the instigation of Satan and interpolated in the divine revelation. As they were inconsistent with the Quranic concept of monotheism, Muhammad was 'reproofed' and they were later 'expunged'.

Maududi asks: But does this interpolation make sense? Was the Prophet so naïve as not to have seen through it? The relevant verses (53:19-23) in the chapter *Al-Najm* ('The Star'), with the Satanic interpolation, will read thus: 'Have you considered about Lat, Uzza and the third goddess Manat? These are exalted birds whose intercession may be hoped for. Is God to have daughters and you sons?

This is, indeed, an unfair division.' Is the interpolation not contradicted by the subsequent verses? Maududi then refers to another aspect:

Were the Quraish, his inveterate enemies, who listened to Muhammad, so stupid as not to see through the contradiction in these verses and prostrate along with the Prophet and declare that all differences between them were over? Is it a rational interpretation of the event?[12]

Then there is the 'reproof' which is supposed to have been made by Allah to the Prophet in connection with these verses; it appears in the chapter Banu Isra'il (17:72–5). Thereafter, the interpolation was expunged in the chapter Al-Hajj (22:52–3). The first set of verses in the form of the 'reproof' came six years after the incident of the 'Satanic Verses'; the 'expunction' nine years later. Isn't it strange that Allah should have waited so long to give this 'reproof'? Whereas, in a small incident concerning the blind man, the reproof was instant, in so grave a matter with such damaging implications, why was there such a long lapse?

Maududi rightly asks:

Why were these revelations held in abeyance for six years and then inserted in the chapter Banu Isra'il (17), through verses (73–5) (containing the reproof) and thereafter the 'abrogation' through verses (52–53) in chapter Al-Hajj (22) after a further period of three years? Does it mean that the verses containing the 'reproof' were sent down on one occasion and thereafter the 'abrogation' on another occasion? [13]

Moreover, none of these verses are interconnected; they seem haphazard and disjoined and they are patently out of context in the chapters. The whole explanation seems to be so contrived that no reasonable or prudent man can accept it. Muir as well as Watt have indulged in conjectural deduction; their observations are expressions of prejudiced minds. Rushdie has, on his own admission, drawn on the version as given by Watt and then allowed his imagination to run wild to ridicule Muhammad's integrity.

Maududi has exposed systematically the hollowness of the tradition on which Ibn Ishaq, Ibn Sa'd, Waqidi, Tabari and a host of other recounters have relied; he regrets that some of them, with

perhaps pious intentions, failed to see its incongruity and contradictory nature. They were taken in by the gossip spread by the pagans
and repeated by some unthinking and gullible Muslims.

Maududi has reconstructed the broad outlines of the incident,
which seems more in conformity with what actually happened than
the distorted version as reported by Ibn Ishaq and repeated by other
Muslim commentators and historians who followed him. He said
that one day, while the Prophet was reciting the particular verses of
the chapter *Al-Najm*, referring to the three goddesses, the entire
congregation in the Kaaba, which at that time comprised more
pagans than Muslims, was moved by the eloquence of the Prophet
and the majesty of the words in which the three goddesses al-Lat,
al-Uzza and Manat were mentioned. The pagans were elated at the
reference to their favourite deities, and in the midst of the jubilant
upsurge the verses were not properly heard. The pagans believed
that Muhammad had praised their goddesses; hence when he prostrated they too prostrated along with him. The Muslims present on
the occasion also thought that a settlement between their leader and
the Quraish had been effected. But as soon as the pagans realized
their mistake, they invented the story that Muhammad had at first
extolled the intercession of their goddesses and later retracted his
statement. Meanwhile, the news that the Muslims had reached some
kind of reconciliation with the Quraish spread to places as far as
Abyssinia, from where many Muslim migrants returned to Mecca.
Maududi concludes:

Naturally these three things: (1) prostration by the pagan Quraish; (2) their
wrong understanding of the 'Satanic Verses', and (3) the return of the
Muslim migrants from Abyssinia, combined to make up the story. So
much so that some responsible people were also deluded by it, for to err is
human, and even the pious and the learned among the Muslims were
caught in its trap.[14]

Maududi states rightly that even those Muslim commentators,
however eminent, who have rejected the incident, have failed to
apply their minds to its implication. Some of them dismiss it on the
ground that the 'links connecting one version with another are
weak' while some others refer to 'contradictory interpretations by

different commentators' and conclude that its occurrence is doubtful. To quote Maududi, 'This kind of reasoning may satisfy believers but not those who are sceptical of the divinity of the Quran or intend to research the facts and make a correct appraisal of Islam.'[15] There is much more to the baselessness of this incident and its deliberate distortion by Muhammad's critics.

First, apart from the time factor and the manifest contradictions in the 'Satanic Verses', there are the verses of the 'reproof', as contained in the chapter *Banu Isra'il*, which need to be considered:

> But those who were blind to our signs here,
> They will be blind to them in the Hereafter
> And will continue to go astray from the right path.
> Their purpose was to tempt you, O Muhammad,
> From what had been revealed to you,
> To substitute something different in our name.
> Had you listened to them, they would certainly
>   have been your friends.
>
> (17:72–4)

Maududi points out that even a cursory reading of these verses makes it clear that the Prophet was not tempted by Satan or the disbelievers. On the contrary, as the Quran points out, he remained steadfast in his loyalty to God. Hence where was the necessity for reproof, direct or indirect?

The verses which are said to have abrogated the 'Satanic Verses' are contained in the chapter *Al-Hajj*:

> Never did We send before you a messenger or apostle
> Who out of his desire allowed Satan to tamper with
>   Our revelations.
> Yet God abrogates what Satan interpolates
> And confirms His own revelations.
> For God is Most Wise, All-Knowing.
> He makes this a trial for those
> Whose hearts are hardened and diseased,
> For assuredly, in this the sinners go far.
>
> (22:52–3)

A critical study of these verses and of those which immediately precede and follow them will make it abundantly clear to an

unbiased reader that they are of a general nature, having a bearing
on all the messengers and apostles of God; there is no reference in
them to a particular incident. Hence where is the question of
abrogation of the 'Satanic Verses'? Professor Kenneth Cragg of
Cambridge, a Christian scholar deeply involved in 'reckoning with
his neighbour's scripture', asks, 'In a situation so charged, in any
event, with ambiguity, will the theory of deliberate, almost negoti-
ated, compromise, made and withdrawn, be the only or the likeliest
hypothesis? Did the Quraish *think* Muhammad was still negotiable?'
Cragg answers it himself. 'It would not have been the first time that
worship was at once common and contrasted. Certainly in the
sequel the struggle continued with Muhammad resolute and paganism stubborn.'[16]

Besides, if some verses here and there are to be interlinked as in
the above case, then why should the following verses in the chapter
Yunus ('Jonah'), which convey exactly the opposite and prove the
Prophet's unflinching adherence to monotheism, not also be linked
with the 'Satanic Verses'?

> And even when our clear verses are read to them
> They persist in saying:
> 'This is not enough,
> Bring something else or change this.'
> Tell them, O Muhammad!
> 'It is not for me to replace or change them.
> If I were to disobey my Lord
> I would suffer the severest punishment
> On the Day of Judgement.'
>
> (10:15)

In another passage, Muhammad was clearly told that if he were
to resort to any kind of forgery, either of his own accord or at the
instance of Satan, God would 'take him by the right hand, then cut
his heart-vein, and none would dare to protect him' (69:44–7).
Muhammad swore, all the time, by the Quran; his loyalty to it was
never in question. How could he then have contemplated, leave
aside made or accepted, the slightest change in any revelation either
at the prompting of Satan or out of his own desire? The classic
theory of *nashk* or *mansukh*, 'abrogation' or 'abrogated', has no

relevance here; it is meant to explain the replacement of one verse by another, where no contradiction is involved; it is part of the gradual evolution of the Quran.

The traditional form of the episode of the 'Satanic Verses' has also been rejected by the Italian scholar Caetani, in his *Annali dell'Islam*. He is of the view that

when one considers the contempt and enmity which the Quraish tribe, who inhabited Mecca, showed toward Mohammed on other occasions, it would seem highly improbable that they ever condescended to listen to the Prophet's reading of the Koran, to say nothing of acknowledging him as a prophet on account of an insignificant concession. Furthermore, such a sudden abandonment of a principle which he had previously championed so energetically would have utterly cancelled his previous success, and entirely undermined the prestige which he had gained among his followers. And one might add that a compromise with the Quraish tribe could not possibly have been reached by merely changing a few lines of the Koran at a time when a large portion of it was filled with bitter attacks upon the Meccan pagans and their gods.

After quoting Caetani, Tor Andrae, in his book *Muhammad: The Man and his Faith*, points out that the narration of the episode, as given by Ibn Sa'd was hardly reliable, and he observes, 'It is very apparent that in this form the whole narrative is historically and psychologically contradictory.' [17]

Muhammad has been reviled by his detractors as much when he was alive as after his death. His enemies in Mecca said to him that he was 'a man possessed', 'a sooth-sayer' and 'a poet'. They condemned the Quran as 'a forgery' or 'sorcery' containing old stories stolen by him. The Quran refers to these allegations again and again and asks Muhammad not to be dismayed, assuring him that he was, indeed, the messenger of God.

Apart from these charges, he suffered physical harassment at the hands of the Quraish; they subjected his followers to so much torture that he advised many of them to migrate to Abyssinia. He left for Mecca with his followers and settled in Medina. It was only after his final victory over the pagans in 630 that the situation changed and Islam became universally accepted in Arabia. Its rapid spread subsequently to other parts of the world, however, intensified the hatred against it among non-Muslims, especially Christians, who began losing their dominions to the advancing Muslims in most of Asia and Africa. They almost reached the very heart of Europe. Hichem Djait, the well-known historian attached to the universities of McGill and Berkeley, writes:

Over the centuries Christian tradition came to look upon Islam as a disturbing upstart movement that awakened such bitter passion precisely because it laid claim to the same territory as Christianity.[18]

Frustrated, Christian monks hurled the vilest abuses on Muhammad and the Quran. The situation became even worse after the Crusades. The Church led the campaign of hate, with Christian writers and poets following suit. The anti-Islamic literature of Medieval times is a painful and pathetic reflection on Christian bigotry. The Italian scholar Professor Francesco Gabrieli puts it succinctly:

We find it in various versions, inconsistent in their content, but entirely consistent in their spirit of vituperation and hatred, in the writing of chroniclers, apologists, hagiographers and encyclopaedists of the Latin Middle Ages; Guibert of Nogent and Hildebert of Tours in the eleventh century, Peter the Venerable in the twelfth, Jacques de Vitry, Martinus Polonus, Vincent of Beauvais and Jacobus, a Varagine, in the thirteenth, up to Brunetto Latini and his imitators, and Dante and his commentators.[19]

In Dante's *Divine Comedy*, Muhammad is put in the inferno, torn to pieces by pigs; Professor Gabrieli describes it as 'this grotesque fiction, the product of ignorance, fantasy and *odium theologicum*' and observes that 'the evil weed' that Dante sowed 'did not die with him but grew to become the *flagellum dei* both in the East and the West.'[20]

Even after the advent of the Age of Enlightenment in Europe, there was not much change in the Christian attitude; Luther bracketed Muhammad with his enemy the Pope and described them as 'the two arch-enemies of Christ'. On the other hand, Catholics bracketed Muslims with Protestants and denounced both.

Now and then, an attempt was made to understand the faith of the millions of Muslims who had spread all over the world; their power was on the increase and accommodation with them had become inevitable. Translations of the Quran in European languages started appearing, notably by Sale in English and Savary in French. Boulainvilliers and Goethe made sincere efforts to understand Muhammad and his mission, helping to give a more sympathetic picture of Islam. But there were others like Voltaire, whose play *Mahomet*, written in 1742, was a grotesque presentation of the Prophet; the prejudice was so deep-rooted that it affected the thinking of even the best minds in the Christian West. It was left to Carlyle to repair the damage: in a lecture on 'Heroes and Hero-worship' in 1840, almost a hundred years after Voltaire's vitriolic attack on the Prophet, he selected Muhammad as the hero among the Prophets. He declared:

Our current hypothesis about Mahomet, that he was a scheming Imposter, a Falsehood incarnate, that his religion is a mere mass of quackery and fatuity, begins really to be now untenable to anyone. The lies, which well-meaning zeal has heaped round this man, are disgraceful to ourselves only.[21]

About the Quran, which he found difficult to read, he asked:

Are we to suppose that it was a miserable piece of spiritual *legerdemain*, this which so many creatures of the Almighty have lived by and died by? I, for my part, cannot form any such supposition . . . 'One would be entirely at a loss what to think of this world at all, if quackery so grew and were sanctioned here.'[22]

He explained the true meaning of Islam, 'surrendering oneself to God', and quoted Goethe, who had remarked, 'If this is Islam, then we all live in Islam.'[23]

The more the Quran is studied with an unprejudiced mind, the more this truth emerges, for Islam is nothing but a confirmation of all the earlier messages sent by God through His messengers, who came among one people after another. The Quran reiterates the eternal truth about the unity of God and calls upon His creatures to have unshakeable and absolute faith in Him and to do good deeds. These are the two cardinal principles which it enjoins upon Muslims, and these form the bedrock of Islam.

WARS AND ENCOUNTERS

The divinity of the Quran, which some of the characters in Salman Rushdie's book *The Satanic Verses* have ridiculed, has been under attack from the inception of Muhammad's mission. The Jews and the Christians, who were the first to encounter its thrust, carried on a systematic campaign of denunciation, against both the revelations and the character of their conveyor. They allowed the Prophet no peace and took every opportunity to provoke his followers, with the result that a peaceful pursuit often turned into a bloody encounter. The Jews gave up their hostility, to a large extent, soon after their subjugation by the Muslims and their expulsion from Medina. The Christians continued their opposition, with greater vengeance and more vulgar abuse than the Jews ever resorted to. They directed their ire at the Prophet from various angles. First, they said that Muhammad could show no sign of divine sanction for the Quran. Second, that the revelations seemed more the outcome of an epileptic mind than the expression of a real prophet. Third, that the stories he narrated were just a repetition of tales borrowed from the Old Testament, or that they were fables collected by him from the bazaars of Syria which he frequented as a young boy. And finally, that he could perform no miracles. They contended that while Abraham walked on fire, Moses changed a stick into a serpent and Jesus raised the dead, Muhammad possessed no supernatural power.

The pagans of Mecca made the same charges, in almost identical terms, as some of the orientalists are now doing. They told Muhammad that if he were a Prophet, then like the prophets of old, he should cause winds to blow or rain to fall, or he should revive the dead. To all this Muhammad replied, in all humility, 'The only miracles I have are the revèlations of God, who has chosen me, in His infinite wisdom, to be His messenger.' So they damned him, and dismissed him as an impostor. Unmindful, he continued to pursue his mission. The Quran asked him to tell the disbelievers:

> I have no power to do any good or bad, even to myself.
> Only God has the power and does as He pleases.
> If I had the knowledge about the unseen
> I would have enjoyed abundance of good,
> And no evil would have befallen me.
> Verily, I am just a warner
> And a bringer of glad tidings
> To those who believe in God.

(7:188)

There could not have been a more straightforward and honest explanation of his position. And yet, while other prophets, whose miracles can at best be matters of belief and at worst flights of fancy on the part of their followers, are glorified and revered, Muhammad is denounced. This despite the fact that neither science nor philosophy gives much credence to miracles. Even in classical antiquity, many thinkers have expressed serious doubts about them. For instance, Cicero declared that 'there are no such things as miracles'; they were invented 'for the piety of the ignorant folk'. Celsus said that miracles, whether attributed to Christ or Moses, were 'insufficiently attested and most improbable'. Even in the Middle Ages, many questioned their veracity. In the eighteenth and nineteenth centuries, the doctrine of miracles was publicly denounced. David Hume shred it to pieces in his work *Enquiry concerning Human Understanding*. There was no scientific evidence to establish their authenticity. Even some of the Christian priests, such as Rudolf Buttman, discarded them and preached that Christianity was more a moral than a supernatural force.

To the end of his prophetic mission, Muhammad disclaimed the power to perform miracles; he asserted that these could be performed by Allah alone. Though subsequent traditions attributed supernatural acts to him, they were indeed the handiwork of his followers. Several Muslim theologians held that these could not be accepted as valid because they contradicted statements in the Quran and went against the tenor of the teachings of the Prophet. George

Bernard Shaw has written on this issue in his inimitable style:

No one is ever tired of stories of miracles. In vain did Mahomet repudiate the miracles ascribed to him: in vain did Christ furiously scold those who asked him to give them an exhibition as a conjurer: in vain did the saints declare that God chose them not for their powers but for their weaknesses; that the humble might be exalted, and the proud rebuked. People will have their miracles, their stories, their heroes and heroines and saints and martyrs and divinities to exercise their gifts of affection, admiration, wonder, and worship, and their Judases and devils to enable them to be angry and yet feel that they do well to be angry. Every one of these legends is the common heritage of the human race; and there is only one inexorable condition attached to their healthy enjoyment, which is that no cne shall believe them literally.[1]

Even the Age of Enlightenment or the advent of Marxism made no difference to this attitude. As Professor Bernard Lewis has observed, 'Apart from the work of a few scholarly broad-church Western Marxists, the literature of polemic, whether Marxist or Christian, shows little sign of intellectual curiosity or detachment – a quality which was indeed regarded by the one as a sin, by the other as an ideological error.'[2]

Muhammad could have easily given to himself the aura of divinity and his followers would have been all too happy to hail him for it. Instead, he curbed them and warned them not to deify him. As the Prophet lay critically ill, he was informed that a rumour had spread among the faithful that he was dead. This caused wide consternation among them. Muhammad mustered all the strength at his disposal, walked to the mosque and addressed the congregation. 'I am told that rumour of the death of your Prophet has filled you with alarm, but has any prophet before me lived forever? Everything happens according to God's will and has its appointed time which can neither be hastened nor avoided. I will return to my Lord who has sent me.'

Despite this clarification, when Muhammad died, Umar, who later became the second caliph, could not believe it. Abu Bakr had to recite the Quranic verse which clearly stated that Muhammad was mortal and only Allah was immortal.

All through his life, Muhammad reasoned with the people and

tried to convert them. He did not resort to force, magic or any hypnotic method to gather followers. He valued the intellect and emphasized the role of reason in human development. There are numerous verses in the Quran which admonish him to shun coercion and exercise persuasion and patience:

> Call all to accept
> The way of the Lord,
> But do it with wisdom
> And use persuasion.
>
> (16:125)

He was a simple man, who never ceased to be human and refused to be regarded as divine. And for that he was maligned. Instead of looking at his life in its proper historical perspective, orientalists have devoted pages and pages to spurious traditions, concocted by the hired theologians of Muslim rulers who sought justification for their own corrupt and immoral acts in alleged sayings and practices of the Prophet. Millions of such traditions were thus coined and passed on from decade to decade. In the process, more concoction was added to them. On the basis of these traditions many an Ibn Ishaq or Waqidi wrote their histories, spicing them up with gossip and scandal. After almost two centuries, Bukhari and Muslim – the two most reliable of the recorders – rejected ninety per cent of such traditions as totally false; even some of those which they found reliable are of doubtful nature. With no proper research facilities, historians like Ibn Sa'd and Tabari gathered whatever they heard about the Prophet and put them in their works. In their excessive zeal they turned Muhammad into a God on the one hand and a lover of all worldly pleasures on the other. His Christian and Jewish detractors found in these accounts enough material to indulge in selective quotation-mongering, and with some intelligent distortions of facts they painted the Prophet as a sensual man, an opportunist, a ruthless warrior and a politician rather than a saint.

In his introduction to George Sale's English translation of the Quran, Sir Edward Denison Ross has rightly observed:

For many centuries the acquaintance which the majority of Europeans possessed of Muhammadanism was based almost entirely on distorted reports of fanatical Christians, which led to the dissemination of a multitude of gross calumnies. What was good in Muhammadanism was entirely ignored and what was not good in the eyes of Europe was exaggerated or misinterpreted.[3]

In judging whether the Quran is the Word of God and whether Muhammad is His prophet, arguments don't help; they tie us in knots. This is equally true of other scriptures and other prophets. My point is that if one believes in God, then one cannot disbelieve in His messenger. The one follows from the other. Likewise, if prophets like Abraham, Moses, Jesus, Krishna, Buddha, Zoroaster and many others, who millions of people throughout the world venerate and whose teachings have uplifted mankind, are genuine, then more so was Mohammad, who lived and worked inside history.

Again, if revelations are accepted as true, then you cannot ridicule the medium; Rushdie has sought to do so by caricaturing Gabriel as Gibreel Farishta in his novel. Muslims revere Gabriel as the archangel who brought God's revelations to Muhammad. He is also as much a part of the Judaeo-Christian tradition as of Islam. He is the first among angels, and is regarded real as much by Christians and Jews as Muslims. Satan also belongs to the same species. He is the fallen angel who led the rebellion against God and the embodiment of all that is evil on earth. Even today, he continues to be a vital part of not only religious but also secular literature in practically every language. Consequently, as Satan represents all that is evil, so does Gabriel represent all that is virtuous. He is as much a part of human evolution towards its fulfilment as Satan towards its frustration. Iqbal composed a poetic dialogue between Gabriel and Satan on the conflict between belief and disbelief in God. In the Quran there are many references to Satan and his followers reflecting the fight between good and bad, virtue and vice, as has existed throughout history. The central theme is the belief in the oneness of God. In the concluding part of the poem, Iqbal depicts Gabriel's unalterable faith in God and Satan's unbending defiance of His authority:

GABRIEL
Our high estate is humbled by
your ancient mutiny;

What credit have the angels now
in the sight of the Most High?

SATAN

My rebel spirit has filled Man's pinch
of dust with fierce ambition,
The warp and woof of Mind and Reason
are woven of my sedition.
The deeps of Good and evil you see
but from land's far verge;
On which of us, on you or me,
descends the tempest's scourge?
Khizar and all your guardians are pale shades:
the storms I teem
Roll down ocean by ocean, river by river,
stream by stream!
But ask of God this question,
when His audience you shall find –
Whose blood is it has coloured bright
the history of mankind?
In the heart of the Almighty
like a pricking thorn I wait;
You only cry forever
God is *great* and God is *great*.[4]

At another place Iqbal says to the non-believers:

This one prostration which you find so burdensome
It frees you of a thousand prostrations.

Rushdie's novel, which mocks at many such beliefs, has attracted
universal attention; it has naturally infuriated Muslims everywhere.
But this kind of calumny against Islam, as I have mentioned earlier,
has been an ongoing process, ever since the birth of Islam. To non-
Muslims, whether Christians, Jews, Hindus or Buddhists, Muslims
have been followers of Mahound, which means the devil or the
spirit of darkness. This attitude continues till today; it has not
substantially changed, even if a Margaret Thatcher or a George
Bush may, in order to appease Muslim sentiments, pay lip-service

to Islam. Muslims are regarded by many non-Muslims as either fundamentalists or terrorists, an attitude stemming from the same old prejudices of the past. For long there was the common belief that Muhammad gave to non-Muslims only two choices, the Quran or the Sword, and further that Islam spread through the Sword. Sir Thomas Arnold, after much painstaking research, collected facts and figures for his monumental work *The Preaching of Islam* and proved that Islam was spread, not by 'the exploits of that mythical personage – the Muslim warrior with the sword in one hand and the Quran in the other', but by the force of the teachings of the Quran and the character of the Prophet.[5]

Sir Thomas's has remained, however, a voice in the wilderness; there are many other persons, no less distinguished, who persist in presenting the Prophet as a ruthless warrior. They ignore the very basis of his faith; they are not impressed by the fact that he abhorred violence and preached compassion. When his detractors scorned him, he did not react, and when they persecuted him, he bore it patiently. They tortured his followers, but instead of retaliating he advised them to migrate to Abyssinia. However, the more he humbled himself before his enemies, the Quraish of Mecca, the more they harassed him. They pelted him with stones, threw rubbish at him, and even worked out a plan to murder him. To frustrate their evil designs, he migrated along with his followers to Yathrib (later to be called Medina), a city 300 miles from Mecca. There he carried on with his mission peacefully. Although he was accepted by the majority of the people there as their leader, he did not impose his will on the rest of the population. He brought together the various tribes, the Muslims as well as the Jews and the pagans, and arrived at a working arrangement with them for the conduct of day-to-day affairs.

He entered into a covenant with them, which came to be called the 'Constitution of Medina' and formed the basis of a composite state. It guaranteed, in particular, that the Jews 'who attached themselves to our Commonwealth ... shall be protected from all insults and vexations ... they shall have an equal right with our own people to our assistance and good offices.' It also provided that 'the Jews shall practise their religion as freely as the Muslims; their clients and allies shall enjoy the same security and freedom; the guilty shall be pursued and punished.' The Jews were required to join 'Muslims in defending Medina against all enemies; the interior of Medina shall be sacred to all those who accept this document.' Further, it was specified that those 'who join us are entitled to our aid and support so long as they shall not have wronged us or lent assistance to any enemies against us'.[6]

A similar assurance was later given to the Christians, who inhabited Najran and the neighbouring territories. Muhammad gave his pledge to them that he would safeguard 'their lives, their religion and their property' and that 'there shall be no interference with the practice of their faith or their observances; nor any change in their rights or privileges'. They were assured that 'no bishop shall be removed from his bishopric, nor any monk from his monastery, nor any priest from his priesthood, and they shall continue to enjoy everything great and small . . . not oppress or be oppressed.'[7]

Despite these guarantees and assurances, the Prophet and his small band of followers were confronted, right from the beginning, by powerful forces determined to destroy them. These groups thrived on violence. Their favourite song was

> If an enemy tribe we do not find,
> We go to war with a friendly tribe;
> Thus our lust for war is quenched.

The Battle of Badr in 624 was forced on Muhammad; he had to contain the animosity of the Quraish, who were secretly plotting his extermination. The highly exaggerated accounts of the battle and the circumstances preceding it, told by Muslim chroniclers who wanted to boast of the valour of their co-religionists, cannot transform it from a defensive to an aggressive encounter. Orientalists have distorted their versions and presented a picture of the Prophet-in-arms. But the truth is different. The Quraish were spoiling for a fight, and were determined not to leave Muhammad in peace. To escape persecution from them, the Prophet sent his people away to Abyssinia; but the Quraish followed them and asked King Nagus to hand over the migrants to them.

Similarly, when the Muslims took refuge in Yathrib the chief of the Quraish, Abu Sufiyan, threatened punitive action against the leaders of Aas and Khazraj, its two main tribes, if they did not throw Muhammad and his followers out of the city. Against this background, how was it conceivable that the Prophet would take on the mighty Quraish, knowing well their enormous fighting resources? And that, too, at a time when he was bedevilled with conflicts between the *muhajirun*, or Meccan migrants, and *ansar*, or the Medinian helpers. The Jews and Christians were hostile towards him despite his best efforts to be friends with them. Among the *ansar* there were many *munafiqun*, ready to stab him in the back; their leader, Abdullah ibn Ubayy, dreamt of becoming the ruler of Medina and saw a threat in Muhammad's growing strength. Under these circumstances, why would the Prophet have embarked on an expedition at Badr, a place 85 miles from Medina, and provoked the Quraish? And what was the strength of his force? Barely 300 untrained and poorly equipped Muslims for taking on the powerful Abu Jahl, who had come with more than a thousand well-trained men-at-arms! If Muhammad was the aggressor, what could have been his motive? Booty, say his detractors. But there is nothing in the Prophet's character to suggest that he was a marauder. Why, even a marauder would not have ventured on such a perilous adventure! The fact that he won the battle was, indeed, a miracle. That is why he attributed it entirely to God.

The furious Quraish began feverish preparations for avenging their defeat. They had to humble Muhammad as a matter of honour. The Battle of Uhud, which took place a year later (625), was the result of the search for vengeance against the Muslims by the redoubtable Abu Sufiyan and his pagan followers. The Meccan chief had vowed that he would not cohabit with his wife, Hind, until he had settled scores with the Muslims; Hind, on her part, had vowed that she would not rest until Badr was avenged. Muhammad, who had no choice but to defend Medina, asked the Jews to fulfil their commitment under the covenant, but they refused. The leader of the *munafiqun*, Abdullah ibn Ubayy also betrayed the Prophet. At first, he gave 300 men, but at the eleventh hour withdrew them. Moreover, Muhammad's Companions were divided on the military strategy to be adopted against the enemy; he had to hammer out a consensus among them. On the battlefield confusion was created when a section of Muslims, thinking that they had won, abandoned their post and started gathering the booty. The archers, who were monitoring troop movements, left the top of the hill, came down and joined in the collection of the spoils. Thus the Prophet faced heavy odds all around; yet he managed to put up strong resistance. The war seemed to be going in his favour until indiscretion on the part of his archers and some clever moves by the enemy general, Khalid bin Walid, turned the tables and victory slipped out of Muhammad's hands.

The triumphant Quraish were far too exhausted at the time to capture Medina; invasion would have been a long drawn-out affair, and they were not prepared for it. They returned, therefore, to Mecca, hoping to take on Medina sometime later; for the present, they were content with avenging their defeat at Badr. Their victory emboldened the neighbouring tribes to make forays upon Medina and encouraged the Jews to join hands against Muhammad's enemies. The faithful were at first demoralized by the defeat; but Muhammad's indomitable courage and dynamic leadership revived their spirit. Both the victory at Badr and the defeat at Uhud reinforced the belief among the Muslims that the Prophet and his followers were being tested by God. If Allah had willed it, they could have easily won at Uhud; but He wanted the Muslims to prove their mettle as much in defeat as in victory. They had to steel themselves to face any eventuality; therein lay the secret of the success of their mission. They realized that adversity was as important for human development as prosperity, and that defeat was as necessary for cleansing the soul as victory was for advancing their cause.

Much has been made by the enemies of Islam against the treatment meted out by the Prophet to the Jews of Medina; but the adverse role of the Jews has been underplayed. Watt has grudgingly admitted that 'The Jews were attacking the whole set of ideas on which Muhammad's position was based.'[8] During the Battle of Badr, many of them had actively encouraged the Quraish to avenge their defeat; there is enough evidence to this effect. Their chief, Ka'b bin al-Asraf, had visited Mecca to pledge his support, haranguing the

Meccans; in a song of vengeance, which he himself had composed, he asked them to rise and fight the Muslims:

> At events like Badr you should weep and cry
> The best of the people were slain . . .
> How many noble handsome men,
>   the refuge of the homeless were slain
>
> . . .
>
> I was told that al-Harith ibn Hisham
> Is doing well and gathering troops
> To visit Yathrib with armies
> For only the noble, handsome men protect
>   the loftiest reputation.[9]

The Jews of Medina comprised mainly three tribes, Banu Qaynuqa, Banu Nadir and Banu Qurayzah. Of them the most powerful was Banu Qaynuqa, who had pledged their support to the Prophet but had never accepted his leadership; they secretly plotted against him. They were in constant touch with the Quraish and helped them whenever and wherever they could. Hence the relations between the Jews and the Muslims were always strained, and as time passed, they worsened. The immediate cause of the trouble that arose between them at this time was the molesting of a Muslim woman by a Jewish shopkeeper; the subsequent siege of the fortress of Banu Qaynuqa and the latter's expulsion by the Muslims out of Medina showed the depth to which their relationship had sunk.

There was also the wholesale exile of the tribe Banu Nadir. They were in the forefront of the campaign against the Prophet and had openly lamented the defeat of the Quraish at Badr and urged them to murder Muhammad. They had also conspired with Abdullah bin Ubayy to help the Quraish in their evil designs. As a result, the Muslims were determined to punish Banu Nadir. They besieged their fortress and stopped all their provisions. Their departure has been vividly described by Ibn Ishaq: he writes that they left Medina in a procession 'with such pomp and pleasure as had never been seen before'; Waqidi goes a step further and reveals that 'their women wore the finest dresses and the costliest jewels'. They must, indeed, have been out of their minds to rejoice while being uprooted from their hearths and homes. The truth is that soon after settling down at Khaibar they began making frantic preparations to avenge their humiliation. Their favourite poet, Samanak, incited the Jews:

> For killing al-Nadir and their confederates
> And for cutting down the palms, their dates ungathered
> Unless I die we will come at you with lances
> And every sharp sword that we have! [10]

The Jews were advantageously placed; they had plenty of resources to fight and their fortresses were well guarded. They were also able to entice the neighbouring tribes, particularly the Gátfan, to join them. So reinforced, they planned to invade Medina. The Muslims became nervous and initiated negotiations, but these failed.

The Prophet decided to take the offensive. He marched to Khaibar and after several encounters with the enemy gained the upper hand. When the encircled Jews sued for peace, Muhammad allowed them to keep their fertile lands provided they gave the Muslims half the produce. The Jews agreed and invited Muhammad and his companions for a feast to celebrate the occasion. When a shoulder of lamb was brought and served to Muhammad, he took a mouthful but, noticing the strange taste of the meat, immediately spat it out. He tried to warn one of his Companions who had already started to eat, but it was too late. The Companion died instantly. The woman who had cooked the lamb was summoned, and she admitted that the meat had been poisoned. The Muslims were furious; they wanted to repudiate the agreement and resume fighting. But the Prophet forgave the Jews and honoured the terms of the agreement.

Despite Muhammad's best efforts, the Jews did not reconcile themselves to his leadership and were always working against him. In this the Banu Qurayzah played the most sinister role. After the victory of Quraish in the Battle of Uhud, they were convinced that Muhammad and his followers could easily be wiped out. Towards this end, they conspired not only with Abu Sufiyan, the leader of the Meccans, but also with the other neighbouring tribal chiefs to invade Medina from different directions. Their aim was to encircle the city and entrap the Prophet and his men, but Muhammad's strategy of digging deep trenches on the northern side spoilt their game. The invasion did not take place and the Meccans and their 'confederates' retreated. The 'Battle of the Trenches', as it is called in Muslim annals, finally sealed the fate of Muhammad's enemies.

In the plotting of the invasion, Banu Qurayzah had played an important role; it was also a treasonable one, since they had pledged to defend the city under the Constitution of Medina. The Muslims were furious and were determined to punish them. Consequently, as soon as the threat of invasion was over, the Muslims laid a siege on the fortress where Banu Qurayzah lived. 'Trenches were dug in the market of Medina,' Ibn Ishaq tells us. 'The Jews were brought out in batches and were struck off in those trenches . . . They were 600 or 700 in all, though some put the figure as high as 800 to 900.'[11] After they had surrendered and the siege was lifted. Banu Qurayzah were put on trial. At their request, Said bin Muadh, the leader of Aas and one of the confederates of the Jews, was appointed as the arbiter. The judge gave his verdict on the basis of the Jewish Law, as enumerated in Deuteronomy: if the enemy makes peace after defeat, then 'you shall put all its males to the sword'. Banu Qurayzah were held guilty of treason and their men were ordered to be beheaded. All 900, it is said, were thus executed – only women and children were spared.

These gory accounts are to be found in the work not only of Ibn Ishaq but also of Waqidi and Ibn Sa'd. But they do not seem to be based on carefully scrutinized evidence. A few years ago Barakat Ahmad, a scholar and diplomat, carried out extensive research on the original sources, for his book *Muhammad and the Jews*, and produced startling disclosures which establish that much of what these chroniclers have recounted is not only unauthentic but also baseless. He has shown that several contemporary reporters, such as al-Zuhri and Qatadah, make no mention of these events, and that the traditions on which Ibn Ishaq and the other chroniclers have based their reports are unreliable. Significantly, there are no Jewish versions of these atrocities. As Ahmad puts it, 'It is not normal with the Jews not to record their misfortunes.'[12] There is not a word about the massacre in Samuel Usque's book *A Consolidation for Tribulations of Israel: Third Dialogue*, which is a classic of Jewish martyrology. Furthermore, while the number of Jews killed is said to be 900, the total number of both Muslims and non-Muslims killed during the Prophet's lifetime, in all the wars, big and small, did not amount to even five hundred. Finally, if Muhammad wanted to exterminate the whole tribe of the Jews of Banu Qurayzah, why would he have spared the Jews at Khaiber who had plotted to poison him?

Further evidence of Muhammad's attitude to the Jews is given by an incident that occurred as he and his followers were leaving Khaiber for Medina. A rabbi noticed that some Muslims had taken with them, as spoils of war, copies of the Torah. The rabbi protested to Muhammad, who ordered the Muslims to return every copy of the sacred book and apologized for their misdemeanour. Commenting on this, Dr Israel Welphenson, a Jewish scholar of repute, writes,

The event shows what a high regard the Prophet had for their scriptures. His tolerant and considerate behaviour impressed the Jews, who could never forget that the Prophet did nothing which trifled with their sacred scriptures. The Jews knew how the Romans had, when they captured Jerusalem in 70 B.C., burnt their scriptures and trampled them underfoot. The fanatic Christians persecuting the Jews of Spain had likewise consigned their scriptures to fire. This is the great difference we find between these conquerors and the Prophet of Islam.[13]

I don't propose to discuss the various other battles or expeditions in which Muhammad was involved, because they don't have the same significance; but it is clear that in every case he acted under provocation. His general attitude was that of reconciliation. He did not approve of aggression, because the Quran has warned the faithful that 'God does not love the aggressors'; nor could he encourage looting, since the Quran specifically prohibits it.

The best proof of Muhammad's abhorrence of aggression is the treaty which the Prophet entered into with the pagan leaders of Mecca at Hudaybiyah, a place nine miles from the city. After the 'confederates' (the Meccans and their allies) failed to capture Medina, the Prophet gathered more than 1400 of his followers and asked them to accompany him to Mecca to perform the pilgrimage. They wore the pilgrim's robe and took no arms. On reaching Hudaybiyah, the Prophet asked the Quraish to allow them to enter Mecca, but the leaders of the Quraish refused. After much persuasion they agreed to sign a treaty. The terms were quite obviously humiliating to the Muslims, the worst part being the loss of face they would suffer because they would have to return to Medina without performing the pilgrimage. The Meccans told them that they could come back the next year and Muhammad agreed. There was one condition that seemed apparently favourable to the Meccans but which, in effect, helped the cause of Islam; that was the free movement that was to be permitted to the Meccans and the Muslims of Medina. The migrants were allowed to return to Mecca, where the renewing of contacts with relations and mingling freely with the Meccans furthered the process of conversion. Similarly, the visits of the pagans to Medina had a beneficial effect: it encouraged their conversion. Among those who thus became Muslims were the two redoubtable warriors Khalid bin Walid and Amar bin Aas.

Initially, many Companions returned to Medina unhappy; Umar indignantly called the treaty a 'humiliating retreat'. But Muhammad was a man of vision; he knew that it would pave the way for the expansion of Islam. And so it did. Allah acclaimed it in the Quran as 'a great victory'. In accordance with the treaty, the Muslims, under Muhammad's leadership, visited Mecca the following year, performed the pilgrimage and returned peacefully to Medina. The spectacle of more than 2000 pilgrims observing the religious rites in a sombre and disciplined manner had a remarkable effect on the Meccans, who left their houses and pitched tents on the neighbouring hills, from where they watched the Muslims. It was a moving spectacle of Islam in action in its pristine simplicity and spiritual glory.

After the lapse of a year, Banu Khuza'a, an Arab tribe which had aligned itself with the Muslims, were attacked without cause by Banu Bakr, a tribe aligned with the Quraish. Banu Khuza'a asked the Prophet, as was provided for in the treaty, for aid and protection. Muhammad called upon the Quraish to fulfil their obligations or repudiate the treaty. Foolishly, they took the latter course. Muhammad realized that their intentions were not honourable. He therefore prepared his people for the final confrontation with the enemy. He drafted 10,000 of his followers, armed them fully, equipped them with all the necessities, and marched them towards Mecca. They camped a short distance from the city. From the spirit that enthused them and the sense of dedication to the cause that inspired them, their victory seemed assured. The pagans, on the other hand were in disarray; some of their military leaders had already joined the fold of Islam; even their chief, Abu Sufiyan, had lost heart and was anxious to come to terms with the Prophet. Only his wife, the fiery Hind, was unbending; but her defiance gained her no popular support. The rank and file among the pagans lacked the will to fight and began to perceive Muhammad as the saviour of the Arabs. They were convinced that the Muslims had become invincible; Abu Sufiyan, therefore, sued for peace. Muhammad offered him the most generous terms: every pagan was given a pardon, except the three or four who were accused of naked treason, no house was allowed to be looted, no man to be robbed and no woman to be molested. General clemency and a public guarantee of equality of treatment to friend and foe alike was announced. The Meccans who had migrated to Medina were not to take back their houses from those who occupied them. Not only Abu Sufiyan but even his wife, Hind, who had openly abused and plotted against the Prophet, was forgiven. The Quranic injunction was clear:

> When, with God's help, victory comes,
> And you see men in hordes
> Accepting His way,
> Then glorify the Lord
> And ask for His forgiveness
> And proclaim
> His grace and mercy.

(110:1–3)

Muhammad and his followers entered the Kaaba in all solemnity and cleansed the House of God of the idols. They prayed and thanked the Lord for the final victory. Muhammad addressed the Meccans, who had gathered within the precincts of the Kaaba:

There is no god but God. He has no partners. He has fulfilled His promise and helped His slave and defeated all coalitions against him. Revenge and blood reparations are swept off under my feet. The Kaaba will be properly guarded and the supply of water to pilgrims will be provided free. O! You Quraish! God has wiped out the arrogance of the heathen days and all the pride of your ancestry. Remember that all mankind has descended from Adam and Adam was made of clay.

Reciting the following Quranic Verses, he told them that all human beings were one:

> People are created
> > in pairs
> As males and
> > females,
> And from their
> > union
> Are formed nations
> > and tribes,
> So that they may
> > know
> One another
> > properly.
> However, in the
> > sight of God,
> The most honourable
> > of them
> Are those who are
> The most righteous.
> God is, indeed,
> > All-Knowing
> > and Fully-Informed.

He then called together all the leaders, big and small, of the Quraish and granted them pardon, assuring them that once they joined the fold they would be no different from the other Muslims and, in fact, would become their equal.

Every Prophet had his own approach and own style of functioning; each came in different times and worked among different people. To compare one with the other would be of no avail, and indeed the Quran specifically forbids it. True, Christ fought no wars, but there was no need for him to do so. But Muhammad, as we have seen, had to fight to survive. His wars have, therefore, to be viewed from the larger historical perspective. They were, no doubt, religious wars because it was his religion that was constantly attacked. As the *Encyclopaedia Britannica* has observed,

However much the concept and practice of holy warfare is repugnant to many minds today, in the context of Islam it implies a sensitivity to evil and a conviction that evil has to be resisted and overcome in a total dedication. In this way the faith of Islam has shaped human history by obedience to a resolute and powerful God. Islam also illustrates the point that predestination need not bring with it a submissive fatalism.[14]

In terms of modern warfare, 'wars' is a misnomer for the battles that Muhammad and his followers fought. In truth, they can hardly be called battles: they were mere skirmishes. An analysis of the figures of the dead in the conflicts between 622 and 632 shows that in all, no more than 500 people died on both sides. In the 'War of the Trenches', for instance, the 'confederates' had brought more than 10,000 armed men to invade Medina, while on the other side an almost equal number of Muslims were arrayed, defending the frontiers. Their encounter lasted a month, but as H. Lammens points out, 'Adding the losses on both sides, it is impossible to make up a total of twenty dead.'[15] In the Middle Ages, when wars devoured thousands of men on either side, these figures indicate the restraint, compassion and consideration for human life that Muhammad exercised. He cannot, therefore, be termed a warrior. He held every life sacred, and he abhorred the shedding of blood unless for a just cause. His life was dedicated to peace.

In the supreme hour of his glory, when Mecca lay at his feet and the defeated pagans came forward one after another to take the oath of fealty, he saw an old man approaching him rather timidly with faltering steps. Muhammad asked him, 'Of what do you stand in awe? I am not a king, I am as humble as you are, born of a mother, who ate flesh dried in the sun.' Washington Irving, in his *Life of Mahomet*, has commented:

His military triumphs awakened no pride nor vain glory, as they would have done had they been effected for selfish purposes. In the time of his greatest power he maintained the same simplicity of manners and appearance as in the days of his adversity. So far from affecting regal state, he was displeased if, on entering a room, any unusual testimonial of respect were shown him. If he aimed at universal dominion, it was the dominion of the faith; as to the temporal rule which grew up in his hands, as he used it without ostentation, so he took no step to perpetuate it in his family.[16]

MUHAMMAD'S MARRIAGES

Like the wars, Muhammad's marriages have been a subject of vilification by his detractors. The modern protagonists of monogamy find them reprehensible; they have provided critics with enough material to cast slurs on his character. Rushdie has used them to paint a lurid picture showing twelve prostitutes in a brothel, bearing the same names as the wives of Muhammad and attributing to them the same habits and mannerisms. Still worse, they are made to utter obscenities and indulge in vulgar sexual practices. This has justifiably hurt the sentiments of the faithful, who regard the wives of the Prophet as their mothers. True, some writers in the West have been no less offensive: a typical example is the observation by Muir, who wrote, 'The numerous marriages of Mahomet failed to confine his inclinations within the ample circuit of his harem. Rather, its multiplied attraction weakened restraint, and stimulated desire after new and varied charms.'[1] But Muir, who was ruthlessly attacked by the Muslims in his day, was neither as vulgar or offensive as Rushdie has been in his fictional characterization.

Once again, the source material comes from Muslim traditionists and Arab historians, many of whom seemed intent on presenting the Prophet as a superman endowed with enormous sexual powers. Ibn Sa'd in his *Tabaqaat* even quotes a tradition (obviously concocted to justify the sexual exploits of a caliph) that Muhammad was able to satisfy all his wives in one night. Watt condescendingly comments, 'This looks like an invention, for the usual account is that he gave his wives a night each in turn.'[2]

All this is worse than invention; it is libel of the worst kind, against a man who was pious and ascetic, who lived simply, worked hard, and devoted most of his time to reforming his people. Carlyle rightly observed, 'Mahomet . . . was not a sensual man. We shall err widely if we consider this man as a common voluptuary intent mainly on base enjoyments, nay, on enjoyments of any kind.'[3] Let us test this statement on the basis of available evidence; recent research has cleared many cobwebs.

At the outset we must not forget that monogamy, a Christian weapon for enforcement of morality, is a recent phenomenon; in the Middle Ages, polygamy was prevalent in most parts of the world. Men took hundreds of wives as a measure of social status. Except for Christ, who was celibate, most prophets were much-married men – even saints kept concubines. In Arabia, women were treated worse than chattels; fathers buried their new-born daughters alive. Marriages were contracted for social convenience, and divorces were common and were not looked down upon. Hence the marriages of the Prophet have to be viewed in this larger historical perspective. The concepts of morality have been changing; in Egypt, brothers married sisters; in today's West, sexual promiscuity has become a norm. In seventh-century Arabia, marriage was a means of cementing tribal affiliation.

It is true that Muhammad had many wives, though there is a dispute about the number. According to most classical biographers, there were eleven, excluding the Jew Rehana and the Christian Maria. Rehana, haughty, proud and unbending, was brought to Muhammad as a prisoner of war after the surrender of Banu Qurayzah. Hafiz ibn Hajar has written that she 'was manumitted and then sent back to her family, where she lived in seclusion'. Shibli Nu'mani finds this version most reliable. According to Ibn Sa'd, however, she was married to the Prophet, but he has produced no concrete evidence.

Maria's case is different: she gave birth to Muhammad's son Ibrahim (who died in infancy), and has, therefore, been regarded by a majority of jurists as his wife. The highly respected modern biographer M. N. Haykal has pointed out that after the birth of Ibrahim all doubts about her status were cleared.

The moot point is not the number of wives Muhammad had, but

why he married them and, above all, what his attitude was to women.

Several traditions were circulated two or more centuries after Muhammad's death purporting to show that he was attracted to them in a physical sense. There seems to be no truth in this assumption. I am not prepared to accept that the Prophet would ever have had physical relations with women other than his wives. It is not in conformity with his character or the tenor of his teachings. Rather, Muslim rulers, who enjoyed having concubines, had traditions concocted in the Prophet's name in order to give a certain sanction to their own misdemeanours in the eyes of the faithful.

The Quran, in any case, restricts the number of wives to four, and that, too, is hedged with several conditions. A man must treat all his wives equally, even in love and affection, and this instruction was accompanied by an explicit assertion that it was not possible to do so. After the promulgation of the restriction to four wives, Muhammad never took another wife. So the charge that he had eleven or twelve wives while his followers were allowed only four is baseless; surely his critics did not expect him to divorce some of his wives to bring down their number to four! Though the number is large, it can be easily proved that none of his marriages were either for personal gain or carnal pleasure; each was contracted with a definite purpose and for a just cause.

Muhammad's first wife, Khadijah, had been twice or thrice widowed. She was forty when the Prophet married her. He was then just twenty-five. By all accounts, they led an extremely happy married life. Khadijah bore him four daughters and two sons, though the sons died in infancy.

Muhammad first worked with Khadijah as her trade agent, but his adroitness and transparent sincerity so impressed her that she took him as her husband. He was a great comfort to her, and she a tower of strength for him. When he received his first revelation in the cave of Mount Hira and was much shaken, it was Khadijah who gave him courage; she stood by him and enlisted herself as his first disciple. All through his life, he cherished the memory of their relationship, and until her death he did not take another wife. In later years, when Aisha, his youngest wife, expressed jealousy about his lasting fondness for Khadijah he rebuked her and said, 'I cherish her memory because she was so loyal to me. When people belied me, she believed in me, when people were afraid to help me, she stood by me like a rock; she was my best companion and bore my children.' Was he then a sensuous man? Or a caring husband?

After the death of Khadijah, Muhammad was in great distress. On the one hand, he was harassed and persecuted by the pagan leaders of Mecca, and on the other his domestic life was in a shambles. The children were young, and there was no one to look after them. Friends prevailed upon him to take another wife, and though he hesitated at first, he eventually agreed. His second wife, Sauda, was also a widow. Along with her late husband, she was one of Muhammad's early followers and, on his advice, had migrated to Abyssinia. On their return, the husband died. Sauda was past forty when the Prophet took her as his wife to look after his young daughters. She had a son from her first husband but had no children by the Prophet.

His third wife, Aisha, was the daughter of his closest Companion, Abu Bakr, the first caliph. Abu Bakr wanted to thus cement their friendship, but was hesitant because Aisha was very young. Muhammad was also reluctant, but he finally agreed to marry her. According to Ibn Sa'd, Aisha was nine years old when the betrothal took place, and they were married a few years later when Aisha reached puberty. Aisha's age at the time of the marriage is disputed, but recent analysis puts it at fifteen and not, as some have suggested, eleven. However, what is important to note is that what pleased the Prophet was her intelligence and not her beauty.

On one occasion, Aisha briefly left the caravan in which she was accompanying the Prophet, to answer the call of nature; while returning she lost her necklace. As she went in search of it, the caravan departed without anyone realizing that she was left behind. A young Arab, Safwan, found her waiting on one side of the road; recognizing who she was, he gave her a lift on his camel. Her detractors spread the scandal that Aisha had deliberately stayed behind; false allegations were whispered against her character. On hearing these, the Prophet was much distressed; for almost a month he did not speak to her. Then the revelation came exonerating Aisha; it contained not only punishment for adultery but also for slanderers, who attacked the character of a chaste woman. This incident created quite a crisis in the Prophet's life; its implications were serious enough for Allah to give the guidelines to the faithful.

Muhammad's relationship with Aisha was different from that of his other wives; it was more intellectual than sensuous. Traditionists describe her as the Prophet's favourite wife, but that is wrong. The Quran enjoins that all wives are to be treated equally. Muhammad was indulgent towards her because Aisha loved to talk and argue with her husband, of whom she was an eager pupil. She took pride in the fact that most of the revelations in Medina came while she was with the Prophet, which she saw as a special favour from Allah. She narrated more than two thousand sayings and anecdotes of the Prophet, and these form the bedrock of traditional Islam. A lady of strong will and iron determination, she was possessed of sterling character which she guarded even after her husband's death. Rushdie's depiction of her in his novel is, therefore, not only baseless and unfair but also highly defamatory. She was at times impulsive and occasionally abrasive; her wit and sarcasm often had the better of her wisdom. But she was a good companion, a devoted wife, and even after Muhammad's death continued to be a great source of strength and inspiration to Muslims. She bore no children and died at the age of sixty-six. According to the orientalist D. S. Margoliouth, 'Of the entire number of inmates, Aisha alone, by force of character and keenness of wit, won for herself a place in the political and religious history of Islam.'[4]

Muhammad's fourth wife was Hafsa, the widowed daughter of Umar, the second caliph, who was one of his most trusted Companions. Her first husband was fatally wounded in the Battle of Badr. Umar was extremely attached to her, and he asked his friend Uthman, who later became the third Caliph, to marry her, but he refused. He then asked Abu Bakr, but he also declined. Finding Umar in acute distress, the Prophet took Hafsa as his wife. She was temperamental and prone to fits of jealousy and anger. She did not have a particularly striking disposition, and she did not get on well with the other wives, at times losing her temper even with the Prophet. This is recorded by her father, Umar, in *Sahi al-Bukhari*, the most revered book of traditions. In the words of Umar:

Once my wife argued about a certain matter. I told her 'Who are you to advise me?' She replied, 'You do not allow me to talk about a trifling matter but your daughter has angry exchanges with the Holy Prophet (peace and blessings of Allah be upon him) on all sorts of matters and distresses him all the time.' I got up and went straight to Hafsa and asked her: 'Is it true that you talk angrily with the Holy Prophet (Peace and blessings of Allah be upon him)'. 'Yes, I do,' she replied. I said, 'I warn you against it; Allah will punish you. You should not compete with Aisha.'[5]

Muhammad's fifth wife was Zainab, another widow whose husband died fighting in the cause of God in the Battle of Uhud, which had resulted in the defeat of the Muslims by the Quraish. She was good and kind hearted, devoting herself to the welfare of the poor. She spent most of her time in feeding the destitutes and came to be known as *Umul Masakin*, or mother of the downtrodden. The Prophet was much impressed by her sense of dedication to the cause of the unfortunate Muslims. He took her as a wife, but she died within three months of their marriage, when she was hardly thirty.

The Prophet's sixth wife, Salama, was also a widow. Her husband had succumbed to the injuries he had received during the Battle of Uhud. She came from a distinguished family belonging to Banu Firas. One of the earliest converts to Islam, she did not accompany her husband to Medina because she was not allowed by the Quraish to take her child. It was one of the forms of persecution which the enemies of the Prophet resorted to. After some time she managed to escape, but soon after her migration her husband died, a martyr to the cause of Islam. Pregnant with another child, Salama was heartbroken and distressed. The Prophet sympathized with her lot and offered his hand in marriage. A self-respecting lady, Salama hesitated at first, as she had children by her late husband. The Prophet assured her that he would take care of them as his own. She was touched by his thoughtfulness and married him.

Despite the fact that she was attractive, Salama never bothered about her appearance or worldly comforts; her sole concern in life was to practise piety. She fasted three days in a month and often spent the whole night in prayers. She listened to the Prophet with great respect and obeyed him implicitly. On one occasion, he saw her wearing a gold necklace which had been given to her by her parents. When Muhammad showed disapproval of it, she promptly broke it into pieces and distributed the gold among the poor.

Salama was straightforward and outspoken. A friend asked her once about the private life of the Prophet; she said that his private life was no different from his public life. She was the last of the Prophet's wives to die and was witness to the internecine warfare that had gripped the world of Islam.

Muhammad's seventh wife was Zainab. She was a young widow when she migrated to Medina and the Prophet married her to his adopted son, Zaid bin Harith. On their divorce, the Prophet himself married Zainab, who was then thirty-eight years old. This marriage has irked most of Muhammad's detractors, who have criticized it as morally wrong on two grounds. First, it is argued that Zainab, being the wife of the Prophet's adopted son, was like a daughter to him. Second, it is claimed that Muhammad manipulated her divorce so that he could marry her. However, a careful analysis will show that these criticisms are unfounded.

Zaid came as a slave to the Prophet, who emancipated him and declared him his adopted son. He was so fond of Zaid that he even arranged his marriage with the beautiful Zainab, who was a granddaughter of his uncle Abu Talib. Later, it so transpired that Zainab was not happy with her marriage to Zaid because of the disparity in their social status.

The charge that the Prophet was responsible for the divorce is based on a patently unreliable tradition. According to this, the Prophet went to Zaid's house one day, unannounced, and found Zainab on her own. The Prophet was so bewitched by her beauty that he was unable to restrain himself and abruptly left Zaid's house. Since that time he is said to have wanted to marry her. But nothing could be further from the truth. Zainab was no stranger to Muhammad; she was his cousin and he had known her since childhood. It was because of the loss of her first husband that he was keen to rehabilitate her. Had he been so attracted by her beauty, he would not have arranged her marriage with Zaid. Zainab was indeed not happy with Zaid: she resented the fact that she was married to a slave, and looked down upon him and treated him shabbily. Zaid often complained to the Prophet about her behaviour but the

Prophet always cautioned patience. Zainab held the Prophet responsible for her humiliation and pleaded with him that he should marry her to retrieve her position in the eyes of her tribe. So incensed was Zaid with her overbearing manner, that one day in a fit of temper, he divorced her. Zainab's relatives pressed the Prophet to marry her. Muhammad did not agree saying it was unthinkable for him to do so. She was the wife of his son, he said, for among the pagans an adopted son was equal to a natural son. It was then that a revelation came, clarifying the position that an adopted son cannot be a son: filial affiliation has to be natural. Muhammad was thus given permission by Allah to marry Zainab. Until her last days, Zainab retained her pride, refusing to accept help from anyone, not even from the second caliph, Umar, and looking after herself by sewing clothes.

Muhammad's eighth wife, Juwairiya, was the daughter of Harith bin Abi Dirbar, the chief of the powerful tribe of Banu Mustaliq. She was married to a scion of the same tribe, and both her father and husband were inveterate enemies of Muhammad. The father, in particular, had participated in the attack on Medina in the 'Battle of the Trenches'. Juwairiya was obtained as a prisoner of war from this battle. Her father, Harith, approached several Companions to release her on payment of a ransom, but no one obliged him. Finally, he went, rather hesitantly, to Muhammad and told him: 'O Muhammad! it does not behove me, as one of the chiefs of my people, that my daughter should become a maidservant. I beseech you, therefore, to release her. I am prepared to pay the ransom amount.' 'Is this your wish also?' Muhammad asked Juwairiya. Harith turned to her and pleaded that she should not agree to anything that would disgrace her family. 'The best course then will be for the Prophet to marry me,' replied Juwairiya. Harith was pleased with her reply and paid the release money instantly. The Prophet then took her as his wife. The marriage created a reservoir of goodwill among the Muslims for her tribe, and all the other prisoners of war were set free. Aisha grew very fond of Juwairiya and helped her to learn the tenets of Islam. She was a quick learner and she soon became a great devotee of the new faith. Of her personality, Aisha said, 'She exudes charm which no one can resist.'

Ramalah, better known as Umm Habiba, was the ninth wife of Muhammad; she was a daughter of his inveterate enemy Abu Sufiyan, the leader of the pagans of Mecca, and his wife, the fiery Hind. Ramalah and her husband had embraced Islam in defiance of the wishes of her parents. To escape harassment by them, the couple migrated to Abyssinia. There, the husband became a Christian, but Ramalah refused to give up Islam. In the course of time, the husband began leading a life of ease and pleasure; he took to heavy drinking, which resulted in his death. On her return to Mecca, the Prophet felt sorry for Ramalah's plight and married her. He also realized that marriage with her would help the cause of Islam.

He was impressed by the strength of her convictions. She held the Prophet in such reverence that she refused to allow her father to sit on the same bed on which the Prophet sat, thus showing her resentment towards her father for his continued hostility to the Prophet. At the time of their marriage, Ramalah was thirty-eight, and she dedicated every moment of her life to Muhammad's service. She outlived him by more than two decades and died at the age of seventy-three, when her brother Muawiya had taken over the caliphate. Ramalah had two sons from her first husband; she had no children from the Prophet.

Muhammad's tenth wife was Safiyah, who was taken as a prisoner of war in the Battle of Khyber. Her father and mother were Jews belonging to the two leading Jewish families. The father traced his ancestry to the Prophet Aaron, while the mother was a descendant of the famous Jewish tribe of Quraisa. Safiyah, whose original name was Zainab, was married to a well-known Jewish poet Salm bin Mishkam. But they could not get on, so the husband divorced her. Safiyah married again, this time to a Jewish warrior of great repute. She lost him, too, when he was killed in the Battle of Khyber, along with Safiyah's father and the other male members of her family. Safiyah was taken as a prisoner of war and became the maid of one of the Companions. Other Companions objected to this on the grounds that she was the daughter of one of the tribal chiefs and, therefore, she could only be assigned to the Prophet. Zainab also expressed her desire to become a Muslim and marry the chief of the Muslims. That alone, she said, would help restore her dignity and status among her people. The Prophet then mounted her on his camel, covered her with his robe and accepted her as his wife. It was then that he gave her the name Safiyah.

On her arrival in the Prophet's house in Medina, Muhammad asked Aisha if she liked her.

'But she is Jewish!' Aisha replied.

The Prophet reprimanded her: 'So what? She is as good a Muslim as anyone else.'

Once, Umar, during the Prophet's lifetime, asked Safiyah whether she still maintained her Jewish links.

'I observe Friday and not Saturday,' Safiyah told him bluntly, 'but I continue to have affection for my Jewish kith and kin. Islam does not prohibit that.'

Umar was speechless. According to one account, she was very close to Fatimah, the Prophet's daughter and the wife of Ali, the fourth caliph. She bore the Prophet no children and died at the age of sixty. According to another account she had supported Ali's rival, Uthman, the third caliph, in their political wrangling. Safiyah had a mind of her own and maintained her dignity to the last.

Maymunah bin Harith was the eleventh wife of the Prophet. Her first husband divorced her, and her second husband died in tragic circumstances when Maymunah was fifty-one years of age; her condition was thus pitiable. She was the sister-in-law of the Prophet's uncle Abbas, who had been loyal and faithful to the Prophet. Abbas approached Muhammad with the proposal of marriage; Muhammad hesitated but, seeing the disappointment on his uncle's face, he gave in. Khalid bin Walid, the great warrior, who came go be known as the 'Sword of Islam', was Maymunah's nephew. He was also extremely fond of her and wanted her to be properly rehabilitated. This marriage between members of two leading Quraish families created a stir among the pagans, who prevented it being solemnized in Mecca. The ceremony, therefore, did not take place in Mecca but in Sarif, 15 kilometres from Mecca on the road to Medina.

The marriage had special political significance, since it broke the barriers between the various leading tribes. After this union, a number of relatives and supporters of Abbas and Abu Rahim,

Maymunah's deceased husband, embraced Islam, thus swelling the ranks of Muslims. Many of them were warriors. Furthermore, Maymunah, who was of a kind and charitable disposition, liberated many slaves and helped the Prophet in his efforts to bring about an egalitarian society.

The story of Mary, or Maria Qibtiyah, who was presented to the Prophet as a slave by the Archbishop of Alexandria, and whom Muhammad subsequently married, has provided much ammunition for his critics. Sir William Muir, in his *Life of Mahomet*, devoted a chapter to it. He mentions that Muckouckas, the Governor of Alexandria, had sent Muhammad 'two Coptic maids, Shirin and Mary, as a gift' and further that 'the beauty of Mary, whose fair complexion and delicate features were adorned by a profusion of black curling hair, fascinated Mahomet.'[6] It is not known from what source Muir obtained this description of Maria, or Mariyah as she was called after her marriage with the Prophet. Nor is there any evidence that she and her sister Shirin were the gift of the Governor. This again is the invention of Waqidi. The Egyptian biographer of the Prophet, M. H. Haykal, categorically states on the basis of historical data from early Arab sources that the two sisters were the daughters of one of the most respected Coptic leaders, Simon, and were sent to Muhammad by the Archbishop with the request that they should be treated with all the honour due to them. Hence the Prophet married Maria and gave Shirin in marriage to one of his Companions, Hassan ibn Thabit. It would have been an act of discourtesy on Muhammad's part to have kept them as slaves. After Khadijah, Maria was the only other wife who bore him a child, a son named Ibrahim, who died within two months of his birth. Maria could not bear the loss, and died a few years later.[7]

From these accounts it can be seen that none of the Prophet's marriages was for carnal pleasure. His first wife, Khadijah, was fifteen years older than him; his second, Sauda, was nearing forty when he married her to provide a mother for his four daughters, who were then very young; Aisha and Hafsa were the daughters of his closest Companions, Abu Bakr and Umar, who, following Arab custom, wished to thus cement their close relationship with the Prophet. Zainab bint Khusaymah was the widow of one of the martyrs in the Battle of Uhud, in which seventy Muslim wives had become widows. Muhammad wanted to set an example for the faithful to follow. Salama was the first Muslim woman to migrate to Medina; her husband gave his life in the Battle of Uhud, and their first child had been tortured by the pagans. Zainab bint Jahsh, a cousin, had been given in marriage by the Prophet to his slave Zaid. Zainab could not get on with Zaid, and insisted on Muhammad marrying her to restore her status. Juwairiya and Safiyah were Jewish prisoners of war belonging to two of the most distinguished Jewish tribes; Ramalah was the daughter of Abu Sufiyan, the leader of the pagan Quraish; and Maymunah was the widowed sister-in-law of his uncle Abbas and the aunt of one of the greatest army commanders of Islam. Maria came from the Archbishop of Alexander and was the daughter of one of the foremost Copt leaders. Most of these women were around forty or fifty and were thus past their prime when Muhammad married them; they had been divorced or widowed two or three times, and most of them had children from their previous husbands. Except Khadijah and Maria, none of the wives bore Muhammad any children.

These facts conclusively establish that the marriages of the Prophet were contracted for social or political purposes or on humanitarian grounds to further the cause which was closest to his heart.

The Prophet treated his wives well; he met every wife in turn, alloting a day to each. He also took each of them in turn on his journeys outside Medina. By his conduct, he set an example to Muslims in equality of treatment to their wives, which the Quran enjoins upon them. His wives lived with him in mud houses on a diet of water and dates. Very often there was nothing to eat in the house, but he told them that if they wanted comforts he would gladly release them of their marital bonds. However, they preferred suffering hardship to leaving him.

Professor Hitti writes: 'Even in the height of his glory Muhammad led, as in his days of obscurity, an unpretentious life. He was often seen mending his own clothes and was at all times within the reach of his people.' [8] When did he have the time for pleasure? Even Watt had to concede, although grudgingly, that 'Though later Muslims might produce colourful stories of Muhammad's susceptibility to feminine charm, and though there is no reason to suppose that he disregarded the factor of physical attraction, it is practically certain that he had his feelings towards the fair sex well under control, and that he did not enter into marriages except when they were politically and socially desirable.'[9]

To accuse such a man of being a voluptuary is patently unfair. The Prophet's wives, from all the evidence we have, were women of character; they led a pious life and many of them were of noble lineage. Even after the Prophet's death, they lived simply and practised utmost piety. No scandal has ever been reported about any of them, yet Rushdie links their names to the inmates of a brothel. Is it freedom of expression or licence to wound the hearts of those who revere these simple, pious wives of their Prophet as their mothers?

Unfortunately, Rushdie has taken advantage of spurious traditions concocted by some Muslim traditionists, ever eager to emphasize the manliness of the Prophet; they were also trying to provide a religious cover for the sexual pursuits of their patrons. These traditions conform neither to the nature of the Prophet's marriages, nor to the reality of his relationship with his wives. As a result of these spurious versions, on which the orientalists have feasted, there has been a strong reaction among a section of Muslims. Imam Rashad Khalifa, a Saudi Arabian theologian, has gone to the extent of opining, after considerable research in original sources, that 'the extremely popular *Hadith* [Traditions] and *Sunna* [Practices] have nothing to do with Prophet Muhammad', and further that obedience to them is tantamount to a 'flagrant disobedience of God and His final Prophet'. He quotes the verses 6:112 and 25:31 of the Quran in his support and contends that these 'traditions are "Satanic inventions"'.[10]

The charge that Muhammad had concubines is preposterous; this would have been a negation of the Quranic injunction, which provides the harshest punishment for illegitimate fornication; even in respect of slave-girls, marriage is compulsory for sexual gratification. Some jurists have relied on certain earlier verses of the Quran (23:5–6 and 70:29,30) for permission to have concubines, but most jurists are of the firm view that these were superseded by later verses, which declared every illegitimate sexual act punishable as a sin. One of these is categorical:

> The woman and the man
> Guilty of adultery or fornication,
> Flog each of them with a hundred stripes.
> Let not compassion deter you
> In a matter prescribed by Allah
> If you believe in Him and the Last Day.
> And let a party of believers
> witness their punishment.
>
> (24:2)

Unfortunately for Islam, what the Quran prescribed and the Prophet practised most Muslim rulers defied with impunity, and to ease their conscience had traditions concocted in Muhammad's name, which did considerable damage to his image and provided colourful material for slander.

We must not forget that the Quran dealt as much with current problems as with issues of fundamental and lasting significance. The 'occasions of revelations', to which I have referred earlier, give a key to the understanding of the situations as they prevailed at that time. Hence Muhammad's multiple marriages have to be viewed in the light of the circumstances and the requirements of the times in which he lived. To quote the British biographer of the Prophet, R. V. C. Bodley:

Muhammad's married life must not be looked at from an occidental point of view or from that set by Christians. They were living at a period and in a country where the only known ethical standards were theirs.

Bodley asks why the codes of Europe and America should be considered superior to those of Asia and Africa. He comments that until the people in the West 'can prove that their way of living is on a higher moral standard than anybody else's they should reserve judgement on other creeds and castes and countries.'[11]

The problem is that even now, when a lot of objective and sympathetic works on Islam, based on the latest research, have been published, the mind of the common non-Muslim is not yet free of old prejudices. The Christian, in particular, is far from convinced of

Muhammad's status as a prophet. He continues to believe that while Christ was a celibate, Muhammad was a polygamist; while Christ was sincere, Muhammad was a hypocrite; while Christ preached love and peace, Muhammad propagated hatred and war; while Christ laid down his life for the redemption of the human race, Muhammad resorted to violence to suppress his fellow beings. Rushdie has reinforced these prejudices and given them a new and more alluring form.

These prejudices are also a result of the rather lopsided emphasis that Christian clerics have placed on certain values such as love, compassion and celibacy, to the detriment of a holistic view of human life. These are, no doubt, worthy ideals, but human experience over the millennia has shown that their opposites, too, cannot be ignored. Human 'weaknesses' have often kept pace with human 'strengths' in the progress of mankind. History is indeed the product of the interaction between them. Many of the greatest warriors have not only brought glory to their communities but have also promoted intercourse between diverse peoples by the very fact of their conquests, and therefore the rise of great civilizations has, sometimes, been due to their cruel and ruthless adventures. Likewise, several poets, writers, scientists and explorers can be condemned as profligates, if we take a one-sided, supposedly moral view of their personal lives.

Similarly, there exists racial discrimination in the same West and its offshoots that proclaim and seek to practise the noble concepts of love and brotherhood. It also cannot be seriously disputed that one reason for widespread promiscuity in Europe and America is the Christian insistence on the laudable principle of monogamy. Indeed, it will not be much of an exaggeration to say that Christian beliefs are cracking up more among Christians than non-Christians. The value of celibacy among the Catholic clergy itself has, for instance, come to be challenged and so also the Vatican's continuing opposition to abortion and other birth-control measures. It is notable that despite the experience of two millennia and contact with other civilizations, Christian theology refuses to recognize that spirit and matter are not opposites but complementary to each other, and that both are the gifts of God in his munificence. The result is that redemption continues to be regarded in the Christian West as being contingent on the spirit of man freeing itself from the clutches of matter. St Peter preached that flesh is the source of all evils; but without flesh, man would not be there. And why did God create matter if matter was all evil? As E. Barker and R. Preston have asserted, like many other earnest Christian thinkers before them, the standards affirmed in the New Testament 'are unattainable'; they are inapplicable 'to our everyday concerns'.

Islam, on the other hand, takes a more holistic and realistic view of life. It rejects the doctrine of the Original Sin and all that goes with it. The Prophet himself lived in a way that his followers could emulate. According to one tradition, some of his Companions boasted of leading pious lives. The first said he did not marry; the second that he did not eat meat; the third that he slept on bare ground; and the fourth that he fasted all the time. The Prophet told them, 'Praise be to Allah! I am married and I lead a pious life. I eat meat and I also fast. I sleep and I also keep awake.'

Thus he struck a balance and emphasized that religious activity had to be combined with worldly pursuits. He neither gave excessive credence to material things nor did he undermine the significance of spiritual bliss. He deprecated the acquisition of wealth and 'the glitter of the world' but did not favour asceticism or renunciation. He did not divide life between God and Caesar. That is the basic difference in the approaches of Muhammad and Christ. Islam does not encourage extremism in human behaviour; it favours neither mortification of the flesh nor indulgence; it prefers monogamy but does not insist on it; it allows war under certain conditions but its central message is one of submission to God and of peace. In short, it seeks to regulate human conduct according to man's inherent capacity, requirement and limitation, but it refuses to radically transform human nature, as it is neither physically feasible nor spiritually desirable.

As I have said earlier, scholars and historians from Raymond to Mark of Toledo, from Roger Bacon to William Muir, from Dante to Voltaire, have cast aspersions on the Prophet's divine mission and painted him in the worst colours. To many of them, he was not only not a man of God – much less a prophet – but also not a desirable human being. The list of his detractors is long; it includes some of the greatest names in the West. However, both Muhammad and his religion have survived their onslaught; in the last fifteen hundred years Islam has attracted more converts in every age and in every land than any other religion. History shows that the more Islam is suppressed the stronger it becomes.

One of the best tributes to the role of Muhammad in the uplift of man has been paid by the highly respected French scholar Regis Blachere, in his book *Le probleme de Mahomet*:

Neither indifference, nor wounds to his self-respect, nor wrong done to his material interests, nor intrigues nor threats, nor above all, the many offers of compromise made by the pagans, were able to deflect him from his mission. In the gravest hour – the Quran bears witness – he could retain his balanced judgement, revive the courage of his followers, and close his eyes to slight faults in order the better to destroy treason. As a true leader of men, he knew how to choose his advisers, turning to account the faithfulness of 'Ali, the moderation of Abu Bakr, the energy of 'Umar and the resilience of Uthman. He had no illusions about men, and never failed to remind them of their duty and their vocation. Better than anyone, too, he knew the faults and virtues of the people among whom he was born. This inspired man, who never for a day had thought of succeeding without God's help, yet knew how to look into the future and to measure the strength and weakness of his adversary. Whatever may be said of him, he was a good and generous man. At the taking of Mecca, his clemency was more than a political act. Hagiography, as always, has done a bad turn to its hero. With its *naïveté*, its miracles to order and its insipidity, it is forced, in order to satisfy popular needs, to raise to the role of miracle-worker, one who, the Quran never ceased to repeat, was a mortal like all other men. If, at his last hour, Muhammad had asked himself about the success of his mission, he could have passed to his rest in the serenity of knowing that he had fulfilled his task.[12]

In fulfilling that task, his best instrument has been the Quran, which he bequeathed to his followers so that they could mould their lives in accordance with its precepts. However, it was this Book that William Gladstone, the British Prime Minister, held in his hand and declared in the House of Commons: 'So long as there is this book, there will be no peace in the world.' His wrath was on the Ottoman Turks, who were challenging the might of Christian

Europe, but he visited it on the Quran which he admitted he had not read. Prejudices do not die; they thrive on hostility and affect the judgement of even the best of persons. Ignorance breeds them.

PART II

QURANIC VERSES

In the name of Allah, the
Beneficent, the Merciful

AN EXPLANATORY STATEMENT

The Quran literally means 'Reading'; it is a collection of the revelations that descended from God to Muhammad through arch-angel Gabriel. The total reverence of Muslims for their Holy Book baffles non-Muslims. However, this has to be seen in the context of the unflinching faith in God that is the basis of Islam. As Professor Caesar E. Farah of the University of Minnesota points out,

it would be difficult to observe a more thorough manifestation of devotion to God than is evinced by the followers of Islam. No other religion appears to inculcate as much dependence on God in the trivia of daily life; nor does God figure so centrally among other religious groups in the ups and downs of ordinary living. Indeed, no task, commitment, performance, journey or repose, however minute or momentous, pleasurable or unpleasurable, is undertaken without the involvement of Allah. No blessing or bounty of any sort is received except through the grace of Allah. Misfortunes are endured with passivity and resignation, but faith in Allah remains unwavering, as it is His sole prerogative to bestow or withhold as He sees fit.[1]

The Quran was revealed in the Arabic language, and its immediate audience were the Arabs of west-central Arabia in the seventh century. But it has universal appeal; even the admonitions and injunctions that were issued for local consumption contain a moral or a message which conforms to the basic approach of the Quran, as do the historical sections, in which stories regarding previous prophets are told so as to draw lasting ethical or moral conclusions. There is, however, a juxtaposition of the local, historical, allegorical and fundamental verses, which often confuses the uninitiated reader.

The Quran is not a conventional book. Its contents are not

arranged in a systematic manner, and there is repetition of topics, ideas and arguments. Sometimes a new theme is introduced without any apparent connection to the preceding text. The problems of philosophy and metaphysics are dealt with from an uncommon angle, as are historical events. As Maulana Maududi explains, 'That is why an unwary reader is baffled and puzzled when he finds all these things contrary to his preconceived notion of a book.' This happens because he is unaware of the historical relevance of its promulgation and its unique nature. Hence it is necessary to understand properly the Quran's background and the method and manner of its teachings.

The Quran is a mingling of the spiritual and the material, the divine and the mundane; it covers everything from the sun to the moth. It explains a moral in a verse, which might ordinarily take a whole book, it enunciates a principle from several angles and attacks a wrong from a multitude of directions. And yet its main values are put forth not only unambiguously but in a forceful manner. These are, in a sense its quintessence. They symbolize the spirit of its teachings. The Quran itself puts it thus:

> God has sent down the Book,
> In it, are verses, basic or fundamental,
> That form its foundation.
> There are others
> Which are allegorical.
>
> (3:7)

This passage gives us an important clue to the interpretation of the Quran. Broadly speaking, the Quranic verses, which are intertwined and are not in any specific order, have to be separated so as to classify them under two broad categories: (1) the nucleus or foundation of the Book, literally 'the mother of the Book'; and (2) the part that is figurative, metaphorical, allegorical or historical. The first part contains principles and morals, injunctions and directions, warnings and blessings. They embody universal truths, though they were given a local colour so as to be comprehensible to those to whom they were addressed. The second part is the more difficult to follow. Some theologians describe it as mysterious, and it needs the exercise of ingenuity by the reader to understand its inner meaning.

It has parables, allegories and anecdotes that need to be explained and interpreted, and from which moral guidance again emerges. It is in the nature of a covering for the kernel of the Quran.

The fundamental verses constitute what is called *muhkamat*, or precise, exact and clear pieces which contain a definite approach or direction. As Maududi explains, these are

those verses of the Quran which have been so couched as to make their meaning quite plain without any shade or ambiguity. They have been purposely so worded; hence there is little scope for misinterpretation. These verses constitute the fundamental principles of the Book; they and they alone determine the aim and object for which the Quran has been sent down. They invite the world to the true path of Islam, teach the believers morals and give them warnings and directions. They refute wrong beliefs and practices and lay down the right way of living. They expound the principles of religion and its beliefs and practices, morals and duties, commandments and prohibitions. Therefore, a seeker of truth should turn to these verses as these alone can satisfy his needs. Naturally, such a person will concentrate on these verses and endeavour to derive the greatest benefit from them.[2]

Professor Mahmud Shaltout of Al-Azhar, Cairo, is equally unequivocal:

The texts which could have more than one meaning are concerned with subsidiary aspects of Islam but not its fundamentals and have given rise to a plurality of Muslim theories and attitudes which are more or less personal points of view and are far from being obligatory.[3]

The allegorical or mysterious verses are called *mutashabihat*. Their main object is to bring home to the reader the reality of the existence of God and man's obligation to Him through historical events, allegorical anecdotes and interesting parables, and by the interaction of natural and supernatural objects. They compress within a few verses a mine of information dealing with a variety of subjects, expressed in sometimes vague, sometimes transcendental, language. Maulana Abul Kalam Azad, the great Muslim savant of the Indo-Pakistan subcontinent, has explained it thus:

What come under *mutashabihat* are all those aspects of life which are beyond the reach of human intellect and cannot be perceived through the senses, or brought within the purview of positive knowledge.[4]

Most commentators have warned that any disquisition on *mutashabihat* invariably leads to misinterpretations. How then do we get to the real meaning? That is a task for the learned exegetists and commentators, but even they have not always been successful. The best course, therefore, for those who are interested in the essence and the basic teachings of the Quran, is to concentrate, as both Maududi and Azad have advised, on the fundamental verses, which are clear and unambiguous and within the comprehension of the ordinary reader, leaving the complex verses to the learned to unravel. 'Instead of hair-splitting and probing into their meaning,' to quote Maududi, the reader should look at the Quran as a whole and draw the best out of it for his guidance.

Maulana Rumi, whose *Mathnavi*, or book of mystical poems, has been characterized as 'the Quran in the Persian language', has been of the same view, though he has expressed it in words which may shock the faithful:

> Out of the Quran I draw the marrow
> And throw away the bones to the dogs.[5]

The reference to 'dogs' is to those who quibble unnecessarily on superficial issues; it is not used in a derogatory sense.

I have tried to make a selection of those verses of the Quran which, I feel, are basic and fundamental; I may have erred in doing so. The selection is, I admit, not traditional. From each of the 114 chapters of the Quran I have selected verses that reflect, in my opinion, the spirit of Islam. In all, there are 6,666 verses in the Quran, divided into chapters that are of varying length.

The Book, as has already been noted, was sent down in stages; as soon as the revelations were received by Muhammad, he repeated them word by word to his followers. They were immediately learnt by heart by those who heard them. Hence, it is proudly claimed by Muslims that they were preserved in the hearts of the faithful. Apart from this, they were also written on stone, parchment, papyrus, palm leaves, and even on ribs of animals and pieces of leather, after they had been dictated by the Prophet to some of his Companions.

Salman Rushdie makes a reference in *Satanic Verses* to one

occasion, when Abdallah ibn Abisarah, one of the five scribes to whom the Prophet had entrusted the task of taking down the revelations in Medina, inserted a few words of his own into the revelation, pointing out to Muhammad that it sounded better thus. Muhammad, it is reported, accepted the change. As a result, Abdallah lost faith in the divinity of the Quran, gave up Islam, returned to Mecca and joined the pagans. However, on the conquest of Mecca, he expressed regret to the Prophet, who pardoned him on the intervention of his son-in-law, Uthman. This is a story based on a tradition recorded by Ibn Hisham. But there is no corroboration of it. None of the four other scribes ever made such a charge against the Prophet. Richard Bell relies on Ibn Hisham and says, 'That does not look like an invented story'. But that is precisely what it is. Bukhari and Muslim, the two most reliable recorders of the traditions, have shown that out of every hundred traditions, current in their times, ninety-nine were invented and did not have the remotest basis in fact. Alfred Guillaume mentions in his book *The Traditions of Islam* that Abu Daud (817–888), a pupil of Imam Hanbal and one of the six most respected recorders of traditions, 'wrote down half a million Hadith, from which he selected 4,800'. Spurious traditions make a mockery of history; the one in question was obviously circulated by the Prophet's detractors, and some of the traditionists, unwittingly, recorded it without a proper check. The pity is that the orientalists have pounced upon it to cast doubt on the divinity of the Quran.

During the Prophet's lifetime there was no systematic collection of the revelations: they were not recorded in book form. The revelations were preserved in the memories of the Companions who were aware of the arrangement and the order of their placement. The work of proper collection was started by Abu Bakr, the first caliph (632–634), at the instance of Umar, who later succeeded him as the second caliph (634–644). Umar was alarmed when he found that due to the death of a number of Companions, either in wars or through natural causes, the number of Quran readers had been fast dwindling. This, he feared, might result in an irretrievable loss of the Quranic verses. The task of collation was entrusted to Zaid bin Thabit, who had been the Prophet's secretary and a scribe.

He wrote down the revelations on sheets of equal size, in the order the Prophet had recited them, and handed over the collection to Abu Bakr. On the latter's death, it was taken over by his successor, Umar, who handed it for safe-keeping to his daughter Hafsa, a widow of the Prophet.

On Umar's death, when Uthman became the caliph (644–655), disputes arose in different parts of the Caliphate about the reading of the Quranic verses. As the Quran is the earliest Arabic text committed to writing, the vowels therein were unmarked, with the result that the verses were read by different groups each with their peculiar pronunciation.

Uthman asked Zaid to consult three other leading Companions to finalize the manner of the reading of the Quran by adopting the dialect of Quraish, the tribe to which the Prophet belonged. Thus an official text was prepared and sent to different parts of the Caliphate. Uthman also ordered that all other copies of the Quran that were in circulation should be destroyed. This compilation of the Quran brought about much-needed uniformity not only in the text but also in its reading. It has remained intact ever since, and it is this Quran which has come to us without any change. There was, however, still the problem of the inadequacy of the script, which was set right in the reign of Abdal Malik, the Umayyid caliph (685–690); even then, some differences persisted which were finally sorted out only by the end of the ninth century.

The codification of the Quran, with its emphasis on textual accuracy, helped greatly to eliminate mispronunciations, but it was not possible to impose a uniform chanting style on the faithful in different parts of the Caliphate, consisting now of more non-Arabs than Arabs. The Prophet himself had not encouraged such uniformity, because he was aware that different tribes pronounced words in different ways; he therefore left each tribe to recite the Quran in its own style. By the time of Uthman, diverse styles, both Arab and non-Arab, had developed, and eventually these were reduced to seven *qiraat*, or chanting styles, which have received orthodox recognition. The textual reading had to be the same, although the pronunciation could be different.

The Book has several names, but it is commonly referred to as 'al-Quran'. In the Quran, God mainly addresses Himself to Muhammad. Sometimes, He uses the singular 'I', and sometimes the plural 'We'. Often, He refers to himself as 'Allah' or 'Rehman', or by other names − according to a tradition there are ninety-nine names for Allah. In such cases he speaks in the third person. God also speaks directly to man, both the believer and the non-believer. So the form varies, depending on the situation and the nature of the revelation. Of the verses addressed to the Prophet, some are of a personal nature, but most are of general interest, dealing with ethical principles or fundamental values, outlining a code of human conduct. These are interspersed with parables and tales of earlier prophets.

The language of the Quran is Arabic. Allah says, 'We have made it an Arabic Quran so that you [Arabs] may understand the truth' (43:3). Since the immediate addressees to whom the Message was being transmitted were Arabs, it had to be conveyed in their language. This does not mean that Allah's language is Arabic, as some Muslim theologians claim. He uses whatever instrument He pleases.

There are numerous references in the Quran to earlier prophets, and many of these are familiar from the Old Testament. Because these are recounted in the Quran, the charge is often made by Christian and Jewish clerics that Muhammad borrowed them from their scriptures. This is intended to prove that he was the author of the Quran, and not God. The orientalists have also made similar allegations. But the Quran itself has clarified this to Muhammad: 'Nothing is said to you which was not said by us to apostles before you' (41:43); further, that in the former prophets 'you have a good example to follow' (40:6). As for the stories, God explains:

> Stories of Our apostles
> That We narrate to you,
> All have one object:
> To make your heart stout
> In the pursuit of truth.
> They provide both an exhortation
> And a lesson to believers.

(11:120)

In view of these statements, how would the accounts of the former prophets in the Quran be different from the versions of the Bible and the Torah? The Quran accepts these as divine revelations, though it disapproved of the later accretions in them which dilute the monotheistic creed and their original purity.

After the death of the Prophet, his followers increasingly felt the need to understand correctly the content and context of the various Quranic verses. With every age their interpretations multiplied. Conflicts arose on not only points of language but also of nuance; not only on personal allusions but also on eschatological descriptions. Tabari was one of the first to produce a commentary, thirty volumes long, on the Quran; then there was the work of Waqidi (d. 1075). They were followed by Zamakshari (d. 1143), whose forte was the correct grammarian understanding of the text, and Imam al-Razi (d. 1209), who specialized in philosophical discussion of the inner meanings of Quranic verses. A century later came al-Baidauwi (d. 1286), whose comprehensive commentary, incorporating various interpretations, has become a standard work. Since then, hundreds of *tafsir*, or commentaries, by eminent theologians and scholars have appeared in every country, in every age and in every language, with the result that there is such a mass of literature that the understanding of the Quran is made even more difficult.

The Quran deals with varied subjects. Broadly, they can be classified under three headings: (1) *tauhid*, or the unity of God; (2) *qassasul ambia*, or histories of earlier prophets; and (3) *dinyaat*, or rules and regulations for human behaviour. Some theologians have divided them as *tauhid*, *tadkir* (which means exhortations arising out of the histories of prophets or the crises that Muhammad faced), and *ahkam*, or commandments.

Muslims revere the Quran as a miracle, unmatched and unparalleled; because of its rhymed prose, force of imagery and turns of phrase, its contents are regarded by them as full of wisdom. To quote Imam Ghazzali,

the verses of the Quran, in relation to intelligence, have the value of sunlight in relation to the eyesight, to wit, it is by this sunlight that the act of seeing is accomplished.[6]

The Quran is accepted without qualification by Sunnis as well as

Shias, and by every sect and school in Islam. As G. E. von Grunebaum writes,

Such common ground does not prevent fission, but it does offer a large measure of conceptual and imaginative homogeneity and a universally accepted framework for value judgements. The Book guarantees a measure of mutual understandability, if not understanding, and a spiritual refuge in which to recover from the strain of reality and to gain strength for yet another attempt to reorganize this refractory world under God.[7]

The first revelation descended on Muhammad while he was meditating on Mount Hira, in the month of Ramadan in his fortieth year. He saw before him a dazzling white figure. It was the archangel Gabriel, who said to him, '*Iqra*' ['Read'].

'*Ma ana bi-quari*' ['I am not a reader'], he replied.

Gabriel took hold of him, pressed him hard, and insisted again that he read. Muhammad once again replied that he could not read. Then Gabriel spoke and asked him to repeat after him:

> Proclaim the name of your Lord
> Who is the Creator and
> Cherisher of all.
> He created man
> Out of a clot of blood.
> Proclaim the glory of your Lord
> Who is the most bountiful.
> He taught man the use of his pen.
> Taught him what he did not know.
>
> (96:1–5)

Thus the first revelation extolled the power of the pen. It shook the unlettered man to whom they were addressed. Trembling, he went home and told his wife Khadijah what had happened. A spirit, he said, had gripped him; he felt nervous and distraught. Khadijah comforted him and assured him that he was the chosen one of God, and instantly declared herself his first disciple.

That was the beginning of his divine mission. Thereafter, revelations came to him one after the other. Ali, his first cousin and still in his teens, and the middle-aged Abu Bakr, his closest friend, joined the ranks of his followers. Slowly, others followed in their footsteps, but not until three years had elapsed did God ask Muhammad to publicly proclaim the faith which came to be known as Islam, demanding the worship of only one God and the abjuring of the worship of idols, which was the prevalent religion. His own kith and kin in the tribe of Quraish, who were the leaders of idol-worshippers, mounted a campaign of damnation and persecution against him. He had, so far, been an ordinary member of his family, an orphan, with little resources; his detractors were powerful men of enormous wealth and influence. Despite the odds, Muhammad persisted; God gave him courage through his revelations and assured him:

> By the glorious
>   hours of the dawn
> And the still darkness
>   of the night.
> Your Lord has neither forsaken you,
> Nor is He displeased with you.
> Verily, what is to come
>   in the future
> Is better for you
> Than what has happened.
> For your Lord will give you
> Whatever will please you.
> Did He not find you an orphan
> and provide shelter for you?
> Did He not find you confused
> And show you clear direction?
> You were poor and
> He blessed you with riches.
> Hence do not ill-treat an orphan,
> Nor turn away the beggar.
> Proclaim the favours of your Lord
> And recite His praises.

(93:1–11)

The Prophet was also advised to go about his task unmindful of the attacks on him. He was not to retaliate nor fight his detractors. He was clearly told: 'If they accuse you of imposture, so were prophets who came before you' (3:184). Likewise, the revelations to earlier prophets were confirmed by the Quran:

This Quran given to you, O Muhammad,
Is, indeed, Our creation.
No one else can produce it.
In it is confirmation of Our message
Sent to earlier messengers
And an elaboration of the same truth
That the Lord of the Worlds
Has revealed from time to time.

(10:37)

Belief in life after death is common to all religions; the Quran affirms:

Life of this world attracts disbelievers
And they scoff and mock at believers.
But on the Day of Resurrection
Those who are pious shall rise above them.
For God showers His bounties
On those whom He pleases.

(2:212)

The Quran emphasizes freedom of worship:

Let there be no compulsion in religion.
For this is the truth, which stands
   out from error,
That whoever rejects evil and believes in God
Shall grasp the most dependable handle.

(2:256)

Disbelievers were told that they were free to go their own way:

Tell the
   disbelievers:
'I do not worship
What you worship,
Nor do you worship
What I worship.
I will not worship
What you worship,
Nor will you worship

> What I worship.
> To you, your religion,
> And to me, mine.'
> (109:1–6)

Furthermore, idols were not to be reviled lest the idolaters reviled God in retaliation (6:108).

The faithful are required to fulfil five obligations, called 'the pillars of Islam'. First, *shahada*, or the declaration of belief in the unity of God and the prophethood of Muhammad:

> And your God is one,
> He has no other associate.
> (2:163)

This is to be enforced with belief in His Prophet:

> Muhammad is the Messenger of God.
> (48:29)

These two declarations together constitute the first article of a Muslim's faith.

Second, the faithful must pray, preferably in a mosque, five times a day, at dawn, noon, afternoon, evening and night:

> Celebrate the religious service
> And pray at two ends of the day
> And at the approaches of the night.
> (11:114)

There is a dispute whether prayers are to be performed five times or three times a day: Sunnis believe it to be five; Shias, by and large, consider it is three. The Quran also enjoins that a Muslim should do ablutions and purify himself before he prays:

> O Believers! Before you go for prayers,
> Wash your faces, your arms, including your elbows,
> And also your feet up to your ankles,
> And pass your wet hands over your heads.
> In case you are in a state of pollution,
> Purify yourself before the service.
> (3:6)

Third, a fast must be observed from sunrise to sunset every day in the month of Ramadan, when a Muslim is not to eat food or drink even a drop of water:

> O Believers! It is prescribed for you
> That you should fast a definite number of days.
>
> (2:185)

Ramadan was the month in which the Quran was first revealed. The object of fasting is clearly stated:

> O, you who believe in Us!
> Fasting is prescribed to you
> As it was prescribed to those before,
> So that you may learn
> Self-restraint.
>
> (2:183)

The period of the fast is also mentioned:

> Eat and drink until a white thread from a black one
> Can be distinguished by you at dawn,
> And then continue to fast until the night.
>
> (2:187)

At the end of the month of fasting, Muslims celebrate the completion of their process of purification by the festival of Id, known as *Ramadan Id*, or more correctly, *Idul Fitr*.

Fourth, payment of *zakat*, or alms, must be made for the welfare of the poor, out of a faithful's assets. The Quran explains:

> Alms are meant for the poor and the needy . . .
> This is ordained by God.
>
> (9:60)

There are differences about the exact amount and the manner of its giving, whether an individual has to decide it by himself or whether the State can levy a particular percentage of his assets.

Finally, a pilgrimage to Mecca to perform *Hajj*, or religious rites, in the Kaaba, must be undertaken at least once in a lifetime, unless one is unable to due to financial reasons or physical disability:

> Fulfil the pilgrimage to Mecca
> For the love of your Lord.
>
> (2:196)

The last act of the pilgrimage is to make an offering to Allah in the form of the sacrifice of an animal. However, it is made clear that

> It is not the animal's flesh
> Nor his blood
> That reaches God.
> It is man's piety.
>
> (22:37)

Those Muslims who are away from Mecca, be they anywhere in the world, also make the same offering on the day of *Id* which is the culmination of the pilgrimage. This *Id* is, therefore, called the Festival of Sacrifice, or *Idul Duha* (more popularly, *Id Qurban*).

These are the five main obligatory duties that constitute the spiritual discipline for keeping a Muslim on the right path. There are also some others like praying in a congregation every Friday. The Quranic admonition in this regard is as follows:

> Believers, when the call is given
> For prayers on Friday,
> Hasten in earnest
> To remember your God
> And leave your business.
> That is best for all.
> And when prayers are over
> Then disperse quietly
> And seek Allah's bounty.
> Celebrate His praises
> So that you may prosper.
>
> (62:9–10)

The congregational prayers to celebrate the two festivals of *Id* are not mentioned in the Quran; they are, therefore, not obligatory. However, they have a social significance and are commonly accepted by the faithful as a demonstration of Islam's unity and of Muslim brotherhood.

The forms and rituals are not prescribed by the Quran, but they have come down from traditions and practices of the Prophet and are therefore as compulsory as the requirements mentioned in the Quran. The Quran is not only a spiritual guide, a code of ethics and a handbook of morals, but it also contains rules and regulations for the day-to-day affairs of the world, covering diverse fields, such as social conduct, marriage, divorce, inheritance, usury and even theft, adultery and murder. I have not included the verses pertaining to these in this book, though according to most exegetists they are a vital part of the fundamental verses. However, they are relevant only to Muslims, and I have tried to confine myself in the selection to such verses as will be of interest and benefit to all.

But the salient features of the commandments and rules and regulations of the Quran need to be spelt out, because without them the Quran cannot be fully grasped. They are covered in less than 300 verses. Some of them are mandatory, some optional. Of the verses, thirty contain penal provisions, seventy cover civil offences, thirteen relate to juridical and procedural matters, seventy deal with family and personal laws, and twenty cover economic dealings.

Professor N. J. Coulson has observed that the verses which call for legal action 'are predominantly ethical in quality', but their number is 'extremely limited'. No more than 'approximately eighty verses deal with legal topics in the strict sense of the term'.[8] They are concerned with such offences as murder, armed robbery, apostasy, theft, fornication, adultery and slander against a chaste woman.

As regards the laws pertaining to marriage, divorce and inheritance, which form the basis of Muslim Personal Law, the Quranic directions are rather broad-based; not all of them are easily enforceable. They are capable of complex implications and have resulted in a variety of interpretations, sometimes expressing opposite meanings.

Take, for instance, the verses in respect of polygamy:

> Marry women who seem good to you,
> Two or three or four in number;
> However, if you fear
> That you may not be able to act

> equitably towards all,
> Then marry only one.
>
> (4:3)

Some jurists have held that it is not possible to act equitably towards all the four wives; the Quran allows, therefore, only one wife. Others are of the opinion that it is for the man to decide. But there is another verse which confirms monogamy:

> You will never be able to deal equitably
> With all your wives, however much you may want.
>
> (4.129)

Then there is the provision of *mehr* (dower), the amount which a husband promises to pay to the wife in lieu of marriage; it is the opposite of a dowry, which a wife or her parents pays the husband on marriage and which is prohibited in Islam. The Quran admonishes the faithful:

> Since you have sought marital enjoyment with your wives,
> Give to them their marriage portions as stipulated.
>
> (4:24)

Further, it is declared:

> Seek [them in marriage]
> With gifts from your property,
> Desiring chastity, not lust;
> Seeing that you derive
> Benefit from them, give them
> Their dowers [at least]
> As prescribed; but if,
> After a dower is prescribed, you
> Mutually agree [to vary it],
> There is no blame on you.
>
> (4:24)

It further admonishes:

> Give to the women their marriage portions
> And do not attach thereto any strings
>
> (4:4)

There are also clear instructions about a woman's maintenance in the case of divorce:

> Provide them the means to live properly;
> The well-to-do according to their capacity
> And theh ard-pressed according to their means.
>
> (2:236)

The husbands are told:

> You, who believe!
> You are forbidden to inherit
> Women against their will.
> Nor should you treat them
> With harshness, nor
> Take away part of the dower
> You have given them, except
> Where they have been guilty
> Of open lewdness;
> On the contrary, live with them
> On a footing of kindness and equity.
>
> (4:19)

The wives are told:

> Men are the protectors
> And maintainers of women,
> Because God has given
> The one more [strength]
> Than the other, and because
> They support them
> From their means.
> Therefore, the righteous women
> Are devoutly obedient, and guard
> In [the husband's] absence
> What God would have them guard.
>
> (4:34)

However, if any wife is disloyal or guilty of misconduct then the husband is permitted to 'admonish her first, then stay away from her and finally beat her lightly'. But if she returns to obedience, then 'do not seek a pretext to ill-treat her' (4:34). In the case of

separation between a man and his wife, the Quran instructs that
two arbiters be appointed, one by each family, to settle the dispute:

> If you fear a breach
> Between them,
> Appoint (two) arbiters,
> One from his family
> And the other from hers;
> If they wish for peace,
> God will cause
> Their reconciliation.
>
> (4:35)

The Quran permits divorce, though the Prophet had said that
'Of all the lawful things, God detests nothing more than divorce.'
The manner of divorcing the wife by the husband is explained:

> Divorce may be pronounced;
> Then either your mate should be sent away decently
> Or you should part with her decently.
>
> (2:229)

Again it is prescribed:

> A divorce is only
> Permissible twice: after that,
> The parties should either hold
> Together on equitable terms,
> Or separate with kindness.
> It is not lawful for you, O Men,
> To take back
> Any of your gifts [from your wives],
> Except when both parties
> Fear that they would be
> Unable to keep the limits
> Ordained by God.
>
> (2:229)

But the parting cannot be sudden; there has to be the *iddat*, or
waiting period, 'a supreme innovation of the Quran', as Professor
Coulson describes it. The period has to last until the wife completes
three menstrual circles or, if she is pregnant, until she delivers.

During this time, she is entitled to the husband's financial support. This period can also be used for reconciliation. The Prophet was clearly told in the Quran:

> Whenever you or other men divorce women,
> Take care of them during the waiting period
> Fear the Lord and do not turn them out of their homes.
> Nor should they be made to leave
> Except if guilty of sexual misconduct.

> (65:1)

Another warning given to the husband is that he should not obstruct his divorced wife from marrying someone else:

> That is purer in conduct and more orderly,
> For God knows while you do not
> What is best for you.

> (2:232)

The system of inheritance on the death of a Muslim is a vital part of Muslim Personal Law and is governed almost mathematically by the provisions in the Quran.

Initially, before enunciating the method of sharing out the inheritance, the Quran tells a believer that, while on his death-bed, he must 'bequeath equitably to his parents and kindred' and also 'to his wives'. This is an important admonition, because 'it recognizes the system of exclusive inheritance by the male agnate relatives as well as the capacity of women relatives to succeed'. Later on, it is translated into concrete terms, with the result that, of the nine relatives so recognized, six were women – the wife, the mother, the daughter, the consanguine and the uterine sisters. The Quran states:

> To everyone have We appointed heirs:
> The father, the mother and the near relations
> And those with whom there is a settlement,
> Give each of them their share.
> For God is a witness to what you do.

> (4:33)

There is also the direction:

> To men is due a share
> In the inheritance from their father,
>   mother and kindred;
> To women is due a share
> In the inheritance from their father,
>   mother and kindred.
> Whether little or more,
> Each has a determined share.
>
>   (4:7)

Apart from these general propositions, the Quran also mentions the specifics:

When children come into the heritage of their father or mother, God instructs you to assign to the male child a share equivalent to that of two females; if there be females only, and more than two, they will have two thirds of the inheritance; if there be but one, she will receive a half (4:11).

As regards the share of parents, the provision is clear:

The father and mother of the deceased will inherit a sixth of what he leaves, if he has left an issue. If he has left no issue and his father and mother be his sole heirs, the mother will receive a third; but if he leaves brothers and sisters, the mother will receive a sixth, after payment of the bequests and of the debts (4:12).

If a Muslim dies childless, it is provided that 'your wives shall have one fourth of what you leave', and 'one eighth if you have an issue, after payment of the bequest and of the debts'. Again, there is the direction that 'the brother and the sister on the mother's side of the deceased, man or woman who dies without leaving either parents, grandparents, or any issue will receive each a sixth. If there are more than two, they will share in a third, after payment of the bequests and of the debts.'

Muhammad was given further instructions thus:

God gives you the following instructions concerning the succession of a person who dies without leaving parents, grand parents, or issue: the sister of the man who dies childless will receive half of the inheritance. If otherwise and she dies without progeny, her brother will inherit the lot. If there be two sisters, they will have two thirds of what he leaves. If there are brothers and sisters, the male will have share equivalent to that of two females (4:11–12).

Though precise, this arrangement has numerous implications and connotations for Muslim jurists, with the result that the law of inheritance, which is simple and clear, has been subjected to different computations and permutations. But its base is sacred and has remained so through the ages. No Muslim, however pious or learned, has dared meddle with this, as it is a part of the Quran.

As regards crimes, murder is mentioned in several Quranic verses: 'Nor take life – which God has made sacred, except for a just cause' (17:35). No specific punishment for murder is prescribed, but a general rule is stated: 'A life for a life, an eye for an eye, a nose for a nose, an ear for an ear, and a tooth for a tooth' (5:48). The punishment could be waived by payment of money to the next of kin; it is in fact recommended: 'But whoso remits it as alms, shall have therein the expiation of his sin' (5:48). Occasionally, the Prophet imposed the penalty of death in order to curb the spirit of vengefulness among the Arabs, who took pride in taking revenge against their enemies.

Unintentional murder was more leniently dealt with. The Quran says: 'And whoever kills a believer by mistake should free a believing slave or pay compensation to the family of the deceased unless they remit it freely' (4:92).

There is only one verse in the Quran about theft: 'As to the thief, male or female, cut off his or her hands. A punishment by way of example from God for their crime' (5:41). However, this is immediately followed by a provision for pardon: 'But if the thief repents after his crime, and amends his conduct, God turns to him in forgiveness, for God is Oft-Forgiving, Most Merciful' (5:42). According to some traditions, the Prophet was harsh towards thieves and had their hands cut off, though some cases of pardon are also cited. This should be looked at from a historical standpoint. E. H. Palmer, in the introduction to his English translation of the Quran, points out: 'An Arab looked on work or agriculture as beneath his dignity and thought that he had a prescriptive right to the property of those who condescended to such mean offices.'⁹ Muhammad had to curb this tendency ruthlessly; hence the Quranic prescription.

Allied with theft is the crime of *al-hiraba*, or armed robbery. It also includes treason. The verse relevant to it is broad-based: 'The punishment of those who wage war against Allah and His Apostle and strive with might and mean to spread mischief through the land is execution or crucifixion or the cutting off of the hands and feet from opposite sides or exile from the land' (5:37). According to one tradition, the verse was revealed to the Prophet when he was faced with the question of punishing some people belonging to Ukul, a neighbouring tribe, who came to Medina pretending to become Muslims. When they complained of being in poor health, the Prophet sent them to a healthier spot to recuperate, but there they killed the keeper and ran away with his cattle. They were caught and brought before the Prophet. He punished them by having their hands and feet cut off, exactly as they had done to the keeper. Likewise, the Prophet executed eight persons for treason on the grounds of creating mischief in the land.

In regard to adultery, the admonition is:

> The woman and the man
> Guilty of adultery or fornication,
> Flog each of them with a hundred stripes.
> Let not compassion deter you
> In a matter prescribed by Allah
> If you believe in Him and the Last Day.
> And let a party of believers
>   witness their punishment.

(24:2)

There is no mention of stoning the guilty to death. On the contrary, it is implicit that punishment must not result in death, because the verse that follows immediately is clear:

> Let no man guilty of
> Adultery or fornication marry
> Any, but a woman
> Similarly guilty, or an unbeliever:

> Nor let any but such a man
> Or an unbeliever
> Marry such a woman:
> To the believers, such a thing
> Is forbidden.
>
> (24:3)

People making charges of adultery are to be punished if they cannot substantiate them. The relevant verses are explicit:

> And those who launch
> A charge against chaste women,
> And produce not four witnesses
> Flog them with eighty stripes;
> And reject their evidence
> Ever after; for such men
> Are wicked transgressors.
>
> (24:4)

However, according to Caliph Umar, there was originally a Quranic verse that prescribed stoning to death, but it was later abrogated. Despite the abrogation, Umar insisted that the Prophet had ordered adulterers to be stoned to death. Hence, though not prescribed by the Quran, a majority of purists uphold it as *sunna*, or the practice of the Prophet. This punishment can only be inflicted if four witnesses testify to the act, a proviso most unlikely to be met. The idea appears to be that the death penalty is to be awarded only if adultery is shamelessly committed in public. The interpretation of adultery by Saudi Arabian theologians to European jurists attending a conference in Jeddah on 'Muslim Doctrines and Human Rights in Islam' is worth quoting: 'The primary condition, required by the verse, is the presence at the moment of the act of four witnesses, who can be trusted and have never been indicted.' They went on to add that this was because 'public order [had] been seriously offended'. Even in the present, if such an act was publicly performed, the theologians pointed out that 'passers by would take it upon themselves to lynch the performers'. They argued that there was not one case of adultery which had been brought by witnesses before the Prophet. He had, however, dealt with a case where the culprit, out of a spontaneous urge to confess and purify himself, came to him of his own accord and confessed to his crime. The Prophet turned him away even after this confession, not once but three times. However, the adulterer persisted and demanded to be punished. It was then that the Prophet ordered him to be stoned to death. The Saudi theologians declared, 'Fourteen centuries have elapsed since that most severe penalty was inflicted, and we can strongly affirm that fourteen cases of stoning could hardly be numbered in all that time.'

For an apostate, or *murtadd*, 'one who turns back' from Islam, there is no punishment in the Quran. According to one verse: 'O true believers, whoever of you apostatizes from his religion, God will certainly bring other people to take his place, whom He will love and who will love Him, who shall be humble towards the believers, but severe to the unbelievers. They shall fight for the religion of God and shall not fear the obloquy of the detractor' (5:54). There are no recorded cases of the Prophet punishing those Muslims who renege upon their faith. There is, however, misconception about the punishment for apostasy, which has distorted the image of Islam. It has arisen because of classical jurists who have opined that the punishment for apostasy in Islam is death. But Muslims subscribe to the concept of 'freedom of worship', and demand the right to convert non-Muslims. The Quran makes it clear that 'there is no compulsion in religion'; how then can it pronounce death on those who 'turn away' from Islam or 'turn back' on it? On the contrary, the Quran mentions that in place of those who have given up the right path, God will bring better and more faithful ones.

The Arabic word for apostasy is *irtidad*; there is a mention of it in the Quran: 'anyone who after having accepted faith in Allah, utters unbelief, except under compulsion, though in his heart, he remains firm in faith, on him is the wrath of Allah and he will be punished grievously' (16:106).

But the punishment, as is obvious, is for Allah to decide; it is not to be inflicted by man here. In another verse (2:217), *murtadds* or apostates are referred to as 'companions of fire', fated to go to hell. Some critics have tried to translate the word *fa-yamut* ('then he dies') as 'then he is put to death', but there is no basis for it.

It is true that if, during a war, some Muslims committed treason and went over to the other side, then they were put to death on being captured. But that was for being traitors, not apostates. This is clear from many traditions reported in *Sahi Bukhari*, the most reliable book of traditions. Unfortunately, there is one tradition – 'Whoever changes his religion shall be put to death' – which contradicts the entire tenor of a mass of other traditions and, therefore, cannot be relied upon. It also contradicts the verses in the Quran that speak of freedom of worship. Besides, it makes a general proposition and does not specifically refer to a change of religion by Muslims alone. The *Encyclopedia of Islam* has correctly pointed out: 'In the Quran, the apostate is threatened with punishment in the next world.'[10] He can be killed if he joins the enemies of God and forsakes his religion, but that would not be merely for changing religion.

The verses dealing with usury are quite clear in their contents. First, however, we need to clarify what usury is, since there are considerable differences of opinion on the subject. According to the Arab historian Ibn Kathir, Caliph Umar was doubtful about its import, as the Prophet had not clarified the position. Allama Abdullah Yusuf Ali, the eminent exegetist, observes:

Our ulama, ancient and modern, have worked out a great body of literature on usury, based on economic conditions as they existed at the rise of Islam. I agree with them on the main principles, but respectfully differ from them on the definition of usury. The definition I would accept would be: undue profit made, not in the way of legitimate trade, out of loans of gold and silver and necessary articles of food, such as wheat, barley, dates and salt (according to the list mentioned by the Holy Apostle himself). My definition would include profiteering of all kinds, but exclude economic credit, the creature of modern banking and finance.[11]

The relevant Quranic verses read:

> O Believers! Fear God and forego usurious earnings.
> In case you disobey, you will be deemed to be at war
> With God and His Prophet.
>
> (2:278–9)

There is also another admonition:

> Those who practise usury shall rise again as under Satan's influence;
> They pretend that usury is like trade
> But trade is permitted and usury, forbidden.
>
> (2:275)

There is also much debate about slavery: does the Quran sanction its continuation? There are several verses which have been so interpreted, but Professor Fazlur Rahman has explained:

To insist on a liberal implementation of the rules of the Quran, shutting one's eyes to the social change that has occurred and that is palpably occurring before our eyes, is tantamount to deliberately defeating its moral-social purposes and objectives. It is just as though, in view of the Quranic emphasis on freeing slaves, one were to insist on preserving the institution of slavery so that one could earn merit in the sight of God by freeing slaves. Surely, the whole tenor of the teaching of the Quran is that there should be no slavery at all.[12]

The Quranic approach became clear when, in practice, slaves among Muslims not only acquired equality of status but also became rulers, receiving the same recognition from the Ulama as the most exalted among the faithful.

Though Muslims believe that the Quran is the Word of God, its meaning has been the subject of controversy. The issue, in plain terms, is whether the Quran is created or uncreated. The question was first raised by a group of early Muslims known as the Mutazilites – the pioneers of free thinking in Islam – who laid 'the foundations of the moral law on the concordance of reason with positive revelation'. They believed that 'the Word of God has been created *in subjecto*'. They said that the Quran was first spoken on 'the Night of Power', as mentioned in the Book itself, and could not therefore be regarded as uncreated. Further, they argued that if it was uncreated, then God would be commanding and prohibiting what was non-existent. Referring to the verse, 'There comes not to them a fresh warning from their Lord, but they hear it and mock at it' (21:22), they contended that since everything 'fresh' has to be created, the Quran could not be uncreated. Also, Allah said, 'We have made it an Arabic Quran' (43:3). Everything 'made' is naturally something which has been 'created'. Again, it is said, 'But it is evidential in the breasts of those endowed with knowledge' (29:49). Anything that is in the breasts has to be created. Allah further pronounces, 'We have, without doubt, sent down the Message, and We shall assuredly guard it [from corruption]' (15:9). A message cannot be something which is uncreated. Many other verses can be quoted in support of the idea. So the Mutazilites firmly asserted that the Quran was a created thing.

During the rule of three successive Abbasid caliphs, al-Mamun (813–833), al-Mutasim (833–842) and al-Wathiq (842–847), the Mutazilites gained such power that they could coerce Muslims to accept that the Quran was created. In 833, they made al-Mamun promulgate an edict that a judge who did not subscribe to this doctrine could not hold that office. A *mihnah*, or inquisitorial court, was constituted for trying those who denied this doctrine. Incidently, this was the first and the last inquisition in the annals of Islam.

Thus, strangely enough, the pioneers of free thought and reason in Islam became the instruments for the suppression of freedom. Imam Ahmad ibn Hanbal (780–855) opposed their doctrine. He asserted that the Quran existed in its celestial origin from the beginning and would continue to exist forever. In short, Allah and the Quran were coterminous. He suffered much at the hands of the caliph. He was publicly flogged, tortured and imprisoned. But many leading theologians stood by him; some of them were also humiliated. Their opposition to the Mutazilite doctrine gradually gained popular support, with the result that when Mutawakkil (847–861) became the caliph, he abolished the *mihnah* and abrogated state patronage to the doctrine of the created Quran.

No one, however, has explained more ably, clearly and succinctly the basis of the Quran than that greatest of all Imams, Imam Abu Hanifa (699–767), who possessed the uncanny gift of being able to reconcile the seemingly irreconcilable. He wrote in his *Wasiya*:

We confess that the Quran is the speech of Allah – exalted be He – uncreated, that is His revelation and what He has sent down. It is not He, but neither is it other than He, but in a real sense it is one of His attributes. It is written in exemplars, recited by tongues, memorized in breasts, but is not contained in any of these. The ink, the paper, the writing are created things, for they are the work of men, but the speech of Allah – exalted be He – is uncreated. The writing, the letters, the words, the verses, are an adaptation of the Quran to human needs, but the speech of Allah – exalted be He – exists in itself, though its meaning comes to be understood through these things. Whoever says that the speech of Allah – exalted be He – is created is a disbeliever in Allah, the Mighty One. Allah – exalted be He – is one who is worshipped, who continues ever as He was, so that His speech is recited, is written, is memorized, without ever being separated from Him.

Finally, there are innumerable references to the pleasures in heaven as reward for good deeds and to the tortures in hell as punishment for bad deeds. Graphic descriptions – sensual and fearsome – are found in a number of verses to attract the righteous and warn the wrongdoer. Critics have objected to these lurid descriptions, but there are two viewpoints on this issue. Some Muslim commentators have taken it literally and some metaphorically. According to the eminent Pakistani thinker, the late Dr Khalifa Abdul Hakim, 'The grosser minds have always taken them literally, but the Quran, notwithstanding very vivid physical imagery, warns us that they are to be taken as analogies and parables.'[13] In support of his contention, the Khalifa refers to three Quranic verses:

> There is a Parable
> Of the Garden
> The righteous are promised:
> In it are rivers
> Of water incorruptible;
> Rivers of milk
> of which the taste
> Never changes; rivers
> Of wine, a joy
> To those who drink;
> And rivers of honey
> Pure and clear. In it
> There are for them
> All kinds of fruits;
> And Grace from their Lord.
> (47:15)

> The Parable of the Garden
> Which the righteous are promised!
> Beneath it flow rivers:
> Perpetual in the enjoyment
> And the shade therein.
> Such is the End
> Of the Righteous; and the End
> Of Unbelievers is the Fire.
>
> (13:35)

> Now no person knows
> What delights of the eye
> Are kept hidden [in reserve]
> For them – as a reward
> For their [good] Deeds.
>
> (32:17)

He also quotes a tradition of the Prophet to give further credibility to his view:

The Prophet according to *Sahi Bukhari* is reported to have said: 'Allah says, "I have prepared for my righteous servants what no eye has seen, no ear has heard and no mind can conceive."'

This again is supported by an observation of the Prophet's uncle Ibn Abbas, who was one of his close Companions. He said, 'In paradise there are no foods, as in this life except the name.'[14]

Once, a Companion asked the Prophet what virtue was. He replied, 'That which brings peace to your mind and tranquillity to your soul.' And what was vice, he was asked. 'That which makes your heart flutter and which throws your soul in perturbation,' he explained. Hence, the reward of virtue and the punishment of vice is necessarily not physical; it is inner realization, which can make a man enjoy by himself the pleasures of heaven, if he has done good, and suffer the tortures of hell, if he has done wrong. Several commentators, both Muslim and non-Muslim, are now of the view that the religious terminology of *time* and *space* and even of *the earth below* and *the heaven above* or the *here* and the *hereafter* must be taken as indicative of value judgements.

Professor Victor Danner of Indiana University has lucidly explained the Quranic concept of heaven and hell:

The Heavens and Hells of the Quran are depicted with a concrete and even sensual imagery that must not be taken literally. They are interpreted as actual places by the mass of the faithful and perhaps this has been the inevitable consequence of the imagery itself. The paradisal gardens of Eden, the houris, the chaste mates, the goblets of gold, the fruits and drinks, the cool shades, the flowing rivers, the fountains, the carpets and cushions and thrones, are some of the images for the Heavens. The blazing fire, the boiling water, the shades of dark smoke, the garments of fire, the maces of iron, the roasting skins, the liquid pitch, the bitter food, the marching in chains, are some of the images for Hell ... These are images that seek to picture the Hereafter in sufficiently strong enough colours to awake in the believer a yearning for the celestial regions and a repugnance for the internal ones ... The terrifying descriptions of Hell should block the downward movement of the soul and force it to redirect its will upwards towards Heaven, which is described with attractive colours. [15]

It is not possible to cover all the subjects dealt with in the Quran here; in fact, there is hardly an issue which is not mentioned or discussed in some manner in its verses. Through the Quran, Allah gave Islam to Muhammad; but it was through Muhammad that Islam spread and the Quran lives. Hence, Muhammad and the Quran cannot be separated; they co-exist and their common link is God. As Muhammad is made to proclaim in the Quran:

> Truly, my prayers and my sacrifices,
> My living and my dying,
> Is for God, the Lord of all being.
> I am commanded by Him,
> I am the first of His Muslims.
>
> (6:163–4)

The Quran also makes it clear that Muhammad has been given an exceptional role. It speaks of him as 'an excellent example' of character and conduct (33:21 and 68:4). The Prophet himself told his followers that 'God sent me as an apostle so that I may demonstrate perfection of character, refinement of manners and loftiness of deportment.' He was so conscious that he should be good to all that he often prayed, 'O God! I am but a man. If I hurt anyone in any manner please forgive me.' Allah has designated him as 'the seal of Prophets', on whom He and His angels send their blessings (33:56). Muslims are repeatedly admonished by Allah to obey His messenger. That is why, in one of Iqbal's most popular poems, *Jawab-i-Shikwa*, Allah reminds Muslims:

> If you break not faith with Muhammad, We shall always
> be with you.
> What is this miserable World, to write the world's
> destiny, pen and tablet, We offer you.[16]

The Quran has remained the supreme guide for Muslims ever since it was revealed, and no one could have emphasized its importance more than Muhammad. The Word of God was law to him as it is to a billion of his followers throughout the world today. As Richard Bell has observed in his introduction to the Quran:

Few books have exercised a wider or deeper influence upon the spirit of man than the Quran . . . It is the basis of [Muslims'] religious beliefs, their ritual and their law; the guide of their conduct, both public and private. It moulds their thought and its phrases enter into their literature and their daily speech.[17]

The Quran deals with varied subjects, depending on the occasion when a particular chapter or verse was revealed. The speaker is God and the recipient of His Message is Muhammad. Sometimes, God speaks in the singular and sometimes in the plural. The addressee is often the Prophet, but sometimes believers and sometimes nonbelievers are also addressed. There are times, however, when God speaks in the third person. To an ordinary reader these changes both in the addressee and the form of the addressor cause confusion; but the discerning reader will appreciate the necessity of such changes: they produce their own impact on the mind.

In order to simplify the matter, I have taken the liberty of incorporating in the translated versions the addressee in the particular text. Likewise, to maintain uniformity in the form of the addressor, I have often replaced the word 'We', or 'I', by 'God' or 'Allah'.

SUMMARIES OF CHAPTERS AND SELECTED VERSES

___

SURAH I: AL-FATIHA (THE OPENING)
(7 verses)

___

The importance of this chapter has been emphasized by the Quran itself:

> O Muhammad! Truly have We given you
> Seven oft-repeated verses and the great Quran.
>
> (15:87)

According to one tradition, which is universally accepted as true, the Prophet regarded the Fatiha as 'the greatest and finest' chapter. Its contents, if properly understood, epitomize the Quran: what follows in the Book is more or less a commentary on what this chapter contains. Its form is invocatory and it has to be repeated by the faithful in every prayer and on every occasion. Its salient features are: (1) reiteration of faith in the oneness of God; (2) recognition of God's basic attributes; (3) acceptance of the principle of causation in life as in nature; (4) belief in the Hereafter, accountability for man's deeds and misdeeds, and inevitability of rewards and punishments; and (5) the need of correct guidance for man to avoid wrongdoing.

Though it is the opening chapter, it is not an introduction to the Book as commonly understood; it is man's prayer to God and God's response to it. In other words, man asks his Creator for guidance and the Creator gives him that guidance through the

Quran. (According to Maududi, this was the first complete surah revealed to Muhammad.)

SURAH I

1. In the name of God
  Most Gracious. Most Beneficent.

2. All praise be to God,
  Who is the Cherisher
  And Sustainer of all.

3. He is, indeed, all Compassionate
  And Most Merciful.

4. Master of the Day of Judgement.

5. To You alone, O Lord,
  We offer our prayers
  And from You alone
  We seek all help.

6. Show us, O Lord,
  The right path,

7. The path of those
  Whom You have blessed
  And not of those
  With whom You are wrathful,
  Nor of those who have
  Chosen to go astray.

SURAH II: AL-BAQARA (THE HEIFER)
(286 verses)

This is the longest chapter in the Quran. Some commentators, and exegetists have described it as 'the Quran in miniature', as it deals with most of the important articles of Muslim faith. The Prophet is reported to have said, 'Of everything there is a pinnacle, and the pinnacle of the Quran is *Surat-al-Baqara*.'

The chapter begins with the declaration that the Quran is the Book of guidance and warns its detractors that they are doomed if they reject it. Then it tells the story of Adam, his appointment by God as viceregent on earth, of Adam and Eve eating the forbidden apple at the instigation of Satan and in consequence their fall from the grace of Allah. They were forgiven by God and warned that they should resist henceforth Satan's temptations. The episode brings out the inner struggle that man faces between right and wrong, good and evil. It discounts, however, the Christian theory of the original sin.

Then comes the story of the Children of Israel. The Quran reminds believers that they should not confound truth with falsehood; it enjoins them to be righteous. They must seek His help with patience and through prayers. From the heroic struggle of Moses against the tyranny of the Pharoah of Egypt, several moral lessons are stressed, chiefly that the oppressed shall eventually vanquish the oppressor. Sayyid Qutb, one of the foremost modern exegetists of the Quran, has observed that readers of this passage feel 'as though they themselves were witnessing the splitting of the sea and the salvation of the Children of Israel under the leadership of Moses. This vivid picture is one of the most distinct characteristics of the marvellous Quran.'

Among the prophets, Abraham occupies a unique position. He is the builder of the *Kaaba*, the first House of God. In this chapter, God issues the ordinance of changing the *qiblah*, or the 'pivot of Islam', from Jerusalem to Mecca, requiring Muslims to pray henceforth facing the Kaaba:

> The foolish ones will ask,
> Why is their *qiblah* turned away
> From where they formerly prayed?
> Tell them: 'To God belongs the east and the west
> And He guides whom He will to the straight path.'
>
> (2:142)

This redirection is, of course, more than a simple matter of geography; it marks an important break from the Judaeo-Christian tradition.

The Quran makes it clear that to every land throughout history, God sent his messengers – according to a saying of Muhammad, they numbered 1,024,000. Some of them are mentioned in the Quran, many are not. The prophets from the Old Testament are mentioned here. Muhammad came last and therefore is referred to as 'the Seal of the prophets'. He was sent by God to convey both the final warning and the happiest tidings to mankind.

The chapter continues by giving instructions on what is prohibited and what is permitted with regard to eating. It explains the virtues of fasting and how it is to be observed. It emphasizes the vital role that *Hajj* or the 'Pilgrimage to Mecca' plays in Islam; it lays down the norms that should govern marriage and divorce. There are also references to personal behaviour on the part of believers, particularly about righteous conduct, prayer, kindness, charity, probity and patience in suffering. Here is outlined the need for prohibition against intoxicating drinks, gambling and usury.

The section on *jihad*, or struggle in the way of God, with references to the story of Saul and David and Goliath, highlights the virtues of courage, single-minded devotion and unfaltering faith in God.

The chapter climaxes with *Ayat al Kursi*, or the 'Throne Verse', which Muslims regard as the sublimest expression of the power and glory of God; its imagery and lyrical beauty are unmatched. It has evoked high mystical emotion and is said to ward off all evil if uttered with sincere devotion. Ibn Arabi, the father of Sufism, held the 'Throne Verse' to be the greatest verse in the Quran; it was, according to him, the embodiment of the Prophet's saying: 'In the heart of man lies the throne of God.'

The chapter is called 'The Heifer' because of the parable contained in it that illustrates the miserable end of those who go against the will of God.

SURAH II

2.   This is the Book that provides
Guidance for those who fear God.
Of this, there should be no doubt.

3.   They believe in the Unseen,
And are regular in prayer
And spend from God's gifts
In charity to others.

4.   And who believe in Our Revelations to you,
O Muhammad!
As We had given Our Revelations
to those before you
And were equally assured of the life hereafter.

6.   Don't bother, O Muhammad!, about people
Who reject faith in God.
To them it matters little
Whether they are warned or not.
For they shall never believe
They are indeed the condemned lot.

7.   Your Lord has set a seal on their hearts
So that they remain immune to all pleadings.
Their eyes are covered with a veil
And their punishment is great.

21.   O people, worship your Lord
Who has created you and those before you
So that you may learn to be righteous.

22.   God has made the earth your couch,
And the heavens your canopy;

And sent down rain from the heavens;
And brought forth with it
Fruits for your sustenance.
Then set up no rivals unto Him
As you know the real facts.

28. How can you reject faith in God
Knowing that you were without life,
And He gave you life?
And also He will cause you to die
And raise you again
So that you will return to Him.

29. It is He Who has created for you
All things that exist on earth and in heavens
He has given design and order
To cover the seven firmaments;
He has knowledge of everything.

30. Remember O people! how your Lord told the angels:
'I will create a viceregent on earth.'

They asked:
'Pray, will you put man there
Who will do mischief and shed blood?
Why not send us instead
Who worship and glorify You?'

The Lord replied,
'I know what you know not.'

42. Do not cover truth with falsehood
Nor conceal truth, when you know it.

43. Be steadfast in prayer
Practise regular charity;
And bow down your heads
With those who worship Us.

62.   Those who are believers in the Quran
        And in Jewish, Christian and Sabian scriptures
        And are also believers in God and the Last Day
        And work righteously,
        They are assured of their reward.
        They need not fear
        Nor shall they come to grief.

87.   Moses was granted the Book;
        He was followed by other apostles.
        Then came Jesus with Our clear Signs
        Strengthened by Our holy spirit;
        Yet people rejected them all,
        So puffed up with pride were they.
        Some apostles were called imposters
        And some, the people slayed.

88.   They boasted that their hearts contained
        All the words of God.
        Our curse is on them
        For their blasphemy and ignorance.

106.   God does not abrogate
        Any of His revelations
        Nor does He cause any to be forgotten.
        Instead, He substitutes
        In its place something better.
        He has power over everything.

110.   Be steadfast in prayers
        And do regular charity.
        Whatever good you do,
        It will be accountable,
        For God knows whatever you do.

111.   Some of them boast:
        'No one except Jews or Christians
        Will enter God's paradise.'

These are their vain desires.
They can produce no proof.

112.   On the contrary, whoever submits to God
         And does good deeds,
         He shall have his reward with God.
         He need have no fear
         Nor shall he be grieved.

113.   The Jews say the Christians have nothing
         And the Christians say the Jews have nothing.
         And yet both proclaim to adhere
         To the same Book from Us.
         Indeed, they know not what they say.
         On the Day of Judgement
         God will settle their dispute.

114.   Is it not unjust that believers should be
         Prohibited from entering places of worship
         Or that they should enter them
         With fear in their hearts?
         Those who prevent bring disgrace to themselves
         In this as well as the next world.

138.   Our faith is
         Baptism of God.
         For who can be
         Better invoked than God?
         It is Him whom we worship.

139.   How can you then dispute
         About our faith?
         God is our Lord
         And He is your Lord.
         We are responsible for our acts
         And you for yours.
         We are, indeed, sincere
         In our devotion to God.

140.   Can you really say
That Abraham, Ishmael, Isaac,
Jacob and the Tribes
Were either Jews or Christians?
Can you say that you know better than God?
Are you not being unjust
In concealing God's own testimony?
Remember, He is not unaware of what you do.

148.   To each, God has given a goal
Towards which he must turn,
And then everyone must strive together
To achieve all that is good.
Wherever, whosoever be,
God will bring them together.
For He has power over all things.

155.   God tests people in different ways,
Some with fear, some with hunger,
Some with loss in goods
And some by depriving them
Of the fruits of their labour;
And some even with death.
But let glad tidings go to those
Who patiently persevere.

164.   Behold! the power of God!
He controls the heavens and the earth,
And regulates alternation of night and day;
He commands the sailing of ships
And makes rains pour down from the skies.
He gives life to the dead earth,
And creates beasts of all kinds.
And changes routes of winds and clouds
Between the earth and the skies.
These are, indeed, His Signs
For a people who understand.

172.   Believers! Eat the good things
That God has provided you.

Be grateful for His bounties
And pray to Him.

173. He has only prohibited
The eating of dead meat and blood
And the flesh of pig
And the flesh of such animals
On whom any other name
Save that of God has been invoked.
But if, due to necessity,
Or without wilful disobedience,
You eat whatever is available,
Then you are guiltless.
For God is, indeed, Oft-Forgiving
And He is Most Merciful.

177. It is not righteousness
That turns your faces
Towards East or West
But it is righteousness
To believe in God.
And the Last Day,
And the Angels,
And the Book
And the Messengers;
To spend from what He has given
To maintain your kith and kin,
And also the orphans and the needy,
The wayfarer and for ransoming slaves.
O people, be regular in prayer,
And practise charity;
Fulfil the contracts made.
Be firm and be patient.

In pain and adversity
Face every crisis firmly
For you are people of truth
Who only fear the Lord.

183. O, You who believe in Us!
Fasting is prescribed to you

As it was prescribed to those before,
So that you may learn
Self-restraint.

186.   When My servants ask you about Me
Tell them I am indeed closest to them.
I listen to the prayer of everyone who calls,
Hence let them listen to My call.
They must believe in Me
And walk on the straight path.

190.   Fight in the cause of God
Those who fight you,
But do not transgress,
For God does not love transgressors.

213.   Mankind was one nation.
God sent messengers to it
With glad tidings and warnings.
They were given the Book of Truth
So that they might judge rightly
In matters wherein they differed.
But the people of the Book
After clear Signs came to them
Continued to differ among themselves
Because of their selfish contumacy.
However God through His Grace
Guides believers to the true path
So that they may know where they differ.
For God guides those whom He wills,
To the path that is straight.

216.   Fight in the cause of God
Even if you dislike it.
For you little realize
That what you dislike
May really be for your good
And what you like, may be bad.
For only Allah knows what you do not.

219.   They ask you, O Muhammad!
About intoxicants and gambling.
Tell them there is more loss than gain in them.
However, when they ask you about charity
Tell them to give it in plenty.
That is His clear direction
For those who may reflect.

255.   There is no god but God.
He is the Living,
The Eternal, the Ever-subsisting.
No slumber can seize Him
For He is always awake.
To Him belongs the heavens and the earth.
There is none who can intercede with Him
Except by His leave and pleasure.
He knows all about creation
What came before and after.
Everything unknown to His creatures
Is known to their Creator.
They shall never comprehend
The extent of His knowledge
Save as He wills it.
His throne extends from the heavens to the earth.
And He guards it untiringly
And preserves it with all His might
For He is the Highest and the Sublimest.

256.   Let there be no compulsion in religion.
For this is the truth, which stands out from error,
That whoever rejects evil and believes in God
Shall grasp the most dependable handle.
It shall never break
For Allah knows and hears everything.

257.   For God is the Protector of believers.
From the depths of darkness
He leads them into light.
But those who reject Him
And have as their patrons the evil ones,

They will lead them from light into darkness
And make them companions of fire
To dwell therein for ever.

261.   Those who spend their wealth
In the way of God
Will be rewarded like a grain of corn
Which grows seven ears
And each ear sprouts a hundred grains.
God gives manifold rewards to whom He pleases
For He knows and gives in abundance.

263.   The use of kind words
And indulgence to others
Are better than charity
Or the loss that one may
Suffer in doing so.
God is above all wants
And He is most forbearing.

264.   Those who do charity grudgingly
And do not believe in Allah and the Last Day
Are like a rocky field
In which even heavy rains
Do not produce anything.
They shall gain nothing by their actions.
For God does not guide the wrongdoers.

265.   But those who spend their wealth
To please God and enlighten themselves
Are like the garden, high and fertile,
Upon which heavy rains fall
And yield abundant harvest.
And yet, even if it receives scanty rains
It produces enough to eat
For God sees what man does.

267.   O Believers! Give out of the good things
That you have rightly earned
And out of your own produce.

But do not give what is rotten
Or what you yourself would not eat
Except under compulsion.
Remember that God is most affluent
And is worthy of all praise.

268. The evil one threatens you with dire consequences
And bids you to conduct yourselves in an unseemly manner.
God on the contrary assures you
Of His forgiveness and His bounties,
For He cares and is fully aware.

269. He grants wisdom to whom He pleases
And gives rewards to whom He likes
But only men of understanding can grasp
The real meaning of His message.

270. And whatever you spend in charity
Or of your time in devotion to God;
He knows all that you do.
The wrongdoers do not understand
That apart from Him they have no helper.

272. It is not for you, O Muhammad!
To set right the disbelievers,
For God alone can do this
For those whom He so pleases.
Whatever good one does
Benefits his own soul.
He need not do it
To please God.
And the good he does shall be returned in full
For no one shall be dealt with unjustly by God.

274. Those who spend their wealth in charity
By night or day, whether openly or secretly,
They will be rewarded by their Lord.
They need have no fear and will not be grieved.
For their Lord shall protect them in every way.

275.   The man who indulges in usury and lives on it,
He is like one possessed by the devil.
He is, indeed, demented,
For he thinks usury is trading
But trading is lawful
And usury is not.
However those who desist from usury
After warning has been given
Will be forgiven by their Lord.
But those who continue with it
Will become companions of hell
And they will abide therein
For ever and ever.

284.   To God belongs all that is on earth and in heaven.
Remember whatever enters your mind
Is known to God.
He shall call you to account on the Last Day.

285.   The Apostle believes in what God has revealed,
As do all men of faith.
They believe in God,
His angels, His Book and His apostles.
Among the apostles, make no distinction.
For they have all proclaimed:
'We hear the message and we obey it.
We ask for forgiveness of the One,
To whom is the journey's end.'

286.   On no one does God place
A burden greater than he can bear.
Everyone gets the return of what he earns,
And suffers the ill that he deserves.
Hence pray: 'Our Lord! condemn us not
If we forget You or fall into error.'

'O! Our Lord! Burden us not
As those before us You had burdened.
And let it not be greater than we can bear.
Forgive us our sins

And have mercy on us.
You are our Protector and Helper
Against those who reject the truth.'

SURAH III: ALI IMRAN (FAMILY OF IMRAN)
(200 verses)

This chapter deals with the Battle of Badr, wherein barely 300 followers of the Prophet, inspired by their cause, were not only able to overcome the onslaught of a 1,000-strong, well-equipped army of their inveterate enemy, Abu Sufiyan, but were also able to achieve a spectacular victory. A year later, however, the same men suffered a humiliating defeat at Uhud. Apart from treachery by a certain section of Muslims, whom the Quran calls *munafiqun*, or hypocrites – those who pretended to be Muslims but were really non-believers – and the betrayal by the Jews, the defeat was also due to indiscipline in the ranks of some of Muhammad's followers, particularly the archers. God puts believers to the test in both situations: when they are triumphant and when they are defeated. Both are necessary for preparing them to fulfil the mission entrusted to them.

There are references here to the earlier prophets and their struggles against the forces of evil – from Adam, Noah and Abraham to Imran and Moses. Likewise, the story of Prophet Zachariah is narrated and the work of Jesus is commended. The Quran, however, does not recognize Christ as the son of God. He was, indeed, a prophet, like all other prophets who were granted the divine message; the Bible contained the message of God as given to Christ. He was also given the power to perform miracles. Some of his followers betrayed him and plotted to kill him, but God in His mercy uplifted him to the heavens just as he was being killed on the cross. Here, the Quranic version differs from that of the present-day Bible. Similarly, the Quran points out that the Jews tampered with the Torah, betrayed the teachings of Moses and strayed from the right path as shown by God. Muslims are told to respect all the former prophets and make no distinction between them; each of them was sent by God at different times to different peoples to show them the right path.

In their day-to-day behaviour, Muslims are admonished to observe purity in thought and action in every respect. Just as physical purity is necessary for praying, honesty and integrity are essential in business transactions. Also, charity should not be given from illegitimate funds or with an ulterior motive. The faithful must be united; it is good for them. Because of dissensions, nations in the past had lost their power and glory, and suffered moral and physical degeneration. Piety and purity give a far greater security to a people than worldly grandeur or gains. Believers are told never to succumb to worldly temptations.

God is one and eternal. His way is the right way. Muhammad will not live forever; he will pass away as all other prophets have passed away. As they were human, so is Muhammad. God alone lives forever; He is transcendental. It is faith in Him that sustains mankind. Besides Him, nothing is lasting; everything else is transient. God is the Creator and Destroyer of everything; nothing happens without His will or moves without His direction. Hence the faithful should ignore His detractors and sing praises to God's glory and express gratitude for His favours.

SURAH III

7.   God has sent down the Book,
        In it are verses, basic or fundamental,
        That form its foundation.
        There are others
        Which are allegorical.
        The perverts seek discord
        In searching for hidden meaning.
        But except God, no one knows it.
        Those who are firm in knowledge
        Accept the Book as a whole.
        Its teachings can be fully grasped
        Only by men of understanding.

67.   Abraham was not a Jew
        Nor was he a Christian.

He was true to his faith.
He surrendered to God.
He joined no gods with God.

68.   Among people nearest to Abraham
Are people who follow the true path,
As does this apostle.
They are the real believers,
They take God as their protector.

103.   Hold together the Rope of God
And hold it fast.
Be not divided among yourselves,
And be grateful for His favour.
You were enemies before
But He has made you brethren in faith.
You were on the brink of disaster
And He has rescued you.
He has shown you His signs
So that you may be rightly guided.

104.   Let a band of believers arise among you
To invite people to do good
And to take to the right path
And to refrain from doing wrong.
They will, indeed, be the attainers of salvation.

109.   To God belongs all.
All that is in heaven and on earth.
He alone will decide all matters.

129.   To God belongs all,
All that is in heaven and on earth.
He forgives whom He pleases
And punishes whom He likes,
He is Most Forgiving, All Merciful.

130.   O Believers!
Do not practise usury
And thus multiply your wealth.

Fear God.
Then alone you may prosper.

134. Spend your wealth in charity
Whether you are prosperous or not.
And control your anger
And be forgiving to others.
For God loves those who do good.

135. Even after you have done a wrong
And are ashamed of it,
Remember God and seek His forgiveness.

137. Many were the ways of life
That were shown by Us in the past.
Travel through the earth
And see what was the end
Of those who rejected the truth.

139. So lose not heart, O believers,
Nor fall into despair;
Gain mastery over yourself
If you are true to your faith in God.

141. God's object is to purify
Those who are true to His faith
And deprive His blessings to those
Who resist faith in Him.

144. Muhammad is no more than an apostle;
Many apostles came before him.
If he dies or is slain, will you then
Turn back on your heels?
If any of you were to backtrack
He cannot harm God.
On the contrary, it is God
Who surely rewards those
Who serve Him faithfully.

145. Nor can a soul be extinguished
      Save by God's leave.
      The term of life is fixed and recorded.

      If any of you desire a reward
      Here and in the Hereafter,
      We shall give it to him
      And swiftly shall We reward
      All those who serve Us with gratitude.

146. How many of the prophets
      Fought to uphold God's faith
      Carrying with them
      Hordes of men of faith?
      They never lost heart
      Even if they met with disaster,
      Nor did they weaken or give in.
      For God loves those
      Who are firm in their resolve.

147. They only prayed:
      'O our Lord! forgive us our sins
      And anything we may have done
      To transgress our limits:
      Help us to stand firmly
      Against those who resist You.'

148. And God gave them a reward here
      And an excellent reward in the Hereafter.
      For God loves those who do good.

161. Can a prophet ever betray the trust
      Given to him by his Lord?
      No person can be false
      To what is entrusted to him.
      He shall have to restore
      On the Day of Judgement
      What he had misappropriated.
      Every soul receives on that Day
      Whatever it has earned
      And none shall be dealt with unjustly.

162.   Is the man who cares
For the pleasure of God
Like the man who invites
The wrath of God?
How can this be?
The sinner's abode is indeed hell.

189.   To God belongs
The dominion
Of the heavens
And the earth;
And God has power
Over all things.

190.   Behold! In the creation
Of the heavens and the earth
And the alternation
Of night and day,
There are indeed Signs
For men of understanding.

200.   O Believers, persevere patiently
And be unwavering in your faith.
Vie with one another
In your devotion and fear of God
So that you may prosper.

SURAH IV: AL-NISA (THE WOMEN)
(176 verses)

This chapter reflects mainly on family, marriage, rights of orphans, rules of inheritance, the manner of settling family disputes and other related matters.

In the wake of the two battles of Badr and Uhud, special attention had to be paid to the problems of those who became widows and orphans. It was in this context that permission was given by God for a man to marry four wives on the condition that husbands should treat all of them equally in love and in all other respects. Likewise, provision of *mehr* (dower amount) for wives was made. Adultery was made a capital offence, provided four witnesses to the act could be found. However, if a false charge against a chaste woman was made, punishment for the slanderer was no less severe. If the offender repents, God in His mercy may forgive him. Marriage with a widow is recommended; no tampering with a woman's property is permitted, nor usurping the assets of orphans and servants. In family affairs man does indeed have precedence over woman, but otherwise women's rights need to be properly protected. Divorce is allowed, but, first, efforts at reconciliation between husband and wife should be made; only if these fail should separation be effected.

The Quran repeatedly warns people against associating any deity with God; no compromise on this question is permissible. Obedience to God's commands, and to the clear directives of the Prophet, is obligatory, as is obedience to rulers and others who are put in charge of the faithful.

Jihad in the cause of God is incumbent on believers; they should not be swayed by victories or defeats. To the righteous and the stout-hearted, victory is assured, but the weak and the cowardly must suffer defeat. Muslims must be careful of the intrigues of the hypocrites in their ranks who say one thing and do exactly the opposite; they should be shunned. Fighting to repel aggression is permitted, but, without a cause, a human being is not allowed to take the life of another. If he does, he must pay with his life. Again, migrating from places hostile to the believers is encouraged; attachment to faith is more important than attachment to land.

Muslims are enjoined to conduct themselves with dignity and propriety; they should talk of good things in low, moderate tones and act righteously. Belief in God and virtuous deeds are a passport to heaven. Loyalty to God must have preference over all other loyalties, whether that of son to father, or of wife to husband. His book – the Quran – is the light that brightens the path of everyone in search of truth. His prophet, Muhammad, has been sent not only as a warner but also as a mercy to mankind.

SURAH IV

1.   O mankind! Praise thy Lord!
It is He who created man,
And of like nature, his mate,
And from their union
Brought forth countless multitudes.
Revere and fear the Lord.
It is He who has brought about
This bond between man and his mate.
For God watches over everything.

48.   God forgives not anyone
Who sets up partners with Him.
Everything else can be forgiven,
But not this.
It is the most heinous sin.

59.   O you who believe in God.
Obey Him and obey His Apostle,
And those with authority over you.
If you differ among yourselves
Refer the matter to God and His Apostle.
Believe in God and the Last Day
That is the best and most appropriate
Final determination for you.

64.   Not an apostle did We send
But to be obeyed as We willed.
People may be unjust to themselves
And may not harken to the call.
Still if they come to you, O Apostle,
And ask God's forgiveness,
And if you so recommend
They would find God
To be Most Merciful and Oft-Returning.

65.   They cannot really believe in Us
Until they make you, O Muhammad,
The judge in all their disputes

And do not resist your decisions
And accept them with conviction.

69. All those who obey God and His Apostle
Are blessed by the Lord.
The Prophets, the truthful, the just, the righteous
All of them form a beautiful fellowship!

79. Whatever good you do
Is due to the grace of God
But whatever evil befalls you
Is due to your own misdeeds.
We have sent an Apostle
To instruct you and others,
And of this God Himself is the witness.

80. He who obeys the Apostle, obeys God:
But if anyone turns his back on you
You need not bother, O Muhammad!
You have not been sent
To watch over others' misdeeds.

85. Whoever recommends
And helps a good cause
Becomes a participant in it;
And whoever recommends
And helps an evil deed,
Shares in its burden:
God has power
Over all things.

86. If a greeting is offered
Accept it with grace.
God takes careful account
Of all that people do.

107. Do not plead for those
Who betray their own soul.
God does not forgive
The treacherous and the sinful.

108.   Men may hide their crimes from others
        But how can they hide them from God?
        He sees all that they do,
        Even the plotting in the dark.
        Such acts are not approved by Him.
        He encompasses what they do.

110.   If anyone does evil
        He wrongs his own soul.
        But if he repents
        And asks for forgiveness,
        Allah is Most Forgiving.

111.   If anyone commits a sin
        He does wrong to his soul,
        God has full knowledge
        Of all that he does.

112.   But if anyone commits a sin
        And blames someone innocent
        Then he betrays himself
        And commits a flagrant wrong.

122.   But those who believe
        And do righteous deeds
        We shall soon admit them
        To Gardens beneath which rivers flow
        To dwell therein for ever.
        That is God's promise
        Truer than the truth,
        There can be nothing more true.

124.   If those who do righteous deeds,
        Be they male or female,
        And have faith in God
        They will enter Heaven,
        And not a shred of injustice
        Will be done to them.

135. O you who believe in God
      Stand firmly for justice
      And be witness for God,
      Even if it be against yourselves
      Or your parents or kith and kin.
      Whether they be rich or poor:
      God is their best protector.
      Hence do not succumb to temptations
      Nor fumble or fail
      In giving your evidence.
      Verily, God knows all that you do.

136. O you who believe in God and His Apostle
      And the scripture which has been sent down,
      Also in those which came before.
      Those who deny God,
      His angels, His Books, His apostles
      And the Day of Judgement,
      They have, indeed, gone astray.

137. Those who believe in God
      And then disbelieve in Him
      And again believe and disbelieve
      They are verily unbelievers.
      God will not forgive them
      Or show them the right path.

152. To those who believe in God and His apostles
      And make no distinction between them,
      They shall have their reward;
      Allah is, indeed, Most Merciful.

164. About some of the apostles We have told you,
      But there are others about whom We have not.

173. But to those who believe
      And do righteous deeds
      God will give them their rewards
      And more and more of His bounty.

But the arrogant and the disdainful
God will punish them grievously.
They will have no protector besides Him.

SURAH V: AL-MAIDAH (THE FEAST)
(123 verses)

This is the last revelation that Muhammad received during his farewell pilgrimage to Mecca a few months before his death. It declares to the faithful:

This day, O believers! I have perfected
For you your religion
And completed My favour unto you,
And have chosen for you
Islam as your religion

(5:3)

In this chapter, special directions are given for many different areas of activity. How should a Muslim lead his life? How should he pray? What should he eat? What kind of tax should he pay and in what manner? What sort of relationship should he establish with his relatives, his wives, his servants and orphans entrusted to his charge? Also, how should the inheritance of a deceased Muslim be divided among his heirs?

There is then a reference to jealousy among believers; it warns that jealousy leads to disaster and it fosters evil. Through the parable of Cain and Abel, the Quran shows how this vice should be avoided.

There are several warnings given to the faithful here about hypocrites who pose as friends of Muslims but are in reality their enemies and their patrons, the Jews, who were plotting and conspiring against Muhammad.

Offences against life and property are mentioned and their punishment prescribed. The hand of a thief must be cut off, unless he genuinely repents. Similarly, a murderer has to be killed: life for life, eye for eye, and tooth for tooth. Believers are admonished that the *shariah*, or the Law as revealed by God, should be adhered to. They should not transgress the limits between *halal* and *haram* – what is permitted to be eaten and what is not. They are told to refrain from intoxicating drinks, gambling and games of chance, which are described as acts of Satan.

SURAH V

3.   This day, O Believers! I have perfected
        For you your religion
        And completed My favour unto you,
        And have chosen for you
        Islam as your religion.

9.   O Believers! Stand firmly
        With God as your witness
        For fair dealing among people.
        Your hatred for others
        Should not make you commit
        A wrong or depart from justice.
        For justice is next to piety.
        In whatever you do, fear God;
        He knows what you do.

32.   O Children of Israel! If anyone
        Kills another without a just cause,
        Except in retaliation for murder
        Or for causing corruption in the land,
        It is as if he has killed the whole of mankind.
        And whosoever saves a life,
        It is as if he has saved the whole of mankind.

38.   The punishment for a thief, male or female,
        Is the cutting off of his or her hands.
        God sets it as a deterrent
        And He is exalted in power.

39.   However, if the thief repents
        And mends his ways
        And turns to God,
        God forgives him.
        He is Most Merciful, Oft-Forgiving.

48.   To you, O Apostle,
        We have sent the Scripture
        Which confirms the truth of what
        We sent to other apostles.
        Do not follow the caprices of your detractors
        Lest you turn away from Our Revelations.

        To each people We have prescribed
        A Law and a Way
        Which is open and free.
        If God had so willed,
        He would have made all a single people.
        But he desires to test each one
        In what He has given to them,
        So strive hard and compete
        In righteousness and good deeds.
        For the destination of all
        Is to reach God.
        He alone will show where each one differed.

54.   O Believers, if any of you turns away from his faith
        God will bring in his place
        Others who love Him
        And whom He loves.
        They will be humble with believers
        And firm with disbelievers,
        They shall fight in God's way,
        They will not be deterred by reproaches
        Or the mockery of fault-finders.
        He bestows his favours on whomsoever He pleases
        And He knows and encompasses everything.

57.   O Believers! If any of you
        Goes back on his faith
        And leaves the fold,
        God will replace you with others
        Who will love Him
        And who will be humble with believers
        And defiant with non-believers.

They will fight in the way of God
And will never be afraid of reproaches
By the fault-finders.
God's grace will be on them,
For He encompasses everything
And He knows all.

93. O Believers! Intoxicants and games of chance
Are an abomination.
They are Satan's handiwork.
Hence avoid them
So that you may prosper.

103. Tell the people, O Muhammad,
That the good and the bad
Can never be equal,
Even though abundance of bad
May dazzle their eyes.
Ask them to fear God
So that they may prosper.

105. O Believers, protect your souls
And follow the right path.
Those who stray cannot harm you.
God is your destination:
Unto Him all shall return.
Then He shall show
What each has done.

SURAH VI: AL-ANAM (THE CATTLE)
(165 verses)

In this chapter, stress is laid on the significance of the oneness and
unity of God. There are His signs all around to prove His supremacy.
In the past, all those who disobeyed His commands and refused to
believe in Him suffered humiliation and defeat. The dilapidated
monuments of their times are a testimony to their fall. Believers

must draw the necessary moral from this: those who indulge in the pleasures of this world and are not mindful of the Day of Judgement are bound to come to grief. They should learn from the happenings of the past: how prophets were mocked at, disbelieved and disobeyed by the people and how in the end, due to the wrath of God, they suffered. They should refrain from worldly vices. They are told to avoid tribal and family quarrels, and to strive to remain united and act righteously, whatever the circumstances. They should keep away from the detractors of God and His Prophet and never associate anyone with God.

Through the story of Abraham, who disowned his father to prove his loyalty to his Lord, virtues of religious fidelity are emphasized. Even the stars above point to God's omnipotence. He must be obeyed, for His is the right path. Earlier prophets conveyed the same truth to their peoples; they spoke of the unity of God, righteous conduct and faith in the Day of Judgement. These are the essentials of faith. Man has only to look at the multiplicity of God's creation to realize His majesty and power; no one can interfere in this management and no one has any control over it. God manages it as He likes and He is the best of managers.

However, Muslims are told not to revile those who worship other gods, lest the latter revile their God. They should not argue with unbelievers, because even if angels were to come down or the dead were to rise from their graves, testifying to the supremacy of God, the disbelievers would not believe; on the contrary, they would persist in their unbelief and in the worship of idols and worthless gods and goddesses.

Muslims are told that they should be careful in their eating habits; they should not eat the meat of dead animals, or the flesh of pigs, or that of any live animal on which the name of God is not recited while it is being slaughtered. There are ten commandments, which must be obeyed by the faithful: (1) not to associate anyone with God (2) not to show disrespect to one's parents; (3) not to kill one's children because of poverty; (4) not to commit adultery; (5) not to take the life of anyone without a just cause; (6) not to usurp the property of an orphan; (7) not to defraud anyone by tampering

with weights and measures; (8) not to do injustice; (9) not to break
one's promise; and (10) not to create dissension among believers.

SURAH VI

1. Praise be to God,
   Creator of the heavens and the earth.
   He brought in darkness and light.
   Yet there are those who reject Him
   And hold others equal to Him
   But He is the real Guardian of all.

2. From clay, God created man
   And then gave him a fixed life.

3. The Lord of the heavens and the earth
   Knows what you hide and what you reveal.
   He will give you the recompense
   Of what you have earned by your acts.

10. Messengers were mocked before you, O Muhammad!
    But those who scoffed at them
    Finally were mocked and punished.

32. What is this life on this earth
    But a play and an amusement?
    It is the Hereafter that is the best
    For all who are righteous.
    Will you not then understand?

34. Rejected were the apostles before you.
    With patience and constancy they bore it
    And suffered the wrongs done to them
    Until Our aid reached them.
    There is none who can tamper with Our Words.

38. Animals and birds
    Are part of the living world.
    They are not ignored by God;

They are mentioned in His Book.
In the end, they will also gather
Before the Protector of all.

48.   We sent apostles with glad tidings
To warn their peoples
So that those who believe in Us
Should reform themselves.
For them there be no fear,
Nor will they grieve.

51.   To all those who fear Us
Give them this warning.
That everyone will be brought
Before the Lord on the Judgement Day.
They will have no intercessor or protector
Except their Creator.
Hence they should guard themselves
Against all evils.

52.   Drive not away those
Who worship their Lord,
Morning and evening,
Seeking His grace.
In no way are you accountable
For what they do,
Nor are they accountable
For what you do.
Hence do not drive them away
And become the evil-doers.

70.   Leave them alone
For whom religion is a sport
To be played around.
And the life here,
A delightful delusion.
And let them be told
That everyone is responsible
For his own ruin by his acts.
Besides God, they have no intercessor or protector.

72. Pray regularly
    And fear God.
    For it is before Him
    That you shall be brought together.

73. It is He who created in truth
    The heavens and the earth
    He just declares 'Be' and it is.
    His Word is the truth.
    When the trumpet is sounded
    His dominion emerges.
    He alone knows the hidden
    And the manifest.
    He is the Wise, the All-Knowing.

95. God splits the seed-grain and the date-stone
    And then causes them to sprout;
    Thus He brings the dead to life.
    That is God at His creative best.
    How can you then
    Delude yourself from the truth?

98. God has created you
    Of a single man,
    And made this world
    A place of sojourn
    Until you depart.
    Meanwhile, He provides you
    With rain from the skies
    To give you all kinds of vegetation,
    And out of green crops
    Grains at harvest time.
    Then there are the date-palms
    With clusters of dates
    And gardens of olives and pomegranates
    Similar and yet different in taste,
    Some sweet and some sour;
    Feast on them and enjoy them.
    Behold! In all these are Signs
    For people who believe in Us.

101.   The primal origin of heaven and earth
        Is the handiwork of God.
        How can He have a son
        Who has no consort?
        He is above all things,
        For He is the Creator
        And Knower of everything.

102.   God is your Lord,
        There is no other.
        He has created everything.
        Hence worship Him,
        For He alone has the power
        To deal with all affairs.

103.   No one can comprehend
        What He is.
        But He comprehends everything.
        He is above all comprehension,
        All comprehension is within Him.

107.   If God had so desired,
        Man would have worshipped false gods.
        We have not assigned you, O Muhammad!
        To watch over man's doings.
        Nor have you been entrusted
        The task of settling his affairs.

108.   Do not revile those who worship other gods,
        Lest in their ignorance they revile your God.
        Each people sticks to their beliefs,
        They act as they please.
        But in the end
        All shall return to their Lord
        And will be told of the wrongs they did.

165.   O People! It is God who has made you
        His agents and the inheritors of this earth.
        He has raised one above the other in ranks

So that He may test you
On the basis of His gifts to you.
He is, no doubt, quick in punishment
But He is also Oft-Forgiving, Most Merciful.

SURAH VII: AL-A'RAF (THE HEIGHTS)
(206 verses)

In this chapter we find references to the revelations of God given to his messengers from time to time to convey the true meaning of life. He has all through admonished believers to work for the physical and spiritual welfare of mankind. The Quran cites the story of Adam to show how God made him as His viceregent on earth and ordered the angels to bow before him. Every one obeyed except Satan, who, in his arrogance, thought of himself as superior to Adam and refused to obey God's command. He was banished from the heavens and ever since has been doing his worst to mislead people: first he misled Adam and Eve, and thereafter has been misleading their progeny. His weapons have been vanity, jealousy, discord and mischief. He uses them to spread disbelief in God and encourage vice among people.

On the Day of Judgement the denizens of heaven and hell will confront one another. Those in heaven will live in blissful environs, with gardens full of a variety of fruits and flowing rivers. Those in hell will be burning in eternal fire of which they were duly warned. They disbelieved in the supremacy of God and defied His authority, little realizing that He is omnipotent. He created the heavens and the earth in six days; likewise the movement of the sun, the moon and the stars and the changing of night into day and day into night are His handiwork. Instead of praising God for His gifts to mankind, disbelievers choose the path of *kufr*, or denial of His existence; verily, they have gone astray. They ask for trouble and will face the consequences.

When Noah gave the warning to disbelievers, the people of Aad did not heed it and became the victims of the wrath of God. Hud heeded the warning and God saved him and his tribe from the onslaught of the flood. Likewise, Salih was disbelieved by his people and they faced disaster in the form of an earthquake. He chastised his people for 'practising lust for men in preference to women'. They refused to listen to his advice and met a terrible fate: God 'rained down on them a shower of brimstone'. Shuyab told his people to 'give just measure and weight, and not to indulge in fraudulent dealings' and not to 'withhold from the people the things that are their due', also to create 'no mischief on the earth'. They defied him and an earthquake crushed them.

Moses also faced a similar rebellion when he propounded God's message to the Pharaoh and his chiefs. They denounced him as 'a sorcerer well versed' and challenged him to face the best of sorcerers in Egypt, but as the Quran points out, 'Moses' rod turned into a serpent and swallowed all the falsehoods.' Even so, the Pharaoh and his chiefs would not relent, so God inflicted punishment on them – plagues of locusts, lice and frogs – to bring them to their senses. They promised to believe in God if they were spared punishment; but every time they were forgiven and rescued from disaster they broke their word. The Quran explains

> So we exacted retribution from them.
> And drowned them in the sea.
>
> (7:136)

Moses then took the Children of Israel safely across the sea, and despite their lapses, for which he had to castigate even his brother Harun, his followers were saved from the wrath of God, who told Moses, 'My mercy extends to all things.' He favoured all 'those who do right and practise regular charity' and 'believe in Our Signs'.

After giving examples of different prophets and their struggles to bring them to the right path, God asks Muhammad to speak to the disbelievers:

> Tell them: 'O people I have been sent by God
> To whom belongs the dominion of the heavens and earth
> As His messenger to convey the truth

That there is no god but God.
He gives life and death to all,
So believe in God and His Messenger,
The unlettered Prophet, who believes in His words,
And follows Him so that you may be rightly guided.'

(7:158)

SURAH VII

10.   God has placed you, O Man!
        On seats of authority on earth
        And given you the means
        To fulfil your responsibilities.
        But you give Him no thanks.

26.   O Children of Adam!
        We gave you a raiment
        To cover your private parts
        And to add to your adornment.
        But the raiment of righteousness
        Is your best adornment.
        In that is Our Sign
        To show you the right guidance.

27.   O Children of Adam!
        Let Satan not be your guide
        As he has been of your parents.
        He misled them and drove them out,
        Stripping them of their nakedness.
        He and his tribe watch your people
        From where you can not see them;
        They are the evil ones,
        They make friends with those
        Who have no faith in Us.

33.   Tell them, O Muhammad!
        God has forbidden
        Shameful deeds, overt or covert,
        Falsehood of any kind,

Trespassing against reason,
Associating partners with God,
And saying things about Him
Of which you have no knowledge.

34. Every people has been given a fixed period;
It shall neither be reduced
Nor advanced by one moment,
Nor shall it be delayed
Nor advanced by an hour.

54. God alone is your guardian.
He has created heavens and earth
In six days, while being firmly on the Throne.
He draws night as cover for day
And one follows the other in rapid succession.
He has created the sun, the moon and the stars:
Each is governed by His command.
He creates and He governs.
Blessed is He.
He, indeed, is the Cherisher
And Sustainer of the Worlds!

55. Hearken to your Lord for help
And do so humbly and in privacy,
For God loves not those
Who trespass the limits.

56. Do no mischief on earth
And do not disturb His order
Once it has set in.
Call Him for help
And fear Him but longingly
And seek Him sincerely;
For His Mercy is always there
For those who do good deeds.

58. Out of the land that is clean and fertile
God helps you to produce rich harvest.
But out of the land that is barren

Nothing but rotten harvest comes out.
Thus are Our Signs made clear to you
By these symbols of Our creation
So that you may be grateful to Us.

SURAH VIII: AL-ANFAL (THE SPOILS OF WAR)
(75 verses)

This chapter underlines the virtues of *jihad* (struggle, or war) and the significance of victory, and spells out the manner of distribution of war booty. Muslims are enjoined to consolidate the unity of the community, especially in the face of war, which is to be waged in the service of God and not for personal gains. Award of booty has to be viewed in that light; no soldier has an inherent right to it, though his needs are to be satisfied. Hence certain equitable rules of distribution are to be adhered to. Widows and orphans of those who have laid down their lives in the cause of God are to be provided for first.

The principles governing the treatment of prisoners of war are outlined here; these are both humane and generous. Muslims are warned not to wreak vengeance on enemies but to fight them only to advance the cause of God. They are reminded that their victory in the Battle of Badr against heavy odds became possible because of their resoluteness in the face of adversity and, above all, their unflinching faith in the omnipotence of God.

There is also a reference in this chapter to 'those who believed and adopted exile and fought for the faith'; it has been made clear that they are 'in very truth the believers'. Their migration is commended.

SURAH VIII

2.   Hearts of believers tremble
      On hearing the name of God.
      Their faith in Him

Gets strengthened on seeing His Signs.
Hence put all your trust in Him.

3. Believers pray regularly
And give freely in charity
Out of the bounties
Given by Us for your sustenance.

21. Believers, be not like those who say,
'We hear', but they really do not.

24. Believers, respond to God's call
And to that of the Apostle.
It is the Apostle who makes you realize
That God alone has given life to you
He knows what lies in your heart
To Him alone is your return.

27. O you, who believe in God
Betray not His trust
And that of His Apostle,
Nor misappropriate what has been
Entrusted to your care.

28. Remember that your possession and progeny
Are but a test of your faith in Him.
However, your highest reward
Is your faith in Him.

29. Believers, fear God;
He will grant you the criterion
To distinguish between right and wrong.
He alone cleanses you of all impurities
And forgives you your sins,
For God's grace and mercy are unbounded.

38. Tell the unbelievers
That in case they desist
From the path they have chosen

Their misdeeds will be forgiven.
But if they persist, as did those before them,
Their punishment will be severe.

39.   They have to be fought by you
        Until there is no more tumult or oppression,
        And until justice prevails
        And faith in God is restored
        Everywhere and among all.
        But if they cease their hostility
        Then God will see what to do.

40.   And if they don't, then remember
        God is your Protector.
        He is, indeed, most helpful.

53.   God never changes His grace on a people
        Until they themselves change what is in them.
        Verily, God hears and knows everything.

SURAH IX: AL-TAWBAH (THE REPENTANCE)
(129 verses)

In a sense, there is in this chapter a continuation of the theme
elaborated in the previous one; it deals with treaties entered into
with enemies and their breach by the latter and advises Muslims on
what they should do in such circumstances; they were faced with
this question when pagans of Mecca broke their covenant and
engaged in certain treacherous acts. Even then the Quran did not
suggest prompt retaliation. On the contrary, it told Muslims to give
to the other side four months' notice to honour the agreement and
to guard themselves in the intervening period against any untoward
act by the other side. However, if their conciliatory move were to
fail and the enemy refused to relent, then war must be waged to the
bitter end. Nothing should come in the way of pursuing the right
course.

It is made clear that loyalty to God must have precedence over everything else, including 'your love for your fathers, your sons, your brothers or your kindred', 'the wealth you have earned' or 'the fall in your trade that you fear', or the dispossession of 'the dwellings in which you take delight' or 'the land to which you cling'. None of these can be dearer to a Muslim than his faith in God and His messenger. He must strive relentlessly to uphold his faith in God, knowing full well that 'Allah guides not the rebellious'. The Prophet is warned about the hypocrisy of those who do not believe in Allah and the Last Day and 'whose hearts are in doubt'; it is better that they remain inactive:

> If they had come out on your side, O Muhammad,
> They would not have added to your strength.
> On the contrary, they would have created disorder
> Hurrying hither and thither, trying to create
> Disruption and sedition among your people.
>
> (9:47)

This chapter contains reference to *jizyah* (tax on non-Muslims); it is a much maligned provision, which, in reality, was a compensation paid by non-Muslims for exemption from military service, since the latter could not have been expected to participate in wars on behalf of Islam. The relevant verses read:

> Fight those who do not believe
> In God and the Last Day,
> And those who do forbidden things,
> And who do not acknowledge
> The religion of truth
> Even if they be People of the Book,
> Until they pay jizyah
> And willingly submit and are subdued.
>
> (9:29)

SURAH IX

20.   Believers who suffer exile
   While striving in God's cause
   And sacrifice their goods and persons,
   They shall have the highest rank before God.
   They are indeed among those
   Who will attain salvation.

23.   Believers, do not take as your protectors
   Even your fathers or your brothers
   If they are unfaithful to Us.
   If you trust or listen to them
   Then you are verily in the wrong.

38.   Believers, what is wrong with you?
   Why do you cling to this world
   When you are asked to strive
   In the cause of God?
   Do you prefer this life to the Hereafter?
   You know not how useless are
   This world's comforts
   As compared to what is in the Hereafter.
   Why do you then prefer this life
   To that of the Hereafter?

41.   Go forth, whether you are equipped lightly or heavily,
   Striving with your persons and goods
   In the cause of God.
   That is the best way for you
   If only you will understand.

51.   Tell the people, O Muhammad:
   'Nothing will happen to us
   Except what has been decreed by God.
   He is your Protector and mine.'
   Hence let everyone
   Put his trust in Him.

67.   Hypocrites are men and women.
They understand each other,
They enjoin evil and forbid good.
They have forgotten God
So He has forsaken them.
Verily, they are traitors.

71.   Believers, whether men or women,
Are protectors of one another.
They enjoin what is just
And forbid what is evil.
They pray regularly,
They give in charity,
And they obey God and His Apostle
In everything, at all times.
On them will God shower His mercy,
For He is Exalted in Power
And He is All-Wise.

72.   God has promised to every believer
Gardens around which rivers flow,
To dwell in beautiful mansions
And enjoy ever-lasting bliss.
But their greatest bliss will be
The pleasure of God Himself.

97.   The Arabs of the desert are
The worst of unbelievers.
They are hypocrites
Unaware of God's commands
As sent down through His Apostle.
For He knows what is best for them.
He is, indeed, All-Wise.

104.   Do people not know that God
Forgives those who repent
And are His votaries?
He accepts their offerings of charity.
For verily He is Oft-Rewarding and Most Merciful.

105. Tell them to act righteously,
For God observes what they do,
And so does His Apostle,
And also the believers;
Soon will they be brought back
To the One who knows
The seen and the unseen,
And then He shall show them
All that they have done.

109. Which is better,
The one who lays his foundation on piety
And seeks the pleasure of God,
Or the one who lays his foundation on
A shifting sand cliff
Which cannot but crumble to pieces?
He will, indeed, be burnt by hell.
And God never guides
Those who do wrong.

112. But those who, after repentance, turn to God
And are full of praise for Him
And devotedly serve Him
And prostrate before Him,
Doing good and avoiding evil,
And remain within limits
As set by Him;
They shall receive His blessings.
Proclaim this O Muhammad, to all.

SURAH X: YUNUS (JONAH)
(109 verses)

This chapter is addressed to detractors of the Prophet, who cast
aspersions on him by asking why God should have chosen one from
among them as His warner; and if he truly was the warner, why did

he not perform miracles? God confirms that he was indeed His Messenger. As Muhammad was a truthful man, his people should have known of his character and integrity. He had grown up among them and they were fully aware of everything about him. He had never deceived or cheated anyone.

Unwilling to give up their idols, Meccans continued to ask Muhammad for signs from God to prove his credentials such as predicting the future. The Prophet told them, 'The unseen is known only to God.' There are numerous signs, obvious and clear, which point to the sovereignty of God. For instance, the sun, which is 'a shining glory' of His power; the moon, which is 'a light of beauty'; the alternation of night and day, which indicates his organization; the rain, which waters the plants to sustain human life, and animals, which provide the succour to mankind; in short, everything that exists on earth and in heaven, and the birth and death of creatures and their resurrection, establish the might of God, who is the real Cherisher and Sustainer of all creations. Those who talk of partners with Him are in grievous error and are blind to reality. Most of them just follow their fancy. The truth is that God is one and only: He has no equals.

As for the authenticity of the Quran, God declares unequivocally that it is the Book, 'which cannot be produced by anyone other than God'; in fact it is 'a confirmation of the revelations that came before it and their fuller explanation'. Detractors who alleged that Muhammad had forged it are challenged to produce even a single chapter like the one in the Quran. They cannot do so, even if they took help from others. Hence Muhammad is told to ignore their jibes and attacks and to tell them:

> My taste to me, yours to you.
> You are not accountable for what you do
> Nor am I for what you do.
>
> (10:41)

The detractors have 'a little enjoyment' on this earth; but everyone of them has to return to God:

Then We will make them
Suffer the severest punishment
For all their blasphemies.

(10:70)

Through the stories of Noah and Moses, the plight of the disbelievers is depicted and their doom and destruction described. The ultimate triumph of truth is, once again, graphically explained and lessons are drawn.

SURAH X

2.   Why should people wonder
        That We have sent Our Revelation
        To one from among themselves?
        He has come to warn of dangers ahead
        And to give glad tidings about the truth.
        But unbelievers accuse Our Messenger
        Of being a sorcerer.

3.   Verily your Lord is the Creator
        Of the heavens and the earth.
        He created them in six days.
        He is firmly established on His Throne
        Regulating and governing everything.
        No one can intercede with Him
        Except by His leave.
        Indeed He is the Lord. Serve Him
        And listen to His admonition!

4.   Everyone will return to Him,
        That is His promise.
        He creates, destroys and recreates.
        He rewards those who believe in Him,
        But those who reject Him
        Shall suffer grievous hurt.

5.   God has given the sun a shining glory
        And the moon a wondrous light,
        And through their measured beauty

People have the count of time
And learn the number of years.
He has created these
To advance righteousness and truth,
And to explain His signs
To people who understand.

6. In the alternation of night and day
And in all that God has created
In the heavens and on the earth
There are indeed signs
For those who fear Him.

7. Those who do not hope to meet Us
And those who enjoy this life
In the belief that they will not meet Us,
They are those who heed not Our Signs.

8. Their abode is the fire of hell
Into which they will fall
Because of the evil they have done.

9. The Lord will guide those
Who believe in Him
And work righteously,
They will be blessed with gardens
Underneath which rivers flow.

12. When a man is in trouble
He cries to Us in every situation,
Lying on one side or sitting on the other
Or even while standing.
But when We have eased his trouble
He goes about his way pretending
He had never cried to Us,
And did not do anything unfair.

13. Many generations before you, O people!
Were destroyed when they refused to

Listen to their apostles
And rejected Our clear Signs.
They would not believe in Us
And thus were punished for their sins.

15.   And even when Our clear verses are read to them
They persist in saying:
'This is not enough,
Bring something else or change this.'
Tell them, O Muhammad!
'It is not for me to replace or change them.
If I were to disobey my Lord
I would suffer the severest punishment
On the Day of Judgement.'

16.   Tell them further:
'If God had so willed
I would not have preached as I do.
I have spent a whole lifetime in your midst.
Why can't you then understand my position?'

19.   Mankind was created as one nation,
But it differed subsequently.
Had God wished otherwise
Differences would have been easily settled.

21.   When We show mercy to a people
After they have suffered adversity,
Behold, instead of being grateful
They plot against Us.
Tell them:
'God is a swifter and better planner.'
Verily, Our messengers are aware of
All the plans that are made by Us.

22.   God enables you, O people,
To travel over land and sea.
You rejoice while boarding ships
And are happy with favourable breeze.

But you cry to Us for help
When the waves confront you.
Then you beseech Us and say:
'If you will deliver Us from the calamity
We shall indeed be grateful to you.'

23.   But when We deliver you
Behold! you become insolent and defiant.
This is not good for your souls.
What worth is the enjoyment of this life
When in the end you shall return to Us
And shall be told of all that you did?

24.   Your present life is like the rain
Which We send down from the skies.
Their juxtaposition produces the food
For men, women and animals,
Until the fields look like golden ornaments
And their owners feel content.
But suddenly We dry them up.
In these are Our Signs
For those who can reflect.

25.   God invites you to peace in heaven.
He guides whom He pleases
To the path that is straight.

26.   To those who do righteous deeds
There shall be good reward
Such as cannot be measured.
They shall not be shamed
Nor will their faces be tarred.
They will be companions in heaven
Where they shall abide forever.

27.   But those who do evil,
They will receive ignominy..
Their faces will be blackened
And they shall have no defender

Against the wrath of God.
They shall fall in hell
To burn therein forever.

30.   Every soul will taste
Fruits of its own deeds,
And when people will be brought
In the presence of their Lord
They shall then realize
How false was their belief.

31.   Ask them: 'Who is it that
Sustains you and has the power
Over your hearing and sight?
Who gives you life
And raises you from the dead
And who regulates your affairs?'
They have to admit that it is God.
Ask them then why they do not worship Him
And be pious and do righteous deeds.

32.   God indeed is your Cherisher and Sustainer.
This is the truth which distinguishes right from wrong.
Then why do you turn your back on Him?

33.   The word of God is true
And not of those who refute it
And do not believe in Him.

37.   This Quran given to you, O Muhammad!
Is, indeed, Our creation.
No one else can produce it.
In it is confirmation of Our message
Sent to earlier messengers
And an elaboration of the same truth
That the Lord of the Worlds
Has revealed from time to time.

38.   Unbelievers may say
Muhammad has forged it.

Ask them: 'Can you bring
One surah like this
Even with the help of others?'
The result will be obvious.

41.   If they charge you, O Muhammad, with falsehood
Tell them, 'My task to me, yours to you.
You are not accountable for what I do
Nor am I for what you do.'

42.   Some of them may pretend to listen to you,
But in reality they do not.
How can you make the deaf hear,
Or make sense to the senseless?

43.   And there are some
Who pretend to look to you
For guidance,
But they are blind.
How can you make them see?

44.   Verily God does not wrong man,
It is man who wrongs himself.

47.   Remember: To every nation
We have sent an apostle
For people to be rightly guided.
And then We judge them fairly
And do not wrong them in any way.

56.   It is God who gives life
And who takes it away
And to Him shall we all return.

57.   O people: this is the guidance
That has come to you from your Lord
So that it may heal the wounds in your heart
And you may take to the right path.

58.   Tell the people:
        'Rejoice in the bounty of God.
        It will give you better satisfaction
        Than all the wealth you may possess.'

61.   In whatever state you are,
        Whether reciting the Quran
        Or performing a good deed,
        We see everything.
        Nothing remains hidden from Us.
        Not even the smallest atom or the biggest article;
        Everything is clearly recorded for Us.

99.   Had your Lord so wished,
        All people everywhere
        Would have been believers.
        But that is not His way,
        Hence do not force anyone
        To take to Our path
        Unless they do so willingly.

104.   Tell them O Muhammad:
        'In case you doubt the truth of my way,
        I cannot help you; but remember
        To God alone you will be accountable
        Of all that you do.
        As for me, I offer my gratitude to Him,
        For having put me among His believers.'

108.   But those who are disbelievers
        And choose to go astray,
        The loss will, indeed, be theirs.
        And make it clear to them, O Muhammad,
        That you are not there
        To settle their affairs.

109.   Follow then, O Muhammad, your direction.
        Be patient and constant in your faith.
        God alone will decide your fate,
        For He is the best decision-maker.

SURAH XI: HUD
(123 verses)

Once again in this chapter there is a reference to man's ingratitude to God, his rejection of the true path as shown by successive prophets – Noah, Hud, Abraham, Shuyab and Moses – and the punishments that disbelievers had to go through for their defiance of the divine call in every age.

It begins with the classification of the Quranic verses into two groups: first, basic or fundamental, and second, figurative or allegorical. Their relevance and inter-dependence are explained. The basic verses enjoin the faithful to 'worship none but God', to accept Muhammad as His messenger, sent 'to warn and to bring glad tidings', and to desist from evil and do good deeds.

Believers are asked to 'seek God's forgiveness' and to 'turn to Him in repentance',

> So that He may grant them
> Such pleasures as are good
> And bestow His grace on them
> For performing righteous deeds.
> But if they turn back on Him
> Then they shall be punished
> On the Day of Judgement.
>
> (11:3)

Stories of earlier prophets are recounted in this chapter. The Quran explains:

> Stories of Our apostles
> That We narrate to you
> All have one object:
> To make your heart stout
> In the pursuit of truth.
> They provide both an exhortation
> And a lesson to believers.
>
> (11:120)

SURAH XI

1. This is a Book wherein
   There are verses basic or fundamental.
   They are of permanent value.
   They are made plain by God,
   Who is Wise and All-Aware.

2. It teaches people
   To worship none but God.
   Tell them, O Muhammad:
   'Verily I have been sent by God
   To warn and give glad tidings.'

3. Also to explain to them
   To first seek God's forgiveness
   And turn to Him in repentance,
   So that He may grant them
   Such pleasures as are good
   And bestow His grace on them
   For performing righteous deeds.
   But if they turn back on Him
   Then they shall be punished
   On the Day of Judgement.

9. If We show mercy to man
   And then withdraw it,
   He loses his balance
   And falls into blasphemy.

10. In distress, We come to his rescue.
    He exults then and boasts
    That he is free of all evils.

11. The Believers are righteous,
    They work with patience and constancy.
    They are guaranteed forgiveness
    And promised great reward.

15.   Those who are desirous of this life
          And its glitter and pleasures,
          They shall have to pay
          For what they did.
          But they will not suffer unjustly.

118.   Had your Lord so willed,
          He could have made whole of mankind one,
          But even then disputes among people
          Would not have ceased.

121.   Tell those who do not believe,
          They may do what they can.
          But we shall not desist
          From doing our part.

122.   Let them await the result,
          And so shall God.

123.   God alone knows the unseen
          In the heavens and on the earth,
          To Him alone we shall return
          For adjudication of our affairs.
          Pray to Him then and have faith in Him,
          For He knows all that we have done.

SURAH XII: YUSUF (JOSEPH)
(111 verses)

The story of Joseph, the eleventh of the twelve sons of Patriarch Jacob, is narrated here in detail. It is described as 'the most beautiful of all the stories'. It throws abundant light on all aspects of human relationships: the love of the aged father for his sons, his preference for Joseph, the most innocent and virtuous of them; the jealousy that this creates among Joseph's brothers; their intrigue against him;

and the resultant sale of him as a slave and the grief that this causes to the father.

While on a journey, Joseph is bought by an Egyptian merchant from his brothers and taken to the Court, where the ruler's wife Zulikha falls in love with him. Joseph resists the overtures of the Queen; he is put in prison on the false charge of trying to seduce her. Despite the treatment meted out to him in prison, he steadfastly adheres to the truth, and Joseph's strong convictions impress his co-prisoners. One of them, when released, obtains the favour of the ruler's cup-bearer and through him conveys the truth about Joseph to the ruler. He also informs him that Joseph possessed the ability to interpret dreams and the power to foretell the future and could predict any calamity to befall man.

The ruler summons Joseph and asks him to interpret a dream of his. Joseph agrees on condition that the scandals spread against him should be publicly withdrawn. The ruler orders accordingly; he is pleased with the strong-willed, straightforward Joseph and appoints him his *vazir*, or minister. Meanwhile, Joseph's half-brothers, driven by famine, arrive in Egypt and seek Joseph's help. They do not recognize their brother, but he recognizes them. He asks them to bring Benjamin, his real brother, to him before their plea could be heard; they comply. Joseph keeps Benjamin with him and convicts the others of treachery; but finally he gives in to their pleas and forgives them and treats them with kindness. The whole family, including the patriarch Jacob, is brought from Canaan. They join Joseph and the family is reunited. The moral is clear — those whom God protects, no one can destroy:

> There is in the stories of our apostles
> A lesson for men of understanding.
> These are not tales invented,
> But in them is confirmation
> Of Our guidance and exposition
> Of things revealed by Us
> And assurance of mercy to believers.
>
> (12:111)

SURAH XII

56.   We gave power to Joseph
Whenever it pleased Us,
For we bestow Our mercy
On whosoever We please.
And We do not forget
To reward the righteous.

57.   For those who believe
And work righteously
Their reward is, indeed, the best.

105.   How many of God's marvels
In the heavens and the earth
People see and yet pass by.

106.   Most of them do not believe in Him
Unless they associate some partners with Him.

107.   Do they not realize that Allah's scourge
Will fall on them and the Hour of Doom
Will overtake them unawares?

108.   Tell them, O Muhammad:
'This is my path; I invite you to it.
Have faith in Allah
On the basis of what you see,
And what I and my followers do.
Glory to Our Lord, who is One.
I will never join anyone with Him.'

109.   We sent messengers before you;
They were human like you,
And We inspired them as We inspire you.
They lived and travelled like humans,
And saw the end of those who opposed them.
The Hereafter is best for those
Who do righteous deeds.

111.   There is in the stories of our apostles
         A lesson for men of understanding.
         These are not tales invented,
         But in them is confirmation
         Of Our guidance and exposition
         Of things revealed by Us
         And assurance of mercy to believers.

SURAH XIII: AL-RAD (THE THUNDER)
(43 verses)

This chapter eulogizes the majesty and power of God and explains how signs in nature establish the truth of His existence. Those who respond to His call, as conveyed by His messenger, will be blessed by 'all good things'; but for those who do not, 'the reckoning will be terrible'. The words of the Quran are clear:

         Those who patiently persevere
         And seek the Lord's countenance
         And establish regular prayers
         And do charity out of what they have,
         Either openly or secretly,
         And ward off evil with good;
         For them the final abode will be
         The eternal home in the heavens.

                              (13:23)

This home is beautifully described. It shall be surrounded by 'gardens of perpetual bliss'. Its gates will be open to the righteous, where they will find 'their fathers, their spouses and their offspring'. Angels will salute and greet them thus:

         Peace be upon you
         For you have persevered
         For so long, so patiently.
         But now comes the reward
         In this excellent final home.
                              (13:24)

Muhammad has again been consoled and asked by God not to bother about disbelievers and their tactics:

> Many messengers before you
> Were also mocked by them,
> But I granted them respite first
> And then punished them.
> Indeed, terrible was my requital.
>
> (13:32)

The Prophet's role in this regard was made clear:

> Your duty, O Muhammad, is
> To make My message reach them.
> It is My part then
> To call them to account.
>
> (13:39)

He was told not to worry about their plots:

> Those who came before you also
> Devised plots against My messengers.
> But their plans came to naught,
> For the best planner is Allah:
> He counters all other plans.
>
> (13:42)

SURAH XIII

11.   For each person,
Guards are kept
To watch over them
By command of God.
Verily, Allah never changes
The condition of a people
Unless they change it themselves.
And if He wishes to afflict them with
Misfortune, none can ward it off.
Besides Him, there is no Protector.

14.   Pray to God alone;
        He alone can reply.
        If you pray to others besides Him
        It will be like stretching your hands
        To take water to your mouth.
        But when there is no water,
        What is the use of this stretching?
        So are the prayers of those
        Who have faith in others and not in Us.

38.   Apostles were sent before you, O Muhammad!
        They also had wives and children like you.
        It was not given to any apostle
        To bring a sign except as God willed,
        And for each We revealed a book.

39.   God blots out or confirms what He likes.
        He keeps with Him the Mother of the Book.

SURAH XIV: IBRAHIM (ABRAHAM)
(52 verses)

This chapter lays emphasis on the importance of the Quran, which gives light to people trapped in darkness; it points out that God sent a messenger to every people to teach them the truth in their own language. This was necessary in order to make them understand things well. The implication is clear: no particular language is of God; in fact He speaks every language, depending on the need and the location.

Once again, there is reference to Moses and the way he overcame, through the help of God, the evil forces of Pharaoh. The Egyptian King and his chiefs met a miserable end. People are also reminded of the fate of earlier generations:

        O people, have you not heard
        The tales of those in the past?
        Of Noah and his people who defied him,

> And also of Ad and Thamud
> And those who came after them.
> None is better aware than Allah.
> Messengers were sent with clear signs,
> But they refused to listen to them,
> Casting doubt on their mission.
>
> (14:9)

'Doubt about what?' the disbelievers were asked. About God? The Creator of the heavens and the earth? How foolish they were! They also jeered and mocked at the apostles because they were 'no more than humans like ourselves'. The apostles replied, in the words of the Quran:

> True, we are humans like yourselves
> But Allah has granted His grace to us
> His servants as He has pleased.
>
> (14:11)

Faith in Him has to be implicit.

SURAH XIV

1.   A book has been sent to you
        So that you may lead mankind
        Out of darkness into light,
        And show by His leave
        The way to reach Him,
        The exalted in power.

4.   We sent apostles everywhere
        To teach people in their language
        Things to be made clear,
        So that they may not go astray.
        Those who obey, God blesses them.
        He guides only those whom He pleases,
        For He is, indeed, Exalted and All-Wise.

23.   Those who believe and work righteously
        Will be admitted to gardens in the heavens

Beneath which rivers flow –
To dwell therein for ever
With the leave of their Lord.
Their greeting will be 'Peace'.

24. Do you know of a parable
Sent forth by God
About a healthy tree
Whose roots were firmly fixed,
And its branches reached the heavens?

25. It yielded fruits in every season
As willed by God.
So is it with a good word
Through which admonition comes.

26. However, an evil word is like a rotten tree;
Its roots are all torn apart.
They give no stability to the tree.

32. It is God who has created
The heavens and the earth.
He sends down rains from the skies
And produces food to feed you.
God has made the ships for you
So that you may sail through the seas.
He has also made rivers subservient to you.

33. He has put under your subjugation
The sun and the moon.
They diligently pursue their course
And thus alternate night and day.

34. God gives you
All that you ask.
You cannot count
The favours He does.
For verily, man is ungrateful.

48.   One day this earth will be changed
       To something different,
       And so will be the Heavens,
       By Allah, the One, the Supreme.

49.   The sinners on that day
       Will be chained together.

50.   Their shirts made of pitch,
       Their faces covered with fire.

51.   Thus God will reward each one
       According to his deserts.
       Verily, God is swift in taking accounts.

52.   Our Message is clear for mankind:
       Let people take heed of it.
       That there is no God but One.

SURAH XV: AL-HIJR (THE ROCK)
(99 verses)

In this chapter, believers are told to let unbelievers 'enjoy' and 'please themselves', for their pleasures are illusory; God alone is the reality. They are drawn towards Satan, who, in his arrogance, has defied God's orders and is trying to mislead mankind. He was given a respite, but in his insolence he took the wrong path. He has become vengeful and is struggling to take people away from the right path.

Once, angels came to Abraham as guests and informed him of the impending birth of a son, despite his old age. They also told him that the people of Lot were going to be afflicted by a terrible calamity, because they were indulging in abominations. As predicted, brimstone rained down upon them; even the wife of Lot was not spared, as she too had gone astray. Likewise, 'the companions of Wood' (who were presumably the people of Madyan),

having rebelled against Shuyab, were also destroyed.
From these accounts Muhammad is assured:

> Sufficient are We
> For you, against those
> Who scoff and mock at you.
>
> (15:95)

The Prophet is told that he should not be 'distressed at what they say'. He should 'serve his Lord until there comes to you the Hour that is certain'.

SURAH XV

10. We had sent apostles before you, O Muhammad,
    Amongst various people in the past.

11. But never was an apostle
    Not mocked at by their people.

24. We are, indeed, aware of both:
    People who lag behind
    And people who go forward.

25. God will assuredly bring them together,
    For He is perfect in wisdom, All-Knowing.

28. The Lord said to the angels:
    'I am about to create man from clay
    And mould him into shape.

29. 'After fashioning him in due proportions
    I shall breathe My Spirit into him.
    Hence do obeisance to him.'

30. So all the angels prostrated before man,

31. Except Satan, who refused.

32.   God asked him: 'O Satan!
        Why do you not prostrate
        Along with the angels?'

33.   Satan replied, 'I will not be one
        To prostrate before him,
        Whom you have created out of dust
        And then moulded into shape.'

34.   God thundered: 'Then get out from here!
        You are rejected and accursed.

35.   'And the curse on you
        Shall last till Judgement Day.'

36.   Satan pleaded, 'O my Lord,
        Give me then respite
        Until the dead are raised by you.'

37.   God granted Satan the respite

38.   Till the appointed time.

39.   Satan said, 'Since I am put in the wrong,
        I will see that wrong looks right
        And cause your creatures to deviate from the
            right path,

40.   'Except those who adhere to their faith
        And remain devoted to You.'

41.   God replied, 'That will be My way.

42.   'For over My servants
        You shall have no control.
        But those who go astray
        And follow you,

43.   'Verily, their abode,
           As promised by Me,
           Will, indeed, be hell.'

SURAH XVI: AL NAHL-(THE BEES)
(128 verses)

Here, to begin with, is a reminder that God sends down through his angels 'inspiration to such of his servants as He pleases' to convey to mankind 'that there is no god but God'. He has created man 'from a drop of sperm', but this helpless creature becomes arrogant and even dares to dispute the authority of his Creator. He remains oblivious to the many benefits that God has given: cattle, who carry heavy loads for him; water that he drinks; rains that cause vegetation to grow and provide corn, olives, dates, grapes and other fruits. Likewise, God has made night and day subject to his requirements. The sun, the moon and the stars are signs of God's governance and serve the needs of man, as do the seas and the mountains.

However, worshippers of false gods continue with their infidelity; they turn these signs into gods and worship them. They say, 'If Allah so wanted we would not have worshipped others.' But they don't listen to His messengers, who are sent with a clear message that none but He is worthy of worship. They expect miracles or magical proofs, but that is not the way Allah conveys the truth. It is by preaching that His work has to be carried out, and that is the task entrusted by Him to His messengers.

God shows much patience and forbearance in bringing the truth to the people:

           If Allah were to punish
           People for their wrongdoing,
           Not a living creature
           Would remain unpunished.
           But He gives everyone a respite
           For a specified time.
           And thereafter, the person is not spared

> For a single moment.
> No sinner should expect
> Any delay in punishment.
>
> (16:61)

God admonishes His creatures to be just and do good to one another, and to be kind to their kith and kin. He forbids everyone from indulging in shameful things, from doing mischief and spreading discord. If God wanted he could have made all his creatures as one people, but He allows everyone freedom of action. However, each one will be held accountable on the Day of Judgement. The Prophet is told clearly:

> Call all to accept
> The Way of the Lord,
> But do it with wisdom
> And use persuasion.
> Adopt ways that are gracious,
> For your Lord knows best
> Who strays from His path.
>
> (16:125)

He is asked to be patient with them and not to grieve if they don't listen to him. Also, he should not be distressed by the plots they hatch against him. For God is his protector, and no plot can succeed against His will.

SURAH XVI

4. It is God who has created man.
    He has created him from a sperm ·
    And behold! This same man
    Becomes His open disputer.

19. And God knows what man conceals
     And what he reveals.

41. To those who migrate
     In the cause of God,
     After having suffered oppression,

They will, assuredly, be given
A comfortable home in this world.
But their reward is greater in the Hereafter,
Much greater than they can visualize.

42.   They are, indeed, those who patiently persevere
And put all their faith in their Lord.

49.   In reality, all God's creatures,
Whether on earth or in the heavens,
Whether they are of this earth
Or whether they are angels,
Offer their homage to God humbly
And without a trace of arrogance.

63.   God sent His apostles before you, O Muhammad!
But Satan tempted and misled their people,
And made their own acts alluring.
Even today he is the patron of such people.
They shall all suffer a most grievous penalty.

64.   And we sent down Our Book
To explain matters in which people differed,
So that it may become
A guide and a mercy to believers.

72.   God has created mates for you,
So that you may have your own progeny.
And He has provided sustenance for each.
How can you then believe in false things
And be ungrateful to Him for His favours?

77.   The mysteries of earth and the heavens
Are known only to God,
And He will give His judgement
Quicker than the twinkling of an eye
On the Day of Judgement.

78. It is God who brought you into this world
    From out of the womb of your mother.
    He gave you sight and hearing,
    Intelligence and the capacity to feel.
    Hence, be grateful to Him for His blessings.

79. Who makes birds flutter in the air
    And holds them poised in the sky?
    It is only the power of God.
    These are some of His signs
    For believers to reflect upon.

93. If God had so wanted
    He could have made you one people,
    But He leaves them alone
    To decide for themselves.
    Some go astray and some, right.
    Each will account for his deeds.

96. What is with God endures,
    What is with man perishes.
    He bestows His favours on those
    Who patiently persevere.
    Each will get his reward
    According to his deserts.

97. Whoever works righteously,
    Whether men or women,
    And believe in Us,
    We shall give them
    Purer and better existence
    And bestow on them the best of rewards.

101. Sometimes, when We substitute
    One revelation for another
    For reasons best known to Us,
    They accuse you of forgery.
    But don't bother about them,
    For they know not what they say.

102.   Tell them that God has sent these revelations
    To strengthen the faith of believers,
    In order that these may serve
    As a guide and glad tidings to them.

106.   Anyone who accepts the faith
    And then retracts from it,
    On him will be the wrath of God
    And he will suffer dreadful punishment,
    Except the one who does so under compulsion
    With his heart loyal to the faith.

107.   They go back on their faith
    Because they love this world
    More than the Hereafter.
    These rejectors of faith
    Are devoid of God's guidance.

111.   On the Day of Judgement
    Everyone will struggle
    To save himself.
    There will be justice for all
    And none will be unjustly treated.

125.   Call all to accept
    The way of the Lord,
    But do it with wisdom
    And use persuasion.
    Adopt ways that are gracious,
    For your Lord knows best
    Who strays from His path.

128.   God is always with those
    Who exercise restraint
    And do good in this world.

SURAH XVII: BANU ISRA'IL (THE ISRAELITES)
(111 verses)

At the start of this surah, there is mention of *meraj*, or the ascension of the Prophet to the high heavens when he had the vision of God. It describes his journey from the sacred mosque of Mecca to the farthest mosque at Jerusalem (the Al Aqsa), and from thence to the heavens, where he was given a glimpse of the eternal. It has a mystical significance and provides an insight into the spiritual journey of man in search of God.

The Quran makes it clear that everyone is responsible for his deeds or misdeeds; they will be recorded on a scroll kept by angels at God's command. No one will be allowed to bear the burden of another, nor will God visit his wrath on people unless they are first guided by His messenger and given sufficient warning. Then there are admonitions for the treatment of parents: 'Say not to them a word of contempt; on the contrary be respectful toward them.' Likewise, be good to the kindred and all 'those in want'; do not squander wealth, nor kill children for 'fear of want'. Do not commit adultery, nor 'kill anyone except for just cause'. Do not tamper with the property of an orphan. Fulfil every commitment. Also, be honest and careful when you measure and weigh anything, and do not persist in pursuing things of which you have no knowledge. Never be insolent, because it is hateful to God.

The faithful are told to establish regular prayers to God, morning, evening and night, and to recite the Quran so as to heal the wounds and be the source of mercy to all who struggle in His cause. Muhammad is told:

> Say: 'Everyone acts
> According to his own disposition.
> Only your Lord knows
> Who is the best guided.'
>
> (17:84)

The Quran remains the best guide; nothing can compare to it:

Tell the disbelievers, O Muhammad!
'If the whole of mankind and all Jinns
Were to come and try
They could not produce
Anything like this Quran,
However much they may try
And help one another.'

(17:88)

It is God's Word and He is supreme. He is the Creator, to whom every living creature is beholden:

Call Him Rahman
Or by any other name.
He is the Lord of everyone.
To Him belong the most beautiful names.
Do not pray loudly to Him
Nor in a low tone,
But in moderation
Taking the middle course.

(17:109)

SURAH XVII

1.   Glory be to God
      Who took His servant
      On a journey at night
      From the sacred mosque [at Mecca]
      To the farthest mosque [in Palestine].
      He was blessed by Us
      So that We might show him Our signs,
      For God hears and sees all things.

13.   Everyone's ledger of actions
      Is fastened round his neck;
      It shall be brought out
      On the Day of Judgement.
      Then each will see the scroll –
      It will be opened before him.

14.   He will be asked to read his own record
As evidence of the fate that awaits him.

15.   Those who receive guidance from Us
Do so for their own good.
And those who go astray
Bear the weight of their guilt.
For no man can bear another's burden,
Nor do We ever punish a people
Unless We provide guidance to them.

19.   To those who strive
For the good in the Hereafter
And believe in Us,
To them we shall give
Our acceptance and blessings.

20.   In the grant of our bounties
We make no distinction to start with
Between those who believe in Us
And those who do not.
For our bounties are not closed to anyone.

23.   Your Lord has commanded
That you worship none but Him,
And that you shall be kind to your parents,
Both father and mother,
Especially when they are old.
Do not utter a word of contempt.
Do not repel them in any way.
Always address them with respect.

24.   And be humble and gentle to them.
Pray to the Lord to bestow His mercy on them,
For they cherished you when you were a child
And looked after your utmost needs.

25.   Your Lord knows what lies in your heart.
If you act righteously

You shall be given His grace.
For God is, indeed, most gracious
To those who turn reverently to Him.

26. Give to your relations their due
And to the needy what they need.
And to the wayfarer what you can.
But do not squander what you have
In the manner of a spendthrift.

27. Spendthrifts are the brothers of the Devil
And the Devil remains
Ungrateful to the Lord.

31. Do not kill your children
For fear of want.
We shall provide sustenance
For them as well as you.
Indeed, killing children
Is a great sin.

32. Nor commit adultery.
It is a disgraceful act,
An evil of evils,
For it opens the door
To other evils.

33. Do not kill anyone
But for a just cause,
For life is sacred.
However, if one is killed unjustly,
Then his heir can demand
Redress from the killer
Or grant him forgiveness.
But the heir should not take
The law in his hands
And kill the killer.
Then the law will hold
The heir equally guilty.

34.   Do not tamper with an orphan's property,
Except to improve it till he comes of age.
And fulfil all the commitments by him.
You shall have to account
For each of these
On the Day of Reckoning.

35.   Measure correctly
And weigh properly
With a balance
That is not faulty.
It is not only just to do so,
But also most advantageous.

36.   Do not pursue anything
Of which you have no knowledge,
For God looks to every act,
What you say, or hear or feel,
And it shall be examined
On the Day of Reckoning.

37.   Do not strut about arrogantly
When you walk on the earth.
Remember, you cannot rend the earth asunder
Or measure up to the highest mountain.

53.   Tell the people
That they should speak
The best of things
And not to follow Satan,
Who sows dissensions among them
For Satan is their avowed enemy.

70.   To the Children of Adam
We have given special facilities
On both land and seas,
And bestowed on them
The good things,
Far above the other creations.

80.   Say: 'O My Lord!
        Let me enter this world
        Truthfully and honourably
        And let me also depart
        With truth and honour intact
        And grant me the strength
        To remain as I am.'

81.   And say: 'Truth has come
        And falsehood has gone,
        For falsehood cannot last.'

82.   What we have sent down
        In the form of the Quran
        From time to time
        Is a healing and a grace
        To the believers,
        But to the sinners
        Nothing but loss is in store.

83.   Yet when we shower
        Our blessing on man
        He forgets and goes astray.
        But when evil befalls him
        He begins to despair.

84.   Say: 'Everyone acts
        According to his own disposition.
        Only your Lord knows
        Who is the best guided.'

88.   Tell the disbelievers, O Muhammad!
        'If the whole of mankind and all the Jinns
        Where to come and try
        They could not produce
        Anything like this Quran,
        However much they may try
        And help one another.'

89.   In this Quran
We have explained to man
By citing examples
So that he may follow it.
But still most of them
Persist ungratefully
In their unbelief.

90.   They say: 'We shall not
Accept you, O Muhammad!
Until you cause
A spring to gush forth
From the dry earth

91.   'Or until you
Produce out of it
Date trees and vines
And bring forth
Rivers gushing with water.

92.   'Or make the sky
Come down into pieces,
Or show us your God
And the angels
And make them face us.

93.   'Or show us your house
Adorned with gold,
Or mount a ladder to the skies.
But even then we shall not believe
Unless you bring us a book
Which we can easily read.'
Say: 'Glory to my Lord,
I am but a man,
Who has come to you
As His Messenger.
I am nothing more.'

94.   The trouble with people is
That when guidance comes to them,

Instead of believing it
They question the messenger:
'Isn't it strange that
God has sent a man like us
As His Messenger?'

95.   Tell them, O Muhammad!
'If there were angels on this earth
Walking in peace and tranquillity,
Instead of human beings,
Then certainly God would have sent
An angel as His messenger.'

96.   Tell them: 'God is witness to my mission
And that should be enough,
For He knows all His creatures.
He is well informed
About everything.'

110.   Pray to God
By invoking His name.
Call Him Allah or Rahman
Or by any other name:
Every name fits Him.
However, do not pray
Too loudly or softly,
But adopt a moderate tone.

SURAH XVIII: AL–KAHF (THE CAVE)
(110 verses)

This chapter deals with the story of a people long, long ago, who
lived in a cave and remained in slumber until they were awakened
by their Lord:

We relate to you their story
Because they were the youths

Who believed in their Lord
And We guided and advanced them.

(18:15)

There is a parable narrated here concerning two men: one had two gardens of grapevines, date-palms and corn, with a river flowing in the midst of them. His produce was plentiful and he boasted that it could never perish. The other was his companion, who did not possess any garden but had full faith in the mercy of God. He told the first one, 'It may be that God will give something better to me than what you have.' His friends did not take what he said seriously; in fact they made fun of him. But soon they saw thunderbolts fall on the gardens of the first one, turning them into sandy wastes. The companion, who had put his faith in God, felt sorry for him. The moral is plain: man must not forget that his only protection comes from God, who creates whatever He pleases and destroys whatever He likes.

Your sons and your wealth
Are nothing but allurements;
What counts with the Lord
Are your good deeds.
They will be your best rewards
And the foundation of your hopes.

(18:46)

This is illustrated by a story of Moses on a journey with his servant. They were carrying a fish with them. When Moses asked for it at mealtime, the servant told him that it had slipped into the sea. Moses decided to travel back on the same route in search of the fish. On the way, he met another person blessed by God. Moses asked him whether he could accompany him. The man demurred and said that Moses would not have the patience and would go on asking him all the time about what he did. Moses promised not to ask questions, so the man allowed Moses to accompany him. In the midst of a river, however, he scuttled the boat on which they were travelling, and the other passengers were drowned. Moses was aghast at his action and enquired why he was so cruel. The person reminded Moses that he had promised not to be inquisitive.

The two then took to the road. On the way, the person saw a young man and killed him. Moses could not bear it any more. He protested, but his companion took no notice of it. They then reached a village, where they asked for some food. The villagers did not oblige, but before leaving, the person repaired a crumbling wall and asked for no recompense. 'Why did you do this free of charge?' asked Moses. The man scolded him and said he could not proceed further, as he asked too many questions.

He then explained the three extraordinary events that had taken place. The boat belonged to people who were in dire need of it. By scuttling it, he had made it unserviceable so that the King would not confiscate it. As for the deceased youth, he was a rebel against his parents, whom, had he lived, he would have harmed; in his place God would give them a more faithful son. The wall that the man rebuilt belonged to two orphans, and under it treasure was buried; in order to ensure its safety, he had repaired the wall.

This tale is followed by the story of Dhu al Qarnayan, or the 'Two-horned one'. He was a most powerful king, perhaps Alexander the Great. He erected a barrier to protect the people from Gog and Magog, with the result that no one could scale it. He made it clear:

> This is a mercy from my Lord
> But when the time comes
> As promised by the Lord,
> He will turn this wall into dust.
> (18:98)

No one, not even the messengers or the chosen ones of God, can protect people from calamity; God alone is the protector. But the reward for those who reject faith and jest about His messengers will be hell. On the other hand, those who believe in God and do righteous deeds, their abode will be paradise. Muhammad was asked to tell the people:

> 'I am a man like you,
> I have been honoured by God
> To be the receiver of His Revelations
> And to proclaim
>   the Oneness of God.'

And tell them to work righteously
And not to accept
Anyone as His partner.

(18:110)

SURAH XVIII

7.   We have made
Whatever is on this earth
A glittering show
In order to test
Who conducts themselves
In the best manner.

23.   Do not say: 'I will do it tomorrow'

24.   Without adding:
'If God so pleases.'
And remember Him
In case you forget
By telling yourself,
'Please God, guide me
To come nearer to the right path.'

27.   And recite the revelations
As given to you in the Lord's book.
Remember: none can change His words
Nor can any one have
Shelter other than His.

46.   Your sons and your wealth
Are nothing but allurements;
What counts with your Lord
Are your good deeds.
They will be your best rewards
And the foundation of your hopes

48.   On the Appointed Day,
When people shall be arranged

Before their Lord,
Row after row.
They will be told:
'You have come to Us
As we had created you.
However, when you were told
About this Appointed Day
You thought it would
Never come about.'

49. Then the record of your deeds
Will be placed before you.
The sinners will tremble with fear,
For they will see in it
Everything, big or small,
Nothing will be left out.
And then your Lord will treat
Every case justly and fairly.
But no wrong will be done to anyone.

50. When God asked the angels
To bow before Adam,
All obeyed except Satan.
Though he was one of the Jinns
He broke the Lord's command.
How can man then take Satan and his progeny
As his protectors instead of God?
They are, indeed, his enemies.
They will lead him to evil
And there will be no recompense.

56. We send Our apostles
To give glad tidings
And also to warn people.
But unbelievers dispute
With vain arguments,
Trying to weaken the truth the apostles bring,
Even jesting about Our Signs
Despite the warning to them.

58.   But your Lord is most forgiving
        And ever so merciful;
        If He had so wished
        He would have punished them.
        But He has fixed a day;
        They will not escape it.

110.   Tell the people, O Muhammad!
        'I am a man like you,
        I have been honoured by God
        To be the receiver of His revelations
        And to proclaim
           the oneness of God.'
        And tell them to work righteously
        And not to accept
        Anyone as His partner.

SURAH XIX: MARYAM (MARY)
(98 verses)

This chapter contains stories of some of the prophets. It begins with Zachariah's prayer in which he asks God to give him an heir to carry on the divine mission. This seemed impossible, as he was extremely old and his wife was barren. But his prayer was answered: a son was born to his wife. He was named Yahya.

Likewise, when an angel from God announced to virgin Mary the gift of a son, she was horrified, as no man had touched her. She said, 'Oh! I wish I had died before this.' But the Lord comforted her, and when Jesus was born, the infant spoke to the people from the cradle:

        I am the slave of God.
        The Lord has given me the Book
        And made me His Messenger.
        I am blessed by Him wherever I be.
        He has commanded me to worship Him
        And show compassion to all.

> It is my duty to serve my mother
> And not be overbearing or miserable.
> I am blessed now, at my birth,
> And I shall be blessed on my death
> And on my resurrection.
>
> (19:30–33)

The Quran disclaims that Jesus was the son of God; he was his messenger like other messengers.

Abraham was a man of truth. He pleaded with his father to abjure the worship of idols, 'which cannot see or hear'. The father was adamant, but Abraham asked the Lord to forgive his father's heresy. To Abraham was given Isaac, and to Isaac, Jacob, both of whom were made prophets to serve their Creator and to carry on the line of Abraham. Abraham's other son, Ishmael, whom he had agreed to sacrifice for God, was also made a prophet and entrusted with divine mission. Moses was called to Mount Sinai and was blessed by God. His brother, Aaron, was also made a prophet. However, after they passed away, the people lapsed into corruption and immorality and faced destruction and ruination, except those who continued with their faith in God and worked righteously.

SURAH XIX

66.   Man wonders,
       What would happen to me
       When I am dead?
       Would I, indeed, be made
       Alive again?

67.   But he should know
       That We created him
       Out of nothing.

95.   Each one will come to the Lord
       Singly to give his account.

96.   On those who believe in Him
       And do righteous deeds,

Allah will shower His love.
He is, indeed, Most Gracious.

97.   We have revealed the Quran
In Arabic to you, O Muhammad!
So that you may give glad tidings to the righteous
And warning to the contentious.

SURAH XX: TA HA
(135 verses)

At the outset of this chapter the Prophet is reminded that the Quran was a set of admonitions for the good of mankind. There is no need for him to feel distressed by his detractors mocking him and reviling the revelations. On the contrary, he should draw strength from the fact that God is firmly established in His authority and controls everything on earth and in the heavens and all that lies between them.

The experience of Moses, who went in search of fire but returned with the gift of divine mission, is then narrated. God asked Moses to throw down the rod he carried with him to beat down the fodder for his flock; no sooner did he do it than the rod became a snake. God told him to seize it and not to be afraid. He did as commanded, and no harm came to him. He was then told of the divine mission and asked to confront Pharaoh, who had transgressed all bounds of morality and had become an embodiment of tyranny. Moses prayed to God to make his brother Aaron His messenger, so that he could help him. His request was granted. Moses then proceeded to carry out his mission; in fact, he had been prepared for it from childhood, as his mother had brought him up in the palace of Pharaoh and taught him all the learning that was available there. He also lived with the people of Midyan, with whom he mixed and earned their trust.

At God's command, Moses, along with Aaron, appeared before Pharaoh and asked him not to cause any more affliction to the

Children of Israel and to enable them to follow the guidance of the Lord. Pharaoh laughed and jeeringly enquired which of the two, Moses or Aaron, was the Lord.

'Neither of us,' Moses replied:

> Our Lord is the One
> Who has given to each created thing
> Its shape, form and nature
> And blessed it with His guidance.
>
> (20:50)

Moses showed signs to convince Pharaoh that he was, indeed, the messenger of God; but Pharaoh was not impressed by what he termed 'thy magic', and asked him to match his signs against the Pharaoh's magicians on the Day of the Festival. The contest took place and Moses won easily. However, Pharaoh refused to yield and persisted in his acts of inequity. God then asked Moses to travel by night with his followers to escape the fate that awaited Pharaoh. God struck out a dry path through the Nile. Moses and his followers walked the whole distance on it. Pharaoh's men pursued them, but they were drowned in the waters of the Nile.

As a result of God's dispensations, the Children of Israel were not only freed of their bondage but given enlightenment. However, as time passed and while Moses was away, they relapsed into the old habit of worshipping idols; they began to worship a calf that one of their Samiri had made out of gold taken from the people. When Moses came to know of this, he chastised them and brought them to the realization that the calf was useless, with no power to act, while God alone was all-powerful and supreme. Moses also rebuked his brother Aaron, who had erred in not warning the people against the wrong path they had taken while Moses was away.

SURAH XX

5. God is most gracious
   And firmly in power.

6. To Him belongs whatever is
   On this earth and the heavens,
   And whatever lies in between
   And even underneath the earth.

7. Whatever you utter
   Whether loudly or in whisper
   Openly or in secret
   God knows everything.

8. To God belong
   The most beautiful names.
   He is the Lord of everything.
   There is no one like Him.

110. He knows what happened in the past
   And what will happen in future.
   People cannot grasp
   What is what and where.

111. All will have to bow to Him,
   The self-subsisting and the eternal.
   In His presence whoever bears
   A load of iniquity
   Will be in utter despair.

112. But the man who had done good deeds,
   He need not fear,
   Nor will he be harmed.
   He will not be deprived of his deserts.

114. God is high above all,
   He is the Truth.
   His Revelations are in the Quran,
   But make no haste for it
   Until it is completed.
   Plead with your Lord
   To advance you in knowledge
   By and by.

133.   They say: 'Why does he not
        Bring us a sign from
        His Lord?' Had not
        A Clear Sign come
        Of all that was there
        In earlier books of revelations?

SURAH XXI: AL-ANBIYA (THE PROPHETS)
(112 verses)

This chapter deals with the taunts and jibes that prophets had to face from their detractors. Muhammad was no exception; like them he was accused of indulging in witchcraft and magic and of being a dreamer and a poet. Eventually, non-believers will suffer for it. God destroyed those who had rejected faith in Him in the past and had associated Him with others. God granted, for instance, to Moses and Aaron the divine light so that they could show the people the right path. Likewise, Abraham, who bore hardships but remained firm in his faith, was favoured by the Lord. Lot showed exemplary courage in reproving abominations, and was blessed under the divine dispensation. Noah rescued believers from the great flood. David, faced with difficulties, strove for justice. Solomon by his wisdom subdued enemies of God. Job suffered patiently and refused to give up his faith. Ishmael, Idris and Dhu al-Kifl did not succumb to temptations and kept alive their loyalty to God. Jonah sought refuge in God's mercy. Zachariah was devoted to God and constantly asked for His blessings. Mary, despite her fears of public rebuke, never lost faith in God's mercy. All of them were the chosen ones, who form a brotherhood. They lived and died so that mankind could be free of evil and take to the path of righteousness as shown by the Lord:

> We made them leaders,
> To guide the whole mankind
> Through commands given by Us
> So that people may do good deeds

>And establish regular prayers
>And practise regular charity
>And serve none but their Lord.
>
>(21:73)

To each one of them, God testifies:

>We gave them the power of judgement
>And knowledge to carry forward Our message.
>
>(21:79)

Muhammad was specifically informed:

>We have sent you, O Muhammad,
>As a mercy from Us
>To all Our creatures.
>
>(21:107)

SURAH XXI

7.   Before you also, O Muhammad,
        We sent other messengers
        Who were, like you, men
        Inspired by Us.
        In case you do not know
        Ask those who have been
        The keepers of Our message.

8.   They were subject to the same hunger
        And were not immune from death.

10.   For right guidance to mankind
        We have sent Our Book.
        Why don't you understand?
        It is so obvious.

16.   God did not create
        The heavens and the earth
        And all that lies in between
        Just as a sport.

17.   If We were only interested
In some plaything
We would have
Made it so.

18.   But We wanted to confront
Truth with falsehood
And to destroy falsehood.
Hence woe be to you, O men,
That you ascribe
Such false things to Us.

25.   No messenger did We send
Before you, O Muhammad,
Who did not assert
That I alone am the Lord
To be worshipped and served.

34.   To no man before you, O Muhammad,
Did we grant eternal life.
Hence when you die,
It will be as We wish.

35.   Every man shall taste death
And we shall judge each one
By the good or evil he has done.
To Us, all must return.

37.   Man is a creature in haste,
But soon he will see Our Signs.
Then he will not ask Us to hasten,
Fearing what lies in store for him.

47.   On the Day of Judgement
Everyone will be dealt with
Justly and equitably.
Even the weight of a mustard seed
Will be accounted for,
For God is best in computation.

94.   Whoever has done any good
And believes in Us,
He will be rewarded for
Every bit of his good work
As recorded in his ledger.

106.   In this Quran,
Verily, there is the message
For all those who worship God.

107.   Indeed, God has sent you, O Muhammad,
As a mercy to all His creatures.

SURAH XXII: AL-HAJJ (THE PILGRIMAGE)
(78 verses)

This chapter emphasizes the significance of the Day of Judgement, when, as the Quran describes:

> ... mothers will forget
> To feed their children
> And pregnant women shall abort.
> Men will behave as drunkards
> Without consuming any drink,
> Such will be the wrath of God.
>
> (22:2)

In another verses (22:5), man is told that if he has any doubt about resurrection, he may ponder over the fact of creation: how God creates him out of a sperm, turns it into a clot, which is formed into a lump of flesh and then He gives life to it. For a fixed period, God keeps it in the mother's womb and then brings it out and fosters it. It grows into a man, and man multiplies; some die and some reach old age. Likewise, God gives life by pouring rains on barren fields, enabling them to produce fruits in plenty:

> It is because God is the reality
> He gives life to the dead,

> For His is the power over
> All things on earth and in heaven.
>
> (22:6)

God will be the final arbiter who will judge between followers of different religions, whether they are Muslims, Jews, Sabians, Christians, Magians or even polytheists. For the spiritual growth of people, God has provided symbols, such as the pilgrimage to the Kaaba, where men and women from far and near gather every year to pray and praise the Lord and sacrifice in His name. The faithful are told that by the sacrifice of animals,

> It is not the animal's flesh
> Nor his blood
> That reaches God.
> It is man's piety.
>
> (22:37)

Permission is given here to fight against those who are 'wrong believers' or in defence of those among believers 'who have been expelled from their homes'. Otherwise there should be no war, for had God not controlled one set of people warring against another, all the places of worship, whether churches, synagogues, mosques or monastries, where the name of God is 'commemorated in abundant measure', would have been pulled down. Those who die or are slain in the cause of God will be rewarded by Him in paradise.

Muslims are told that to every people God has prescribed rites and ceremonies which they follow; they are warned not to dispute with them: 'Invite them to take to your religion but do not wrangle with them. In case they do, tell them that God knows what is best for them and that He will judge in matters, in which the two of us differ.'

SURAH XXII

1.   O people! Fear the Lord
      And be prepared for upheaval
      On the Day of Judgement.

2.   On that day mothers will forget
         To feed their children
         And pregnant women shall abort.
         Men will behave as drunkards
         Without consuming any drink,
         Such will be the wrath of God.

3.   And yet there are people
         Who dispute about God
         And without realizing
         Listen to the devil
         And follow his rebellious lead.

5.   O people, how can you doubt
         About Our power of resurrection?
         Think how We raised you out of dust
         And created you out of a sperm,
         And turned it into an embryo
         And then into a lump of flesh,
         First unformed and then formed.
         Whosoever We like
         We give it life for appointed time.
         The child is born, then it grows
         To its full stature.
         Some people die early
         And some reach old age,
         In the same way as we produce
         From barren land,
         By pouring down rains
         And thus stirring the seed to life
         Which then swells to produce
         Beautiful produce in pairs.

11.   There are people
         Who worship God
         Superficially, without conviction.
         If they benefit, they are content.
         However, whenever a test comes
         They turn about
         And in the process lose this world
         As well as the next.

12.   They then call on other deities besides God,
       Little realizing that these have power
       Neither to help nor to harm.
       Indeed, they are going beyond limits
       In straying from the right path.

17.   God is the judge of all those
       Who believe in the Quran
       Or the scriptures of Jews and Christians,
       Or of Sabians and Magians,
       And even those of polytheists.
       Each of them will be judged
       On the Day of Judgement,
       For God alone is the witness
       Of all things.

34.   For every people God has prescribed
       The rites of sacrifice,
       So that they may celebrate
       His name on the animals so sacrificed.
       He is the one and only.
       To Him everyone submits,
       Before Him he gladly humbles.

37.   It is not the animal's flesh
       Nor his blood
       That reaches God.
       It is man's piety.
       Animals are subservient to him,
       So that he may glorify God
       And proclaim His guidance
       And give the good news
       To all those who do right.

39.   Permission to fight is given
       To those who are the victims of aggression.
       Verily, God is powerful
       To provide them the aid,

40.   Especially for those who have been expelled
        From their hearths and homes
        For no cause except
        That they believed in God.
        Had God not checked one set of people
        From interfering in the affairs of another,
        Monastries, churches, synagogues and mosques,
        In which God's name is commemorated,
        Would surely had been pulled down.
        God will certainly help those
        Who believe in His cause,
        For He is, indeed, full of strength
        And exalted in power.

67.   For every group We have
        Prescribed rites and ceremonies.
        Let them not then dispute
        On these matters with you,
        But do invite them to worship the Lord,
        For you are assuredly on the right path.

68.   In case they argue with you, O Muhammad,
        Tell them: 'God knows best
        What you do.

69.   'God will judge between you and us
        On the Day of Judgement
        In regard to all matters of dispute.'

73.   Not all the men together can
        Create even a fly, or take anything
        That the fly had taken from them.
        They are, indeed, so feeble and weak,
        Those who invoke others
        And even those whom they invoke.

77.   Kneel down and prostrate before God
        And do good deeds;
        You will, indeed, prosper.

78.   And strive to further his cause.
        God has chosen you, O Muhammad!
        As His Messenger in religion.
        It is the same which Abraham preached.
        God has named you Muslim,
        As were named your ancestors.
        The Apostle is your witness
        And you, O people, be witnesses to mankind;
        Establish regular prayers,
        Do charity and hold fast to God.
        He alone is your protector,
        He offers you the best help.

SURAH XXIII: AL-MUMINUN (THE BELIEVERS)
(118 verses)

This chapter deals with the essentials of faith and how they are to be practised by good Muslims in the face of persecution. They must be humble in their dealings with others, avoid useless talk, practise charity, avoid sex except with those permitted and observe faithfully their commitments. They should also be ever vigilant about their prayers.

God creates man out of sperm. He is then born, lives for an appointed time and then dies. He will be raised again on the Day of Judgement. For his physical sustenance on earth various facilities have been provided, and for his spiritual uplift prophets have been sent. Noah came to guide them but unbelievers accused him of being 'a man possessed'; to establish his *bona fides*, God asked him to construct

        The Ark with Our guidance and under Our observance,
        And as soon as Our command issues
        With the gushing forth of water all around
        Take on board pairs of every species, male and female,

With their relations except those who reject the faith;
They are, indeed, the wrongdoers, who will be drowned.

(23:27)

After Noah, another prophet was sent by God; but the unbelievers
would not relent. They told him that there was nothing except life
on this earth; in the result a blast of wind overtook them and they
were reduced to a heap of rubbish. Other messengers followed in
succession, and each was accused of falsehood. The case of Moses
and Aaron and the story of Jesus are pointers to the sorry plight of
unbelievers. They found out, at their peril, that evil never triumphs.
The messengers form a brotherhood. They came one after another
to proclaim the supremacy of God and to remind people of His
bounty. Each of them preached the same truth, but their followers
went astray and formed themselves into different sects.

Believers are, therefore, told to follow the messengers and to
work righteously and eschew evil. Avoid temptation, however
great it be. On the Day of Judgement, when accounts are scrutinized,
the good will be rewarded and wrongdoers sent to hell.

SURAH XXIII

51.   O, you Apostle!
        Enjoy the things which are pure
        And things which are good,
        Surely We know what you do.

52.   Verily this brotherhood of yours
        Is a single brotherhood,
        And I am your Lord
        Whom you must fear
        When you do wrong.

53.   People divide themselves
        Into different sects
        And cut themselves off
        From the bonds of unity,
        Rejoicing in their own sects.

54.   It is better
        To leave them
        In this confused state.

55.   They think that
        Because they have
        Abundance of wealth
        And are blessed with sons,

56.   They will be given in haste
        Whatever good they want.
        How little do they know
        What is good for them.

57.   Verily, those
        Who fear their Lord,

58.   And believe in
        His Signs,

59.   And do not join
        Partners with Him,

60.   And practise charity
        With all their hearts,
        They will, indeed, be rewarded
        When they return to their Lord.

61.   For their good work,
        They will be in the forefront
        Before their Lord.

62.   On no one does the Lord place
        A burden greater than he can bear.
        He has a record before Him
        Which clearly brings out the truth
        So that no one is really wronged.

78.   God has given you, O Man,
        All the necessary faculties

Of Hearing, seeing and feeling
And also of understanding.
Surprisingly, you offer no thanks
To your Lord and Benefactor.

79.   He has also multiplied your kind.
To Him you will eventually return.

91.   He did not beget a son,
Nor has He a partner.
Otherwise, each pretender,
Posing as a god,
Would have taken away
A part of the creation,
And tried to lord over others
And to confront each other.
God is above all these things.

SURAH XXIV: AL-NUR (THE LIGHT)
(64 verses)

This chapter throws light on the need for social reforms, particularly
in the wake of allegations of suspicious behaviour between a man
and a woman. This has reference to the scandal spread by certain
powerful people against the Prophet's youngest wife, Aisha. She
had accompanied her husband on a journey. When the caravan
halted on the way, Aisha disembarked from her palanquin, and
went a little distance away to ease herself. No one noticed her
absence, not even the palanquin bearers. Aisha took some time to
return, as she had lost her necklace and had gone back to search for
it. By the time she returned, the caravan, along with her bearers,
had left. She waited in the hope that the bearers would realize their
mistake and come back to fetch her. They did not, however; as she
waited, a young man named Safwaan saw her and offered to take
her on his camel. She accepted the offer and returned with him to

join the caravan. This incident was used by Aisha's detractors to cast aspersions on her character; the Prophet too was affected by the insinuations made against her. He kept away from Aisha for some time, which caused her much distress. Then came the revelation exonerating her and prescribing punishment for slandering a chaste woman and for adultery:

> The woman and the man
> Guilty of adultery or fornication,
> Flog each of them with a hundred stripes.
>
> (24:2)

But those who spread scandal baselessly against a chaste woman and fail to produce four witnesses to the alleged act, were equally guilty and must be flogged with eighty stripes (24:4). In regard to the allegations against Aisha, the believers who spread such an unfounded scandal were sternly warned that they had sinned by their unseemly conduct and would meet with 'a grievous punishment in this life and the Hereafter'.

Privacy is another aspect of human behaviour about which God speaks with concern: a believer must not enter the house of another without the latter's permission. Further, he must observe a certain decorum and dignity in day-to-day dealings. He should lower his gaze while speaking and be modest in behaviour. In the case of women, it is specifically mentioned that they should not display themselves or their ornaments. They should cover their bosoms. Let those who lack 'the wherewithals of marriage remain chaste until Allah gives them the means out of His grace'. Prostitution is prohibited and condemned as sinful.

Believers are admonished to obey God and His Prophet; if anyone disobeys Him and His messengers, the fault lies in the defaulter and not in the Prophet, whose duty is only to preach and not to coerce people into submission.

SURAH XXIV

19.   O Believers! Those among you
Who enjoy spreading scandals
Shall be severely punished

In this world as well as the next.
Allah knows the truth but you do not.

21.   O, you believers!
Do not follow in Satan's footsteps;
That will, indeed, be shameful and wrong.
Remember, but for the grace of God,
None of you will ever be pure;
He purifies whomsoever He pleases
And hears and knows all things.

22.   Let not those among you
Who are possessed of
Abundance of Wealth,
Swear not to help your relatives
Or the poor
And those who have left their homes
In the cause of God.
They should forgive them their failings,
For do you not want that God should forgive you?
He is Most Forgiving and All-Merciful.

23.   Also refrain from
Slandering women
Who believe in Us
And are chaste.
If you slander, you will be cursed
In this life as well as the next
And receive grievous penalty.

24.   On the Day of Judgement, your tongue,
        hands and feet
Will give evidence against you
For your misdeeds.

27.   Believers, do not enter
Others' dwellings
Without their permission.
And when you do,
Offer them greetings.

That is best for you
If only you will heed.

30. Tell the believing men, O Muhammad,
That they should lower their gaze
And guard their modesty.
That is purer and better for them,
For Allah knows what they do.

31. And tell the believing women
That they should lower their gaze
And guard their modesty.
They should not show their adornments
Except what is normally required.
They should draw their veils
Over their bosoms and not display their bodies.

33. Let those who do not have the means to marry
Keep themselves chaste
Until such time as God, in His grace,
Grants them the means.

41. Can you not see how all creatures,
Whether in the heavens or on earth,
Celebrate the glory of God?
How birds with outstretched wings
Pray to Him each in its way.
God is aware of all that you do.

43. Can you also not see
How God makes the clouds come together,
And how He makes them into a heap
And how out of it come rains
Which He then sends down from the sky
And makes it strike whomsoever He likes
With a lightning that blinds?

44. It is God who alternates
Night and Day,

And in this there are
Examples for those
Who are imbued with vision.

45.   God has created
Every kind of animal;
In water some creep on bellies
And some walk on two legs
And others on four.
God creates whatever He likes.
He has power over everything.

46.   In things which are manifest
God has shown His Signs.
He guides whomsoever He wills
To a path that is straight.

SURAH XXV: AL-FURQAN (THE CRITERION)
(77 verses)

God has provided man with a criterion to judge between right and
wrong. The Prophet has been sent by God to help people to take to
the right path; but unbelievers mock at him, questioning what sort
of a messenger is he who eats and walks like them, who possesses no
treasure, no palace, no garden. How can they then follow him? God
asks him to be patient, remininding him that messengers before him
also 'ate food and walked in the streets'. They were similarly
maltreated by unbelievers. This is a test through which each one of
them had to pass; Muhammad is no exception.

One common source of disbelief in former messengers was the
question of why angels were not sent to give the message from
God, or why God himself did not appear before them. Why were
human beings, who were just like them, entrusted with divine
missions instead? They could not understand the working of God,
nor were they appreciative of the miracle of creation, which stared
them in the face. Their conceit and arrogance blinded them to such

obvious occurrences as the rise of the sun, the moon and the stars, the alternation of day and night, the blowing of the wind and the falling of rain, all of which are clear evidence of God's supremacy. On the Day of Judgement they will repent for their unbelief and suffer the penalty for their inequity.

SURAH XXV

1. Blessed is God
   Who sent down the criterion
   To judge right and wrong
   To His Messenger so that
   He may warn the world.

3. People who take, besides God,
   Others as gods, who can create nothing;
   They are themselves the created ones.
   They have no control to do either good or evil,
   Nor have they any say on life or death.

20. We had sent messengers before you, O Muhammad!
    They were also men like you,
    They ate food and walked in streets
    And some We made
    An example for others
    To communicate Our message.
    Hence persevere in your task
    Your Lord is always watchful.

63. God's devotees are those
    Who walk on this earth
    With humility.
    And when they are accosted by the ignorant,
    They plead with them:
    'Peace be between us.'

68. Those who do not
    Invoke other gods
    And do not slay life

Except for a just cause,
And do not fornicate,
Will not receive punishment.

69.   But those who do,
Their punishment will be double;
They will dwell in hell.

70.   Unless they repent
And affirm their faith in God
And work righteously,
Then God will change their evil nature
And make them good.
For God is Ever-Forgiving and Most Merciful.

72.   Also those
Who stick to truth
And do not indulge in falsehood,
Avoiding unbecoming talk.

75.   They will be rewarded
With the highest places in the heavens,
Because of their perseverance,
And greeted with salutations,

76.   Dwelling in a beautiful abode
And a home of eternal peace.

SURAH XXVI: AL-SHUARA (THE POETS)
(227 verses)

Here, the stories of various prophets — Noah, Abraham, Hud, Salih, Lot, Shuyab and Moses — are repeated in different forms, and the moral of the triumph of virtue over vice, of good over evil, and the invincibility of the power of God in crises, are once again underlined, as also is the fact that God's messengers had to face hardships and sufferings while propagating His message. As Pharaoh was helpless before the spiritual might of Moses, so is falsehood before truth; as rejectors of Noah's call perished in the flood, so will disbelievers in the unity of God; as those who did not heed Abraham's plea against idol worship were consequently swept away, so will all evil-doers. Hud warned his people that material prowess could be of no avail against spiritual might. Salih cautioned his people against infidelity and its fatal aftermath, while Lot asked unbelievers to refrain from committing sodomy, to which they were accustomed; they rejected his warning and paid for it with their lives. Shuyab thundered against those who tampered with weights and measures, but they refused to listen and were blasted by the wind.

Similarly, when Muhammad raised his voice at Mecca to convey the message of truth as revealed to him by God, pagans, especially of his own tribe of Quraish, jeered at him. They persecuted his followers and hounded him. But eventually they will repent. His prophethood had been predicted in the books of other prophets, but the learned men of Israel, despite the references in their scriptures, paid no heed to Muhammad's divine mission. They would suffer for this. The pagans, including the Prophet's nearest kinsmen, disobeyed the call; they indulged in vanities and resorted to lies. As for the poets, who ridiculed his mission, they were the evil ones, who wandered distractedly in every valley. They practised not what they preached. Eventually, all oppressors would be overthrown.

SURAH XXVI

221.   Shall I tell you,
O People! on whom
The evils descend?

222.   They descend on all those
Who lie and indulge
In wicked things,

223.   Who mouth heresies,
And are nothing but liars.

224.   As for the poets,
        They are listened to
        Only by those who stray
        From the right path.

225.   Have you not seen
        How they wander
        Aimlessly
        In every valley?

226.   They say in words
        What they do not do
        In action.

227.   Those who believe in God
        And remember Him
        And do righteous deeds,
        And who retaliate only when unjustly attacked,
        They will see how
        The oppressors are overthrown.

SURAH XXVII: AL-NAML (THE ANTS)
(93 verses)

This chapter emphasizes the role of revelation in the life of man. There is at first the reference to the struggle of Moses against Pharaoh and a graphic description of miracles he had to perform in an attempt to convince the Egyptian king and his chiefs of the truth of his mission; but they remained adamant in their refusal. They ultimately perished in the storm that engulfed them. Likewise, in the story of Solomon and his dialogues with the Queen of Sheba, the moral is brought out that faith and persuasion ultimately triumph over unbelief and force. The manner in which Solomon persuaded the Queen to accept the true faith and give up the worship of the sun brings out the qualities of his statesmanship and the excellence of the character of the Queen, who responded promptly to Solomon's call.

Next we are told the story of the nine men of a family, belonging to Thamud, who plotted secretly to kill Salih and his people. By a clever device the prophet, who became aware of the plot, pretended that he knew nothing about it. In the end, God came to his help and Salih was able to turn the tables on the plotters and destroy them. In the same manner, the Prophet Lot was aghast to find that men were lusting for men instead of women. He warned them against this evil practice, but they refused to heed him and were crushed by God.

SURAH XXVII

59.   Tell them, O Muhammad!
        All glory is to God,
        Peace be on His Messengers.
        Ask them who is better,
        The true God or the false ones
        With whom they associate Him?

60.   Ask them:
        Who has created the heavens and the earth?
        Who pours down rain from above
        And causes fulsome orchards to grow
        To delight them with their fruits?
        It is not in their power
        To germinate the trees,
        It is God alone who makes it possible.
        Can there be anyone else besides Him?
        And still there are people
        Who swerve from justice.

62.   Who listens to people in distress
        And relieves them of their suffering?
        And who is it who has made man
        The inheritor of this earth?
        Can there be anyone else besides God?
        And still there are people
        Who heed not His message.

63. Who guides people through the depths of darkness,
Whether on land or sea?
And who sends the winds as heralds
Of glad tidings, reminding of His mercy?
And still there are people
Who associate others with God,
Who is far above everyone else.

64. Who creates and then recreates,
And who provides man with sustenance
From above on the earth?
And still there are people
Who talk of other gods.
Ask them to bring forth their proof
If they are telling the truth.

65. Tell them: There is no one
In the heavens or the earth
Who has knowledge of the unknown
Besides the Lord.
Nor has anyone the perception
Of how the dead will be raised
On the Day of Judgement.

66. Nor has anyone the knowledge
Of what life in the Hereafter will be.
Doubts and uncertainties have blinded them;
They do not see the reality.

88. You see the mountains as fixed
But they shall disappear like clouds.
Perfect is the artistry of God.
He knows best what to do.

89. Whoever has done a good deed,
He will receive his reward
And will be saved from the Last Day's terror.

SURAH XXVIII: AL-QASAS (THE STORIES)
(88 verses)

This chapter refers to the designs of Pharaoh, who decreed that all new-born sons would be put to death. The mother of Moses, who had just given birth to him, was asked by God to put the infant in a basket and cast it in a river. She obeyed the command, and the basket was later picked up by some people who took it to the Queen. Moses' mother pleaded with Pharaoh to allow her to keep the child. He consented, and the Queen then brought him up in the palace. With the passage of time, Moses grew up into a man. One day in a fight between two men, he intervened and killed one of them. Moses asked the Lord for forgiveness, but the chiefs of the city, when informed of the killing, decided to punish him for the murder he had unwittingly committed. His friends prevailed upon the chiefs and were able to obtain a pardon for him. They took him to Madyan, where he could be safe from the clutches of his enemies. Moses appealed to God to show him the straight path. In Madyan he found men watering their flocks and not allowing women to do so until they had finished. Moses boldly took the side of the women and volunteered to water their flocks for them. The women were touched by his gesture and one of them took Moses to her father, who was so impressed by his courage and his spirit of service that he gave his daughter in marriage to him.

After living ten years with his father-in-law, Moses took his wife and family on a journey. Stopping on the way, he saw some fire and went to fetch a firebrand. However, when he reached the spot, Moses heard a voice.

'I am your Lord! I command you to throw away your rod.'

He did as told, and to his amazement the rod turned into a snake. Moses was taken aback, but the Lord told him not to panic. He was then asked to put his hand to his bosom. As he withdrew it, it turned white: this was a guarantee that no harm could come to him nor should he fear anyone. He was then ordered to proceed against Pharaoh and his chiefs and put down their oppression. Moses prayed to God to allow him to take his brother Aaron with him, as 'he is more eloquent than I am'. His wish was granted. The two then went to Egypt, where they asked the people to worship God. In response, the Egyptians rebuked him and called him a sorcerer. Pharaoh was furious and declared that there was no God and that he controlled everything. He decided to build the loftiest palace, from where he could talk to the God of Moses. But nothing that he and his people did proved to be of any avail, and eventually they were all swallowed by the sea.

Moses was given the *Torah* as a guide to the right path. Thereafter, many other messengers were sent to preach the same truth; and now Muhammad has come with a similar mission. He need not be discouraged by opposition; on the contrary, he should concentrate on his preaching, for eventually the truth is bound to prevail. Everything will be clear on the Day of Judgement, when non-believers will see the consequences of their folly and believers will receive their just rewards.

Among the followers of Moses, the richest man was Qarun. His enormous wealth had gone to his head, and he forgot his obligation to the Lord and his duty to his people. As a result, the earth swallowed his palace, his riches and finally himself as well.

> And those who had envied Qarun's riches
> Realized their illusory nature and confessed:
> 'It is indeed Allah who gives to whomsoever He pleases
> And takes from whomsoever He pleases.'
>
> (28:82)

SURAH XXVIII

56.   You will not be able
        To guide everyone you like.
        It is only God's privilege
        That He can guide
        Whomsoever He likes,
        And He knows best
        Who should receive
        What guidance.

60.   The material things of this world
        Are just conveniences,
        Or at best an embellishment.
        But what the Lord gives you
        Is far better and more enduring.
        Will you then not understand
        What is in your best interest?

61.   What is better?
        A divine promise
        Which will be fulfilled
        In the Hereafter,
        Or the little enjoyment
        In this transitory world
        Which will cause you to suffer
        Eternal punishment on Judgement Day?

83.   The mansion in the Hereafter
        Will not be given to those
        Who do mischief on this earth,
        But only to those
        Who do righteous deeds.

84.   Our justice is such
        That those who do good
        We reward them doubly.
        But those who do evil
        Are punished only to the extent
        Of their misdeeds.

86.   You have been given the Book, O Muhammad!
        As a favour from your Lord.
        Hence do not bother about people
        Who reject Our teachings.

87.   Do not turn away
        From what God has
        Revealed to you.
        Remain steadfast and invite

People to believe in God,
And not to join any other gods
With the one and only God.

88.   And do not invoke,
           Anyone besides God.
           For everything will perish
           Except His countenance.
           His alone is the command
           And to Him alone everyone shall return.

SURAH XXIX: AL-ANKABUT (THE SPIDER)
(69 verses)

This chapter stresses the significance of faith in God. It is not enough to believe; man must live up to his belief by doing righteous deeds. He should remember that God does not need anything from His creatures, it is they who need to earn His goodwill. Hence their faith in Him should be absolute; even their parents should not be able to persuade them to give it up. They should remain steadfast and God would be with them. Those who failed to listen to the call of Noah or Abraham were wiped out; those who believed in God prospered. Lot shunned worldly power, denounced the lewd practices of his people, and surrendered to the will of God, who made him a prophet. Abraham's progeny, Isaac and Jacob, were likewise ordained by God; they were granted revelations and the right to preach His message. Shuyab told his people to serve and fear the Lord and give up their evil habits; they refused and were seized by a mighty blast. Similarly, the people of Aad and Thamud, despite their intelligence and skill, were misled and in consequence were ruined. Pharaoh, Haman and Qarun met the same fate; because of their insolence they overreached themselves and were destroyed.

Each of them We punished
For the crimes committed by him.

Against some We unleashed a tornado
And against some a mighty blast.
Some were swallowed by the earth
And some drowned in the flood.
However, it was not Allah who harmed them.
They were harmed because of their own misdeeds.

(29:40)

The house that an unbeliever builds is like the web that a spider makes: it is so fragile and weak that it cannot last. It is Allah alone who is the best provider; to him everyone has to return:

Every man shall taste death
And in the end he will come to Us.

(29:52)

To the believers, a home in the heavens is assured; their righteous deeds will not go unrewarded.

SURAH XXIX

4. People who do wrong
    Think that they will have
    The better of this world.
    How wrong, indeed, is their thinking.

6. Whoever strives
    To do good
    Does so for his own good.
    For God does not need
    Anything from His creatures.

7. To those who believe in Us
    And do righteous deeds,
    We will be indulgent towards them,
    Rewarding them more than they deserve,
    Even more than their best deeds.

8.   God has enjoined man
To be kind to his parents.
But if they compel him
To worship anyone besides God,
Then God's command is:
Do not obey them.
For everyone has to return to God
And each will be held responsible for his deed.

45.   Recite from the Book of Revelations
And establish regular prayers.
For prayers keep people away
From shameful acts
And God's remembrance is,
Indeed, best for them.
Surely, God knows what they do.

46.   Do not dispute, O Muhammad,
With the People of the Book
Except by fair means.
However, those who adopt foul methods
Tell them: 'We believe in the revelations
Sent down to us as also in yours.
Our God and your God are one and the same.
To Him alone we all submit.'

64.   What is this life
But amusement and play?
Man's real home is
In the Hereafter,
If only he knew.

69.   Those who strive in God's cause,
God will certainly guide them to the right path.
For verily, God is with those
Who do right.

SURAH XXX: AL-RUM (THE ROMANS)
(60 verses)

This chapter first traces the causes of the fall of the empires of
Rome and Persia, concluding:

> Of those who do evil
> Evil will be the end,
> Especially of those who deny God
> And hold His Signs to ridicule.
>
> (30:10)

And those who have believed in God and worked righteously:

> Shall have bestowed on them a mead of delight.
>
> (30:15)

God's signs are many: His oneness, His omnipotence, His benevolence; also the manner in which He has created man and woman out of
dust, spread them all over the earth and put love and compassion in
their hearts, taught them different languages and given them a variety
of colours. They are enjoined to do righteous deeds, but non-believers
delight in creating mischief on earth. They will be brought to book.
God will restore the balance and destroy those who disrupt the
harmony and peace of His creation. Believers must exercise patience,
and remain constant in their faith in God. Their reward is assured in
the Hereafter, while wrongdoers will not escape their doom. As soon
as the trumpet is blown everyone's account will be scrutinized.

Allah reminds Muhammad of the fate that awaits them:

> Verily We have propounded in this Quran
> Every parable and all the knowledge.
> But unbelievers will still say
> These are nothing but your vanities.
> Allah has sealed their hearts
> So they cannot understand.
>
> (30:58–9)

On the Day of Judgement they will realize their mistake and
suffer for it.

SURAH XXX

10.   Of those who do evil,
      Evil will be the end,
      Especially of those who deny God
      And hold His Signs to ridicule.

14.   On the Day of Judgement,
      When the Hour comes
      For sorting out
      The deeds of men,

15.   Those who had believed in Us
      And done righteous deeds
      Shall have bestowed on them a mead of delight.

16.   Those who had rejected Us
      And denied Our Signs,
      They will be given the punishment
      That they really deserve.

17.   So glorify God
      At the break of dawn
      And at eventide.

18.   In the heavens and on earth
      His alone is the praise.
      Praise Him hence
      At noon and at night.

20.   He created you out of dust,
      That is one of His Signs,
      And then scattered you far and wide.

21.   Another of His Signs is
      That He creates you in pairs
      So that you may dwell in peace.
      And He has instilled in you
      Love and kindness.
      You must reflect on this.

22.   You can see more of His Signs
        In the creation of the heavens and the earth,
        And in the variety of languages and colours.
        Surely, these are His Signs
        For those who understand.

23.   Among His Signs is the creation of night
        For people to sleep,
        And that of the day
        For pursuit of livelihood.
        To those who pay heed
        These are sure Signs.

24.   Among His other Signs
        Are the flashes of lightning
        Which create both fear and hope.
        God sends down rains and produces
        Life on the earth.
        To the wise, these are Signs enough.

25.   Both the heavens and the earth
        Stand by His command.
        He gives the call,
        And behold!
        Straight away you come to Him.

26.   Every being, whether in the heavens or on earth,
        Belongs to Him and should be
        Devoutly obedient to Him.

30.   Hence remain steadfast in your faith
        And act in accordance with God's pattern,
        After which has been modelled mankind.
        There can be no change in it,
        For that is the standard.
        However, most men do not understand.

31.   Turn to Him and repent for your sins,
        Fear Him and worship Him regularly
        And do not associate others with Him.

37.   God increases or decreases
        Whatever provisions He gives.
        Verily, in this are Signs
        For those who believe.

38.   Hence give whatever is their due
        To your kindred, the needy and the wayfarer,
        For this is best for those
        Who seek the countenance of God.
        They will, surely, prosper.

39.   If you benefit by increase in property
        Entrusted by others to you,
        That will give you no benefit from God.
        But if you give in charity
        Out of your own property,
        God will increase it manifold.

41.   Whatever and whenever corruption appears
        It is because of what men have done.
        They have, therefore, to suffer
        So that they may return to the right path.

47.   We sent before you, O Muhammad, many messengers
        To their respective people,
        And like you they were also given clear Signs.
        But people who did not heed them
        Were inflicted with retribution.
        We help those who believe in Our message.

60.   So persevere in your faith in Us.
        Our promise to you, O Muhammad, is true.
        Let those, who fumble, not make you
        Lax in your endeavours.

SURAH XXXI: LUQMAN
(34 verses)

This chapter narrates the story of Luqman, who impressed upon his son the importance of believing in the unity of God and refraining from associating any other deity with God. 'False worship,' he told his son, 'is, indeed, the highest wrongdoing.' He said that God has authority over every being, animate or inanimate. His is the only right path. He enjoined people to be good to their parents, especially their mothers, who bore them and nursed them. However, if parents join others with God and commit *shirk*, then they need not be obeyed.

Obedience to God is the Supreme Law. Luqman advised his son to refrain from disbelief in God and doing wrong, even if that wrong be as small as 'a mustard seed'. Nor should he be arrogant or 'walk in insolence on the earth, for Allah loves not an arrogant man or a boaster'. He also asked him to practise moderation in his speech and action, and fear the Day of Judgement, when a father will be of no avail to his son, nor a son to his father; nor should the pleasures of the present life delude him from taking the right path. It should not make him forgetful of the Hereafter.

SURAH XXXI

2. In this Book of Wisdom
There are verses

3. Which are a guide
For the seekers of good
And a means for their salvation.

4. For those who are constant in prayer
And regular in giving alms
And believers in the Hereafter;

5.   They are the recipients
         Of true guidance from their Lord.

6.   They are the ones
         Who shall prosper.

7.   However there are some
         Who indulge in idle talk
         To dissuade people
         From the right path
         And ridicule God's direction.
         For them is
         The shameful Nemesis.

8.   For those having faith in Us
         And doing righteous deeds,
         For them there will be
         The Gardens of Bliss
         As their final reward.

10.   God has created the heavens:
         They have no support
         As you can see.
         Likewise, on earth
         He has put up mountains:
         They cannot shake or move.
         He has created creatures:
         They are of all kinds.
         He has poured down rains
         And spread them all over,
         And produced for His creatures
         A variety of splendid things.

11.   Now show Me who else is there
         Who can create such variety
         Except God, the Almighty.
         Those who deny His existence
         Are, indeed, in manifest error.

14.   Man should be good to his parents.
        His mother carries him in her womb
        Through travail upon travail,
        Weaning him in two years.
        As to God, so to his parents,
        Man must remain grateful.
        He has finally to return to God.

15.   In case your parents compel you
        To associate someone with God
        Of which you possess no knowledge,

20.   Do not listen to them
        But still be fair to them.
        Follow only those who turn to God,
        For you have to return to Him.
        He will judge how each one has acted.

22.   He who surrenders to God
        And does good deeds,
        He can hold the handle strong.
        The decision rests with God.

23.   If anyone rejects faith in Us
        Do not be dejected:
        He will eventually come to Us.
        We shall then tell him
        Of what he has done,
        For We know everything
        That is in man's heart.

24.   For a little while people may enjoy
        The pleasures of this life,
        But in the end they return to Us
        And face the consequence of their act.

27.   If all the trees were to be pens
        And all the oceans ink,
        Even then the words of God

Would not be exhausted,
Such is His majesty and wisdom.

29.　It is God who makes night succeed day
And day succeed night.
He harnesses the sun and the moon
To run their appointed course.
God knows what everyone does.

30.　God is, indeed, the only reality.
Hence do not invoke anyone else,
For that is falsehood.
God is the highest and the greatest.

33.　O people! do your duty by your Lord
And fear Him and the Judgement Day.
On that day neither a father can help his son
Nor a son rescue his father.
Verily, what God has promised, shall happen.
Hence, let the present life not delude you
Nor delusion keep you away from God.

SURAH XXXII: AL-SAJDAH (PROSTRATION)
(30 verses)

This chapter once again stresses that the Quran is no forgery but 'the truth from the Lord' to admonish a people to whom no warner had been sent before. It asks them to believe in God and do righteous deeds; the messenger's task is to show people the right path. He is not to force them, but only to preach and persuade them. Had God so willed, says the Quran, He 'could certainly have brought every soul to accept His true guidance', but He has left to people the choice of whether to believe in Him or not. However, those who believe in Him will be suitably rewarded in the Hereafter; and those who do not will get their due punishment. Allah makes it clear:

> Is the man who believes in God
> And does righteous deeds
> The same as the man who rejects the faith?
> Certainly not. They cannot be equal.
>
> (32:18)

Like Muhammad, Moses was also given the book by God: a guide to the Children of Israel. By following it they prospered. But they have now left the true path. God will judge them in matters where they have gone astray and punish them for their wrongdoing.

SURAH XXXII

1.   No one knows
The delights that await him.
They are kept in reserve
For his good deeds by Us.

2.   These revelations
As contained in the Book
Are from the Lord of the worlds.
Of that there should be no doubt.

3.   Do they say that you, O Muhammad,
Have forged these revelations?
Tell them that it is the truth
Revealed to you by your Lord
So that you may admonish the people
To whom no warner has come.
Let them receive
The guidance through you.

4.   God has created the heavens and the earth
And all that lies between them
In only six days.
He is firmly on His Throne,
And you have no protector besides Him,
Nor an interceder on His behalf.
Will you not then heed Him?

5   From the heavens God administers
       The affairs on the earth.
       Finally, everything will return to Him,
       For His decision on the Day of Judgement
       May take a thousand years
       According to man's reckoning.

7   God created man out of clay
       And made him perfect,

8.   And then out of fluid
       Created his progeny.

9.   And He gave him proper shape
       And breathed into him God's spirit,
       And equipped him with
       Hearing, seeing and feeling,
       And still how ungrateful is he to his Creator?

19.   For those who believe in Us
       And do the righteous deeds,
       We provide gardens for their abode
       Commensurate with their deeds.

20.   But for those who are rebellious and wicked,
       Their abode is Hell,
       From where they cannot escape
       However much they may try.
       They will be told every time:
       'Taste now the burning fire
       As punishment for rejecting as false
       What you were told was true.'

21.   Even in this world they will taste
       The affliction for their disbelief,
       Much before the severe torment
       That awaits them in the Hereafter,
       So that they may retract
       And choose the right path.

SURAH XXXIII: AHZAB (THE CONFEDERATES)
(73 verses)

The question of whether truth can be suppressed by force is once again discussed here, with particular reference to the attempted invasion of Medina by the Meccans and their allies – the Jews and the other tribes – and the way in which the Muslims frustrated it. In every such conflict between right and wrong, God uses His power to subdue the wrong. His help comes on the side of right in some form or other – in this instance through a hurricane, which people might not have seen but which proved decisive.

As far as believers are concerned, whether in adversity or prosperity, they are told to follow the Prophet:

> The Messenger of God is
> An excellent example to follow
> (33:21)

Likewise, the wives of the Prophet are reminded that they should conduct themselves in a manner befitting their high status and should be an example for others. Being mothers of believers, they should be a guide for other wives. In their day-to-day behaviour, they must exercise patience, privacy and grace. They should guard their speech and never give in to any kind of temptation. They should remain quietly in their homes and not display themselves to others. They should pray regularly and do charity. They should obey Allah and His Messengers and be pure and spotless in their personal lives.

Men and women should guard themselves against vice; they should be humble and considerate. They should not question the judgement of Allah and His Messenger. Muhammad is 'the Seal of Prophets', and his word is final in determining their affairs. They should remember that he has been commissioned to lead mankind from darkness into light; he is the beacon to guide them to the right path. He is full of mercy and grace. All in all, he is a shining lamp, spreading light all around.

In this chapter, directions are given for divorce and for the maintenance of divorced women: 'Give them a provision and set them free in a handsome manner' (33:49). Also, specific arrangements are given for *mehr*, or dower, for wives.

Believers are also told how to conduct themselves before women, particularly before the Prophet's wives, who in turn are to 'wear their outer garments over their persons' while they appear in public. They must obey Allah and His messenger, in order to attain 'the highest distinction'.

SURAH XXXIII

6.   More than to themselves,
        The Prophet is close to believers.
        His wives are their mothers.
        Blood relations are, no doubt, close
        But so should be friends;
        That is the decree of God.

21.   The Messenger of God is
        An excellent example to follow
        For any one who believes in God
        And the Final Day
        And who always remembers Him.

35.   Verily men and women
        Who submit to God
        And men and women
        Who are devout
        And men and women
        Who are truthful
        And men and women
        Who are patient
        And men and women
        Who are humble
        And men and women
        Who are charitable
        And men and women

Who fast
And men and women
Who are modest
And men and women
Who remember God,
God will forgive them
And give them just rewards.

36.   A believing man or woman
            has no option but to accept
        The decision given by God and His messenger.
        To disobey it is to tread the wrong path.

40.   Muhammad is not the father of any man,
        He is the Messenger of God.
        And the Seal of the Prophets.
        God has knowledge of everything.

41.   O Believers!
        Remember God
        All the time
        And sing His praises.

42.   And glorify Him
        Morning and evening.

43.   He showers His blessings on you
        And so do His angels,
        So that He may bring you
        Out of darkness into light,
        For He is benevolent to believers.

45.   O Prophet! You have been sent by Us
        As Our witness and bearer of glad tidings.
        You are, indeed, a warner to mankind.

46.   And as Our chosen one,
        To invite people
        To God's grace

And shine as a lamp
To spread light all around.

59.   O Prophet! Tell your wives and daughters
        And all the believing women
        To cover their bodies
        Whenever they go out of their homes.
        It is for their own protection
        So that they may not be molested.
        God is, no doubt, kind and merciful.

70.   O Believers! Obey God's commands.
        And say the right things.

71.   So that He may
            straighten your affairs
        And forgive you your sins.
        Whoever obeys God
            and His messenger
        Achieves the highest distinction.

SURAH XXXIV: SABA (SHEBA)
(54 verses)

The main theme tackled in this chapter is the inevitability of resurrection. Non-believers make fun of the Hereafter; they challenge Muhammad to prove it by some visible demonstration. They are blind to God's Signs, but when the time comes they will know the reality and then repent. Like Muhammad, David was also blessed by God: mountains and birds marked the occasion of his prophethood by singing God's praises. So it was the case with Solomon, to whom even the wind paid obeisance and a fount of molten brass heralded his arrival, Jinn obeyed his commands. Solomon lived in palaces especially built for him. But even so, he was helpless when death came.

Saba was a flourishing, agricultural place. But because its people defied the authority of God, they were submerged along with all their possessions by a flood. God had provided all amenities to travellers from Saba and Syria, but they rejected the call; their end was miserable. Their fate provides an object lesson to others: only believers are protected by God.

. Muhammad is told that every warner that God sent was harassed and disbelieved, in particular, 'by the wealthy ones'. They boasted of their wealth and progeny and proclaimed that they were indestructible. But God had warned each of them:

> It is not their wealth or sons
> That will bring them nearer to Us,
> But only those will be blessed
> Who have faith in God and do righteous deeds.
> They will be doubly rewarded
> And their abode will be in paradise.

(34:37)

As for Muhammad, his mission is not limited to a particular people or age: it is universal. He is told that he has been sent as a warner to all mankind.

SURAH XXXIV

1. All praise is to God,
To whom belongs everything
In the heavens and on earth.
His is also the praise in the world to come.
He is, indeed, All-Wise, All-Knowing.

2. He is aware of whatever happens here
And whatever comes from above
And whatever goes above.
He is, indeed, Most Merciful, All-Forgiving.

28. We have not sent you, O Muhammad!
But as a bearer of glad tidings
And a warner against sins

To all mankind.
Still most people do not understand.

34.   Whenever We sent a warner to a people,
       The rich among them never believed him.

35.   They told him, 'We have all the wealth
       And have been blessed with sons.
       Who can then punish us?'

36.   Tell them, O Muhammad:
       'Verily, my Lord enlarges and restricts
       His bounties to whom He pleases.
       But most people do not understand.'

37.   It is not their wealth or sons
       That will bring them nearer to Us,
       But only those will be blessed
       Who have faith in God and do righteous deeds.
       They will be doubly rewarded
       And their abode will be in paradise.

47.   Tell the people, O Muhammad:
       'I ask no reward from you.
       What I ask you is for your good.
       God will reward me,
       For He is the witness to all things.'

SURAH XXXV: FATIR (THE FASHIONER)
(45 verses)

This chapter extols the power of Allah and reminds people that He
is their Creator and that He also sustains them. It is the messengers
He sends who should be listened to, and not Satan, who is their
enemy. To follow the latter is to go to hell. Muhammad is, once
again, reminded:

> Verily, We have sent you, O Muhammad,
> With the truth
> And as a bearer of glad tidings
> And as a warner.
> In fact, there has never been a people
> Without a warner from Us
> And he lived among them.
>
> (35:24)

Also he is told:

> If they reject you, O Muhammad!
> So did their predecessors,
> To whom came their apostles
> With clear Signs from Us,
> With Book of dark warnings
> And bright enlightenment.
>
> (35:25)

People can see for themselves how God has given a multitude of shades and colours to His creatures, whether animate or inanimate, and through His revelations conveyed to them the truth about their existence:

> But there are among them some
> Who wrong their own souls,
> And some who follow a middle course.
> And some who lead in righteous deeds;
> The last one receives God's highest grace.
>
> (35:32)

Finally God talks of His mercy, and says that if He were really to punish every sin committed by a living creature on this earth, then no one would remain unpunished.

SURAH XXXV

2.   None can take away out of His Mercy
     What God bestows on mankind.
     And what He withholds,

None can grant.
He is, indeed, the Most Powerful,
Full of Wisdom.

4.   If they reject you, O Muhammad,
Do not grieve.
Messengers before you
Were also rejected.
However, it is to God
That everything is
Left for decision.

6.   Verily, Satan is your enemy,
So treat him as one.
He calls people
To the path
That can only lead to hell.

7.   Hence, those who reject God
Will face terrible punishment,
But those who believe in Him
Will not only be forgiven
But will receive a magnificent reward.

10.   Whoever runs after
Glory and power
Must remember
That all glory and power
Belong to God.
Hence all praise is
Due to him
Who exalts
Every righteous deed.
But for those who do evil
There is terrible punishment in store.
Their evil designs
Will come to nothing.

11.   From clay, God created you
        And fashioned you out of
        A drop of sperm.
        Then He made pairs.
        No female conceives or delivers
        Without His Knowledge,
        Nor is the duration of life, short or long,
        Decreed except by Him.
        All this is so easy for God.

15.   It is you, O People,
        Who are in need of God.
        God does not need you,
        He is above all wants.

18.   The bearer of one's burden
        Does not carry another's,
        Even if it is heavy.
        Not even of one closely related,
        Even if he cries out to another for help.
        Those who fear God secretly
        And worship him regularly
        Do whatever good they can.
        They do it for their own good.
        To God is the return of all.

19.   The blind and the seeing;
        The two cannot be alike.

20.   As darkness and light
        Can never be the same.

21.   As shade and light
        Can never be the same.

22.   Likewise, the living and the dead,
        They cannot be the same.
        God can make anyone hear Him,
        But men cannot hear those
        Who are buried deep in earth.

23.   You are, remember, O Muhammad!
Only a warner.

24.   Verily, We have sent you, O Muhammad,
With the truth
And as a bearer of glad tidings
And as a warner.
In fact, there has never been a people
Without a warner from Us
And he lived among them.

25.   If they reject you, O Muhammad!
So did their predecessors,
To whom came their apostles
With clear Signs from Us,
With Book of dark warnings
And bright enlightenment.

29.   Surely, those who read Our Book
And worship Us regularly
And spread charity out of their wealth,
Whether overtly or covertly,
They will have commerce with Us.
We shall never fail them.

30.   God will, indeed, reward them fully
And give them even more than what they deserve,
For God is not only most forgiving
But also most generous in rewarding.

38.   Verily God knows everything
Even what is hidden in the heavens and on earth.
He possesses all the knowledge
Of whatsoever is in people's hearts.

45.   If God were to punish people
According to their misdeeds,
Not a single living creature will be spared.
But He gives respite to everyone

For an appointed time.
And when that expires,
He takes account of
What they have done.

SURAH XXXVI: YA SIN
(83 verses)

―――――――――

This chapter eulogizes the attributes of God and his Prophet, Muhammad. It is graphic and moving in its description; the magic of its imagery and the exhortatory narration of the parable of the city, which it details, leave a lasting impact on the reader as well as the listener. It fills, as if in a cup, a whole sea of emotion about the grandeur and majesty of God. It exhorts believers and warns unbelievers. That is why this chapter is highly valued by the exegetists, who have called it 'the Heart of the Quran'. It is read by the faithful on ceremonial occasions and is regarded as the harbinger of glad tidings.

God reiterates that Muhammad is His Apostle and no poet; nor does it become him to be one. The revelations given to him are for the people 'whose fathers had received no admonitions' and have, therefore, remained in a state of ignorance. It refers to a parable, concerning a city, where God had sent His messengers. The first two were rejected by the people; then a third one was sent. He was also jeered at. One of the citizens advised his co-citizens that the last messenger should be listened to, because he was asking nothing for himself but was only trying to convey to them what the Lord had commanded him to do. They did not listen and continued to be defiant, and as a result a mighty blast reduced them and the whole city to ashes. Thus God tests His creatures many times, allows them enough scope to take the right path; if they still persist in wrongdoing, only then does He punish them.

Unbelievers do not give up easily their old rites and practices. They refuse to see light despite the fact that God's power manifests itself in various ways, in the movement of the sun and the moon, and even in the growth of plants on earth. It is manifest in the succession of birth and death and of resurrection and in the manner in which His creation functions. The organization and harmonious artistry of His creation are, indeed, matters of wonder; they provide evidence of the majesty and power of God.

The Quran clarifies that on the Day of Judgement:

> To the righteous, God will grant peace,
> But to the evil ones He will declare:
> 'Sons of Adam, did I not warn you against Satan
> And told you to worship Me alone?
> That was the right path for the virtuous to take,
> But so many of you at Satan's instance went astray
> Despite the warning given to you.
> Therefore burn in the hell you were promised
> For having disbelieved in Me.'
>
> (36:58)

SURAH XXXVI

2.   The Quran is, indeed,
      The custodian of all wisdom.

3.   And you, O Muhammad, are indeed,
      One of My Messengers,

4.   Treading the
          straight path.

5.   The revelation sent down to you,
      Is from God, the Almighty, the Merciful.

36.   Glorify God, who has created in pairs
      Everything on the earth,
      Among humans as well as among other species
      Of which you do not know.

77.   Is it not strange that man,
      Whom God has created out of sperm,

Should stand up to Him
As an open adversary

78.   And associate others with Him,
       Forgetting the fact of his own origin?
       He questions One who resurrects the dead.

81.   How can He, the creator of the heavens and the earth,
       Not be able to put life into the dead?
       God is, indeed, supreme.
       He is full of knowledge and skill.

82.   The truth is, when
       God commands 'Be',
       And lo and behold, it comes into being.

83.   So glorify the Lord
       Who has dominion over everything,
       And to Him all will return.

SURAH XXXVII: AL-SAFFAT (THE ROWS)
(182 verses)

This chapter begins with the reaffirmation that God is one, the ruler of the heavens and the earth. He controls everything and guards against 'all rebellious spirits'. He will punish those who, puffed with arrogance, refuse to give up the worship of their idols 'for the sake of a poet possessed'. Assuredly they will be sent to hell with its blazing fires, while paradise, with all its pleasures, awaits believers.

Prophets were sent from time to time to deliver the message of God to their fellow men; but many flouted their guidance and, in fact, persecuted them. Irrespective of the odds they faced, messengers carried out their task as ordered by God. In the end, virtue triumphed and vice was destroyed. This was seen in the manner in which Noah rescued believers from the onslaught of the flood, while his enemies, Pharaoh and his chiefs, were drowned. Likewise it is shown in the test that Abraham faced, when he was ordered by God to sacrifice his son Ishmael, and Abraham smilingly agreed to it. God then replaced Ishmael with an animal in the nick of time. As a gesture for his supreme sacrifice, God made Abraham a prophet also. Isaac was also blessed by God and entrusted with divine mission. Moses and Aaron and their people were delivered from 'a great calamity' and were guided by God to the straight path:

> Thus, indeed, do We reward
> Those who perform righteous deeds.
>
> (37:121)

Elisha called upon his people to refrain from worshipping Baal and pray to God, 'who is the best of Creators'. Except for the believers, they rejected his call. So also was the case with Lot, who delivered God's message to his adherents but, except for an old woman, all his people rejected it and were, consequently, destroyed.

Similarly, Jonah was entrusted with divine mission, but was cast by his enemies into the sea, where a big fish swallowed him. God rescued him and sent him out to spread the faith. His people responded to his call and were permitted to enjoy life. God is, indeed, the Creator and Cherisher of all. He has no sons nor are angels related to him. Hence the faithful must pray to Him and ask for His benevolence, and invoke His peace and blessings on prophets, who have been sent down by Him to guide mankind to the right path.

SURAH XXXVII

1. All those are My witnesses
   Who range themselves in rows.

2. And who are strong enough
   To repel the evil.

3. And who proclaim
   The Message of God.

4. That God is, indeed, one.

180.   Glorious is your Lord,
         Possessor of all honour
         And of all power.
         He is above whatever
         They ascribe to Him.

181.   And peace be
         On His messengers.

182.   And praise to Him,
         Who is the Cherisher
         Of all the worlds.

SURAH XXXVIII: SAD
(88 verses)

This chapter points out how unbelievers glorify themselves and refuse to accept that one among them can be entrusted with divine mission. Nor are their leaders prepared to give up their idols and worship one God. They condemn Muhammad as a sorcerer who is playing tricks by making their many gods into one God. They tell their followers to stick to their old forms of worship and not believe 'a tale made up' by Muhammad. They attack him, but God asks him not to be dismayed. He is reminded of what happened to David, who was endowed by God with both power and wisdom. Yet when a dispute arose between two factions, he did not give a correct judgement. He was much distressed by his lapse, but God forgave him:

         O David! God made you
         A viceregent on earth
         So that you may judge properly
         Between men and men
         And not be misled
         By lust within your heart.
         Remember, those who stray
         From the right path

> Will suffer grievous penalty
> When accounts are taken.
>
> (38:26)

God has not created the heavens and the earth without a purpose. Hence He cannot treat those who believe in Him and work right-eously in the same way as those who reject Him and do mischief:

> Shall We treat as the same
> Those who believe in Us
> And do righteous deeds,
> And those who do mischief
> On this earth?
>
> (38:28)

David's son Solomon was tested by God; because of his worldly strength and royal glory, he defaulted at first, but eventually he chose to turn to God in true devotion. God granted to him such power that even the wind bent to his will. Job cried to God for help while in distress, and God asked him to strike his foot. This brought forth cool and refreshing water, and the thirst of his people was quenched. God chose Abraham, Isaac and Jacob to proclaim His message to their people and to warn them of what was in store in the Hereafter. Ishmael, Elisha and Dhu al Kifl were also His messengers, and spread goodness all around. On the other hand, in the fall of Satan, a warning was sounded for mankind. He was the archangel who refused to obey God's command to prostrate before Adam, saying,

> I am better than Adam, my Lord.
> You have created me from fire,
> But Adam has been made out of clay.
> How can I then bow to him?
>
> (38:76)

God banished Satan from the heavens and declared that he would be accursed until the Day of Judgement. Satan pleaded for respite until then; this was granted to him. He said to the Lord that he would lead people astray except those who were true and sincere

believers. In that case, the Lord warned, He would fill hell with
those who would follow Satan.

SURAH XXXVIII

26.   O David! God made you
        A viceregent on earth
        So that you may judge properly
        Between men and men
        And not be misled
        By lust within your heart.
        Remember, those who stray
        From the right path
        Will suffer grievous penalty
        When accounts are taken.

28.   Shall We treat as the same
        Those who believe in Us
        And do righteous deeds,
        And those who do mischief
        On this earth?
        Likewise, shall we treat as the same
        Those who guard themselves
            against evil
        And those who turn
            away from the right path?

29.   We have sent down
        A Book for you
        Which is blessed by Us
        So that you may ponder
        Over its teachings
        And as men of wisdom
        Reflect on them.

45.   Commemorate Our Servants
        Abraham, Isaac and Jacob;
        They were, indeed,
        Possessors of power and vision.

46.   They were chosen by Us
        For a special purpose.
        To proclaim to people
        Our warning about the Hereafter.

47.   They truly belonged
        To the elect and the best.

48.   Likewise, commemorate
        Ishmael, Elisha and Dhu al Kifl.
        They were also among the best.

69.   Tell them, O Muhammad,
        'I have no knowledge
        Of what goes on above
        Or what is discussed on high.

70.   'I only know what has been
        Revealed by God to me.
        I am to give warning
        Plainly and publicly.'

SURAH XXXIX: AL-ZUMAR (THE HORDES)
(75 verses)

This chapter dilates on how God creates a definite unity of action despite variety in His creations, and how He sorts out the differences among groups and classes. Everyone and everything is eventually governed by a plan, fashioned by Him. He is, indeed, the controller of everything that proclaims His majesty. His laws are of universal application, because it is He who has created men and women and all living creatures. He is not in need of anything from them, but they are all in need of Him. When people are in trouble they seek His help, but when they are helped, they forget their Benefactor and set up rivals to Him. They may enjoy this blasphemy for a little while, but ultimately they will be companions of the fire of hell.

Those who believe in Him and do good deeds, however, will have their just reward from Him.

God has put forth in the Quran every kind of parable so that people may take lessons from them. It is revealed in Arabic so that those to whom it is sent may understand its meaning and purpose. God warns them about *shirk*, or associating partners with Him. Is not a man with many partners likely to be at odds with them? Will he then not be better off without partners? That is the position of God: He is the one and only. Muhammad is told to convey to his people:

> This Book, which has been
> Sent down to you, O Muhammad,
> Contains the truth for
> All mankind,
> So that whoever is guided
> Does so for his good,
> And whoever goes astray
> Will be the loser and sufferer.
> You will certainly not be blamed
> For what they do or do not do.
>
> (39:41)

God will judge between His creatures in matters in which they differ. Wrongdoers will certainly be punished on the Day of Judgement; but God's mercy also knows no bounds. Hence, they need not despair of His mercy for 'Allah forgives all sins. He is Oft-forgiving, Most Merciful', provided wrongdoers turn to Him in repentance and bow before His will.

SURAH XXXIX

1.   The revelations in this Book
      Are all from God,
      He is exalted in power
      And full of wisdom.

2.   With exactitude, O Muhammad!
      We have revealed this Book to you

So that you may serve God
And offer Him exclusive devotion.

4.   Had God so wished
He could have chosen a son
From among those He has created.
But glory to Him.
He is above all this.
He is only One.
He subdues all.

16.   Those who listen to God's word
And understand its real meaning,
They are the ones best guided.
They have been endowed with the
    best understanding.

32.   No one commits a greater sin
Than the one who lies about God
And refuses to accept the truth
When it comes to him.
Do you think unbelievers
Will not be placed in hell?

33.   Those who bring forth the truth
And those who accept it
Are, indeed, God-fearing!

37.   One who has been guided by God
Cannot go astray,
For God is Almighty,
The Lord of retribution.

39.   Tell them, O Muhammad!
To do what they can
And assure them
That you are doing what you can.

41.   This Book, which has been
    sent down to you, O Muhammad,

Contains the truth for
  all mankind,
So that whoever is guided
Does so for his good,
And whoever goes astray
Will be the loser and sufferer.
You will certainly not be blamed
For what they do or do not do.

SURAH XL: AL-MUMIN (THE BELIEVER)
(85 verses)

Here, once more, the divine nature of the Quran is asserted:

This Book is, indeed,
Revealed by Allah.
He is Exalted in Power
Full of Knowledge.

(40:1)

He forgives sin and accepts repentance, but at the same time He is strict in punishing the guilty. His requital to the enemies of Noah was terrible. So will it be to all unbelievers, who reject faith in Him. Those who refused to listen to God's messengers, even when they had come with clear Signs, were unbelievers who would be called to account for their sins. Moses came with God's authority to guide people, but Pharaoh, Haman and Qarun, mighty, powerful and rich, rejected his call. They were warned but they refused to heed the warning. In the end, each of them perished. A wise man advised Pharaoh to listen to Moses; but the Egyptian king was too full of himself. He did not heed him, and proclaimed instead the invincibility of his own might. He and his chiefs were therefore drowned in the sea. Joseph was disbelieved and the unbelievers had to pay for it. Pharaoh asked Haman to build for him the loftiest palace which could reach up to the heavens so that from there he could talk to the God of Moses; it was a vain desire; it landed him in perdition.

What people must realize is that the creation of the heavens and the earth is a greater miracle than even the creation of man. Because of his arrogance, man may consider himself supreme, but he is nothing before his Creator. He must, therefore, humble himself before God and heed the warning of messengers sent by God from time to time. Muhammad was repeatedly told that other messengers sent by God had preceded him. Stories of some of them had been narrated to him but those of many others were not. However, no messenger came to the people with God's Signs without His leave. Every messenger was at first rejected by the people, who exulted in their own knowledge and skill; but when the wrath of God visited them, they could not save themselves. They repented after seeing what God could do to them, but what was the worth of such repentance? Declaration of faith without conviction is worthless; repentance after persisting in unbelief is of no use.

SURAH XL

15. Raised above all ranks
Is the Lord of the Throne;
By His command is sent
Inspiration to those among His servants
Whom He pleases to choose,
To give warning to people
Of their meeting with the Lord.

17. On that Day everyone
Will be requited for what he has done.
No injustice will be done to anyone,
For God is swift and just in taking account.

56. Those who argue about God's Revelations,
They have no understanding,
They are motivated by pride.
But they will achieve nothing by
such vain endeavours.
You pay no heed to them

And take refuge in God,
For surely He hears and sees everything.

57. Surely the creation of the heavens and the earth
Is of far greater magnitude
Than even the creation of man,
Though most men
Do not understand.

58. The blind and the seeing are not equal.
Similarly those who believe
And do the righteous deeds,
And those who disbelieve and do evil,
They cannot be equal.
Will you then not reflect?

78. Messengers were sent by Us before you,
O Muhammad!
Some we have mentioned to you,
And others we have not.
But none came without Our leave
And none without truth and justice.
Those who denied them were lovers of
vice and vanity.
They will come to grief on the
Day of Judgement.

SURAH XLI: HA MIM
(54 verses)

This chapter extols the merits of the Quran, which is revealed in
Arabic, so that its verses may be understood by the people for
whom it is revealed. Moreover, the Prophet being an Arab, the
Book had to be revealed in Arabic so that he could communicate it
to his people. Unfortunately, instead of welcoming the revelations,
his people turned away from him and refused to heed his warning.
In these revelations the purpose and nature of creation is explained,

and people are warned against snares set up by Satan. It provides hope for their salvation. The stories of what happened to disbelievers in the past are narrated; they show to the present generation how evil can never succeed and that ultimately, whatever the odds, it is virtue that triumphs. Believers are, therefore, admonished:

> Virtue and vice can never be the same.
> Then repel vice by virtue,
> This is, indeed, much better.
> In the end hatred will disappear
> And enemies will become friends.
>
> (41:34)

Among believers, those who exercise patience and self-restraint will be granted 'the greatest good fortune'. They should 'seek refuge in Allah' from the evil ones, who incite people to discord.

SURAH XLI

3.   This is a Book
         containing verses
      Explaining in detail
         the Signs of God
      A Quran sent in
         the Arabic language
      So that the people
         here understand.

4.   It is full of
         glad tidings and admonitions
      And still most people turn away from it
      And do not listen to what it says.

6.   Say, O Muhammad, to your people:
      'I am a man like you
      But it is revealed to me
      To convey to you
      That God is one.
      So be steadfast and true to Him

And ask for His forgiveness.
And do not join others with God.'

8.   Those who believe in God
     And do the righteous deeds,
     For them there is a reward
     Which will never fail them.

34. Virtue and vice can never be the same.
     Then repel vice by virtue,
     This is, indeed, much better.
     In the end hatred will disappear
     And enemies will become friends.

35. Only those can attain virtue
     Who exercise patience and self-restraint.
     They will be the persons of the greatest good fortune.

43. Nothing has been told to you,
         O Muhammad,
     Which was not told to the
         apostles before you.
     Your Lord is, indeed, Most Forgiving
     But He is also Most Exacting.

44. Had we revealed the Quran
     In any other language except Arabic
     People here would have said:
     'Why are its verses not in Arabic?
     How can we understand them?
     Isn't it strange that an Arab messenger
     Should be given revelations not in Arabic?'

46. Whoever does righteous deeds
     Does good to himself,
     And whoever does evil
     Does harm to himself.
     Your Lord is never unjust
     To any of His creatures.

51.   When we bestow Our favours
Man turns away from Us.
But no sooner evil befalls him
Than he comes to Us
With prolonged prayers.

SURAH XLII: AL-SHURA (THE COUNSEL)
(53 verses)

In this chapter, Muhammad is reminded that Allah blessed him with the inspiration to propagate the truth in the same way as He had blessed other prophets before him:

God has given you, O Muhammad!
The same religion as He gave to Noah,
And to Abraham, Moses and Jesus.
He enjoined upon them all
To be steadfast in truth
And not to divide people
Except from those who worship others besides God.
For them it is, hard, indeed, to respond.
But God chooses whomsoever He likes
And guides those who turn to Him.

(42:13)

However, through selfishness and jealousy people became divided into different sects; if God had so willed He would have united them and settled the matters on which they differed. But He leaves people to choose their own way. There are people who express doubt and spread suspicion about the integrity of Muhammad and the authenticity of his mission; but he should remain steadfast and not be bothered about these 'vain attacks'. He should frankly tell them:

I believe in the Book of God.
He has commanded me to judge
Rightly between people and people.

> God is our Lord and your Lord;
> For me my deeds, for you, yours.
> There should be no dispute in this.
> It is for God to bring us together
> For His is the final destiny.

(42:15)

People must realize that whatever misfortune befalls them, it is because of their own doing; they must, therefore, conduct their affairs honestly, trusting in the Lord and avoiding crimes and shameful deeds. They should pray regularly and manage their affairs by mutual consultation. They should not commit aggression against others except in self-defence; in that case no blame will be attached to them. However, those who oppress others and transgress limits, defying right and justice, will be in for a grievous penalty on the Day of Judgement. Muhammad has not been sent by God as a guard over them; his duty is only to preach and convey the message.

SURAH XLII

5.   As the heavens are rent asunder
       And angels sing God's praises,
       They implore Him to forgive
       All the dwellers on earth.
       Verily, He is Most-Forgiving.
       He is ever so Merciful.

6.   Those who look to others for protection,
       God watches them with disdain.
       Why should you bother, O Muhammad?
       You are not the disposer of their affairs.

8.   If God had so willed, He would have made
       The whole of mankind a set of believers.
       But he grants His grace to whomsoever He pleases,
       For the sinners there will be no helper or friend.

12.   To God belongs the keys of heaven and earth,

He enlarges and restricts man's sustenance.
He does what He pleases.
He knows what He should do.

15. Call upon people to believe in Us
And ask them to be steadfast and firm.
That is most assuredly Our command.
Let vain desire not mislead them.
Say: 'I believe in the Book of God.
He has commanded me to judge
Rightly between people and people.
God is our Lord and your Lord;
For me my deeds, for you, yours.
There should be no dispute in this.
It is for God to bring us together
For His is the final destiny.'

30. For misfortunes that befall him
Man is himself to blame.
And still God forgives many wrongs
That he in his folly commits.

31. Man cannot frustrate
The will of God.
He has no protector or helper
Besides God.

36. Whatever you have in this world,
Is temporary and ephemeral.
But whatever God will give Hereafter,
That will be better and permanent
For those who trust Him.

38. And for those who harken to His call
And pray regularly to Him
And conduct their affairs
By mutual consultation,
And do charity regularly
From what God has given them.

40. The recompense for an injury is equal injury
    But forgiveness also is a recompense;
    God does not love the unjust.

41. If a wrong is committed against a person
    And he defends himself,
    Then he commits no wrong
    And no blame attaches to him.

42. Blame-worthy are those who oppress others
    And commit wrong and transgress
    With impunity and without just cause.
    Theirs will, indeed, be grievous penalty.

43. However, if one restrains and forgives
    That is, indeed, courageous on his part.
    It will smooth the conduct of affairs.

SURAH XLIII: AL-ZUKHRUF (ORNAMENTS OF GOLD) (89 verses)

It is here emphasized once again that through revelations God shows the right path. He entrusts this work to His messengers. People mock at them, insisting on following the religion of their forefathers and worshipping deities other than God. But their fate is bound to be miserable. What happened to Pharaoh and his chiefs, who ridiculed Moses and refused to harken to his call? They were drowned in the flood and paid the penalty for disobeying the command of the Lord. Likewise, Jesus was defied when he revealed himself as God's messenger. He was not the son of God, but His true servant, who was 'granted Our favour': 'We made him an example to the Children of Israel.' He told them that God was his Lord and their Lord; hence they should worship God and no one else. 'This is the straight path.' Verily, God reveals the truth to everyone, but most people 'have a hatred for truth'. So leave them to indulge in their vanities. They will realize their folly on the Day of Judgement, when account will be taken of their misdeeds and retribution will follow.

SURAH XLIII

2.   This is the book that makes things
Clear to everyone here.
That is why it is sent in Arabic,
So that people understand its teachings.

4.   And, verily, these teachings are contained
In the Mother of the Book,
Which remains with Us.
It is sublime in its contents
And full of wisdom.

5.   Should We take it away
Because people don't heed it?
Or because they transgress the bounds?

6.   It was no different, O Muhammad,
With the other prophets.

7.   In fact, every one
Whom We sent with the Book,
Their people mocked at them.

SURAH XLIV: AL-DUKHAN (THE SMOKE)
(59 verses)

Unbelievers persist in questioning the mission of Muhammad and the authenticity of the Quran which was revealed to him on a blessed night to forewarn mankind. His detractors will regret this when, on the appointed day, due retribution will be exacted from them. The manner in which Pharaoh and his chiefs were drowned in the sea, for refusing to harken to the call of Moses, should be an eye-opener to all unbelievers:

> Neither the earth nor the heavens
> Shed a tear over their fate.
>
> (44:29)

On the contrary, the Children of Israel were saved by God from the scourge and put above all others. But unbelievers refuse to draw a lesson from these happenings. They ask: 'How can the dead be raised to life? First bring back to us our fathers, if what you say, O Muhammad, is really true.' Muhammad is instructed to tell them that they will know the truth on the Day of Judgement, when no one will help them. They will be given the fruit of the Zaqqum tree, the poisonous one, and their food will be mixed with dregs of oil, which will simmer in their stomachs like scalding water. The righteous, on the other hand, shall be blessed with eternal peace and live in paradise amid gardens and fountains, served by dark-eyed maidens clothed in rich silks and fine brocades. They shall be protected from every calamity by their Lord.

SURAH XLIV

38.   We did not create
      The heavens and the earth
      Just as a plaything.

39.   They were created, in fact,
      With a definite purpose.
      But this, most fail to understand.

40.   On the Day of Judgement,
      As promised by Us,
      Due account will be taken
      Of everyone's deeds and misdeeds.

41.   No friend or protector
      Can rescue anyone
      From the fate that awaits him,

42.   Except God, who is Benevolent
        And may forgive anyone,
        For He alone is All-Powerful
        As well as Most Forgiving.

SURAH XLV: AL-JATHIYAH (KNEELING)
(37 verses)

All over the earth and in the heavens there are Signs of God for
those who can see. Unbelievers may jest about them, but they will
pay for their abomination. To the Children of Israel, God granted
the Book, the power to rule and the gift of prophethood. He sent
clear signs to guide them in the affairs of religion. But they fell into
schisms through jealousy among themselves. They became insolent,
corrupt and disunited, and the result was their fall from His grace.
On the Day of Judgement, God will judge between them and
decide on matters on which they differed.

Muhammad is God's chosen messenger. He is shown the right
path by Him, so all believers should follow what he reveals from
God and not cling to their own desires. Those who persist in doubting his mission and continue with their unbelief will have to suffer the
evil consequences of their actions, which will so encircle them that they
will have no escape from the doom that awaits them.

SURAH XLV

13.   God has made subservient to you
        All that is in heaven and earth.
        In them are His Signs
        For those who reflect.

14.   Tell those who believe in Us
        To forgive those who do not.
        They do not look ahead.
        It is for Us to decide
        About what the people do.

15.   Any one who does a righteous deed
        Does so for his good,
        And any one who does a wrong
        Suffers the result thereof.
        Finally all will be put before the Lord
        And made accountable for what they did.

22.   God created the heavens and the earth
        To promote justice and fair play,
        So that every one
        May get what he deserves
        And no one is unjustly wronged.

SURAH XLVI: AL-AHQAF (THE SAND DUNES)
(35 verses)

God created the earth and the heavens for promoting justice and
fair play among His creatures. Those who reject His call and
worship others besides Him are oblivious to this truth as contained
in the Book. They may describe it as a sorcery or forgery, but the
fact is that Muhammad is no bringer of 'new-fangled doctrines', but
is the conveyor of the same message as was preached by messengers
before him. God asks him to tell his detractors that he does not
know what will happen to him nor to them; no one has knowledge
of the future. The task assigned to him is that of a warner; it is the
same as that given to Moses in the past:

        The Quran in Arabic confirms it.
        It warns the unjust
        And gives glad tidings to the righteous.
                                        (46:12)

Believers are enjoined to be kind to their parents and always
remember the pain that a mother has to go through to bear a child
and nurse it for thirty months. They remain ever anxious about
their children. That is why when a child grows into a man and
becomes a parent, he in turn prays that his sons may be blessed with

wisdom and understanding and be ever grateful to God for His benevolence. He is the giver of all good things.

Hud warned Aad, his people, about the winding sand tracts and beseeched them to fear God, but they did not heed him and were destroyed. Similarly, the people of the tribe of Quraish in Arabia, whom God had not endowed with as much power and wealth as Aad and who did not possess the physical and mental faculties of Aad, would meet a worse fate than Aad's if they rejected the call of Muhammad:

> If any person does not harken to the call
> As given by Us through Our Messenger,
> He only harms himself and no one else;
> He cannot frustrate God's plan
> And he cannot have any protector besides Him;
> Such persons will wander aimlessly
> Committing manifest error.
>
> (46:32)

SURAH XLVI

7.   Even when We show Our signs
     Unbelievers refuse to see them,
     And say: 'Oh! This is nothing but sorcery.'

8.   They tell you, O Muhammad!
     That what you have is forgery.
     Why don't you tell them:
        'You are wrong.
     If I forged His Book,
     No one can save me from His wrath.'
     Hence, ask them to stop talking so glibly.
     No one knows better than God what is what!
     God is, indeed, the witness
     Between Him and His Messenger.

9.   Tell them, O Muhammad!
     'I am only God's Messenger.
     I have not brought new-fangled doctrines,

I do not know what He has in store
For me, for you or for anyone.
I am here to follow His dictates,
And convey His teachings to you
As openly and clearly as He wants.'

12.   The Book of Moses came before this
        As a guidance and mercy to people.
        The Quran in Arabic confirms it.
        It warns the unjust
        And gives glad tidings to the righteous.

19.   For everyone the recompense will be
        According to the degree of his deed;
        Both the good and the bad
        Will be accurately judged
        So that no injustice is done to anyone.

SURAH XLVII: MUHAMMAD
(38 verses)

In this chapter instructions are given to believers in the conduct of both their internal and external affairs. In the case of aggression by enemies, they should not hesitate to strike off the heads of unbelievers, though it is better to capture them alive, if possible. However, on achieving victory against them on the battlefield, they should grant them freedom or take ransom after they have surrendered their arms. If God had so willed, He himself would have vanquished them, but He wanted to test the will and the courage of believers. Those among them who give their lives in His cause will be honoured by Him with martyrdom and placed in paradise. God is the protector of believers in every situation; but unbelievers have no protection. There were many cities in the past, mightier than the city of believers, but, because of their unbelief, what became of them? They were wiped from the surface of this earth.

Muhammad is then warned about the role of the hypocrites

among his followers; they say one thing to his face and do the opposite in his absence:

> Their hearts are sealed by God,
> For they act with the basest of motives.
>
> (47:16)

They are, however, mistaken if they feel that God will not bring to light their misdeeds or treachery and not punish them for the wrong they do. They make take it as a sport or pastime, and amuse themselves for a little while, but when the time comes they will repent. Believers should not, therefore, be deluded by their example; on the contrary, they must guard against temptations. They shall certainly be recompensed for their piety and good deeds.

SURAH XLVII

33.   Believers, obey God and the Apostle
    And let your deeds be fruitful.

35.   In your fight in the cause of God,
    Don't be weary and faint-hearted,
    And be not anxious for peace at any cost.
    Remember that God is with you.
    He will never put you to loss
    For the good that you will do.

36.   The life on this earth
    Is nothing but a play,
    But those who believe in God
    And guard against evil,
    He will recompense them;
    He is not interested
    In worldly gains.

SURAH XLVIII: AL-FATH (THE VICTORY)
(29 verses)

This chapter was revealed after the Prophet had signed the Treaty of Hudaibiya, a place to the west of Mecca on the main road to Medina. The terms of this treaty with the pagans of Mecca had upset many of his Companions. Umar called it 'humiliating'. God reassures the faithful that the treaty was not a defeat for them, but a victory, a precursor of the fulfilment of their cherished desire:

> God has, in fact, fulfilled
> His Apostle's vision:
> You shall, therefore, enter the sacred Mosque
> With hair cut short, and fearlessly,
> For God knows what you know not;
> He has, indeed, granted you a speedy victory.
>
> (48:27)

Believers are told that God has forgiven them all their sins of the past and even those that may be committed in future. He has completed His favour to them and guided them to the right path. However, God will punish hypocrites and polytheists, who defy His authority and speak ill of Him. They think that the Prophet and the believers, who were driven away from their city and their hearths and homes, will never be able to rejoin their families, but they are wicked to think so; they will learn to regret their folly. Believers are assured that their future with Muhammad is safe:

> Those who are with him
> Will be strong and safe
> Against all unbelievers.
>
> (48:29)

SURAH XLVIII

8.   Truly, We have sent you, O Muhammad!
      As a witness and bearer of good news.
      And as a warner to people,

9.   So that they may be helped
        In believing in Us and Our Apostle
        And celebrate Our praises,
        Morning and evening.

10.   Tell the people, O Muhammad!
        That those who swear
            allegiance to you,
        Do in reality swear
            allegiance to Us.
        Over them is Our hand of protection.
        If anyone breaks his oath,
        He will do so at his risk.
        And all those who fulfil their covenant,
        They will be the recipients of Our reward.

SURAH XLIX: AL-HUJURAT (THE APARTMENTS)
(18 verses)

This chapter provides some broad directions to Muslims as to how
they should behave towards one another and particularly towards
the Prophet, who is their chief. They should be respectful towards
him all the time, never raise their voice in his presence, wait
patiently till he comes out of his chamber and listen to what he says
with due deference. They must realize that if he were to listen to
them and go by their wish, it would be a misfortune for everyone.
Muhammad must decide by himself, because God has endowed him
with the best judgement.

Believers should act properly. They should not believe what they
hear from others. They must first ascertain the truth and then react.
Those who act otherwise may hurt innocent people, for which they
will have to repent later. If two groups of believers fight against
each other, a third one must bring peace between them. However,
if one transgresses the limits, then that group must be fought
and subdued, for all believers constitute a single brotherhood.
Believers should not mock one another, nor defame anyone or talk

sarcastically against others. They should not entertain suspicion, spy on each other, or defame or backbite; these are sins that must be avoided. Those who try to impress upon Muhammad that they have done him a favour by embracing Islam are in the wrong; on the contrary God has conferred a favour on them by showing them the right path.

SURAH XLIX

6.   Believers, if a wicked person
      Gives some news to you,
      First ascertain the truth.
      For unwittingly you may harm
      People who are, indeed, innocent,
      And then be full of repentance
      For the wrong you have done.

9.   If one party of believers fights another
      Then try and make peace between them.
      However, if one of them transgresses the bounds
      Then all together should fight it
      And make it obey God's command.
      Be just and fair to all,
      For God loves the just.

10.   Believers in God are a single brotherhood.
      So make peace between disputing brothers.
      And fear God in whatever you do
      So that you may receive His mercy.

11.. Believers, let some of you
      Not laugh at others.
      The latter may, indeed, be better
      Than those who are laughed at.
      Also women should not laugh
      At one another.
      One may be better than the other.
      Do not defame people or talk sarcastically
      Or use offensive nicknames,

Nor express wicked thoughts;
Those who do not desist
Are, indeed, doing wrong.

12.   Avoid suspicion of each other,
       For unfounded suspicion is a sin.
       Also, do not spy on each other
       Nor speak ill of people behind their back.
       It is just like eating a dead brother's flesh.
       Hence fear God,
       For He is Oft-Returning, Most-Merciful.

13.   People are created
           in pairs
       As males and
           females,
       And from their
           union
       Are formed nations
           and tribes,
       So that they may
           know
       One another
           properly.
       However, in the
           sight of God,
       The most honourable
           of them
       Are those who are
       The most righteous.
       God is, indeed,
               All-Knowing
               and Fully-Informed.

17.   They impress upon you, O Muhammad,
       That by accepting Islam they have favoured you.
       Tell them that their acceptance is no favour to you.
       On the contrary, God has favoured them
       By guiding them to the true path,
       Provided they remain sincere in their faith.

SURAH L: QAF
(45 verses)

Once again, in this chapter, the question of life after death is discussed. Its importance has been repeatedly emphasized in the Quran. It is, in fact, one of the fundamentals of the religion. Unbelievers persist in refusing to accept its truth, and mockingly ask:

> What! When we die
> Will we all become dust?
> And then shall we be made alive
> And be brought before God?
> This is nonsense, which we cannot accept.
>
> (50:3)

They have just to look up to the heavens above and to the mysteries of nature below to realize the power of God. They should look to the creation of man himself, about whom no one knows better than God, because 'he is nearer to him than his jugular vein'. Every action of his is recorded by the angels, appointed by God to guard over him. On the Day of Judgement, when the records will be opened, he will find that nothing has remained hidden from the Lord.

Unbelievers cannot, therefore, deceive their Creator; it is for their good that messengers are sent. Muhammad is told by God:

> God knows best what your detractors say
> But do not overawe them by force.
> Admonish them through the Quran,
> Those who fear Our warning.
>
> (50:45)

SURAH L

16.   Man has been created by Us
    And We know what goes on in his mind,
    For surely We are nearer to him
    Than his jugular vein.

17.   There are two angels taking notes
       Of what he does on this earth.
       One is on his right
       The other on his left.

18.   Not a word he utters
       But it is recorded at once.

19.   The stupor of death will make man realize
       That he cannot escape it, whatever he may do.

20.   And when the trumpet blows,
       Heralding the Day of Doom,
       Man will remember
       The warning given.

21.   Then everyone will be brought before Us
       With one angel driving him
       And another as witness of his acts.

22.   The veil shall be removed
       And he will see clearly
       How heedless he has been
       Of the warning given him.

23.   The angel will vouch
       For the record of his deeds.

27.   His companion will disown him, saying:
       'O Lord! I did not lead him astray,
       He himself took the path of wickedness.'

28.   God will ask them
       Not to dispute in His presence;
       He had given the warning
       But they did not heed it.

29.   God's word shall not be changed,
       But He is never unjust to His creatures.

38.   God created the heavens and the earth
       And everything that lies between them,

All in a span of six days.
And in no way did it tire Him.

45.   God knows best what your detractors say
        But do not overawe them by force.
        Admonish them through the Quran,
        Those who fear Our warning.

SURAH LI: AL-DHARIYAT (THE SCATTERING WINDS) (60 Verses)

This chapter elaborates the manner in which earlier prophets propagated the message of God among their peoples, and the humiliation and suffering they had to face. The truth and the promise that they conveyed could not be suppressed; they prevailed despite all the odds.

On the Day of Judgement, non-believers, who had doubted its occurrence, will be put on trial before the Creator. They will suffer the consequence of their unbelief: blazing fires of hell will be their abode. The God-fearing ones, on the other hand, will be assigned gardens and fountains in paradise; even beggars and the outcast among them will be the beneficiaries.

Once, some guests came to Abraham, who in reality were angels. He prepared for them a fattened calf. They did not eat it, but they promised that his old and barren wife would be blessed with a son. Abraham was wonder-struck and pleased. He enquired of the angels why they had descended on earth. They replied that they were harbingers of the worst calamity for Lot, whose people had rejected the faith. Similarly, when Moses went, with light and learning, to Pharaoh and his chiefs, they dismissed him as a magician and 'a man possessed'. Their defiance invited the wrath of God upon them and, in consequence, they were drowned in the sea. Aad was also subjected to a blighting wind; it pounded them into dust for disobedience of God's authority. A similar fate awaited Thamud: a thunderbolt struck them. All in all, the rejecters of the divine message as conveyed from Noah to

Jesus met the same end. They were messengers of God who were denounced as magicians or mad men, and Muhammad is the last of them. He is the chosen one of God, and he should, therefore, not be dismayed by the denunciations of his detractors, who will also suffer grievously, like their forebears in the past.

SURAH LI

1. The winds that scatter dust
   all around

2. And the clouds that bear
   heavy burden

3. And move about with ease and comfort

4. And dispense rains
   by My command;

5. By them I say: 'My warning
   is true.'

6. 'Verily there shall be the Judgement Day
   And Justice shall be done to all.'

7. Heavens with their numerous paths
   are witnesses.

8. But you are caught in a web of
   contradictions.

9. That is the reason
   You are deluded away
   from the truth.

10. Woe to those who spread falsehood,

11. And flounder heedlessly in confusion.

12.   They persist in asking:
        'When will the Day of Judgement come?'

13.   Tell them it will be on the Day
        When they will be consigned to hell.

15.   For the Righteous, there will be
        Gardens of fruits and flowers
        And springs of fresh waters.

16.   They shall enjoy the things
        That their Lord will give them
        As a recompense for the good life
        They lived on the earth.

SURAH LII: AL-TUR (THE MOUNTAIN)
(39 verses)

Unbelievers are bound to meet their doom: no one can prevent it, says the Quran. On the Day when it occurs,

> . . . the firmament will shake
> And mountains
>   will fly away.
> On that Day woe to those
> Who discarded the truth
> And propagated falsehood,
> Indulging in shallow trifles.
> On the Day they shall be thrown
> Into the fires of hell.

(52:9–13)

On the other hand, believers will be allotted gardens where they will enjoy the bliss of paradise. They will be given the best of pleasures including the company of wide-eyed *houris* and handsome youths. God will shower His graciousness on them, and they will be protected by Him from every calamity. Unbelievers, however, will be in the dock. Their guile shall be of no avail, nor will they receive help from anyone. So thunderstruck will they be by what they will see that they will be dumb-founded.

SURAH LII

9.   On the Day when
         the firmament will shake

10.   And mountains
         will fly away.

11.   On that Day woe to those
         Who discarded the truth
         And propagated falsehood,

12.   Indulging in shallow trifles.

13.   On the Day they shall be thrown
         Into the fire of hell.

17.   As for the righteous,
         they will be
         In the gardens of bliss.

18.   Enjoying what the Lord provides,
         Keeping them away from hell.

SURAH LIII: AL-NAJM (THE STAR)
(62 verses)

In this chapter, Muhammad is again assured that he neither errs nor speaks out of caprice. He only conveys God's Word. Then follows the allegedly favourable reference to the three goddesses, al-Lat, al-Uzza and Manat, whom the pagans of Mecca worshipped; this reference forms the basis of the charge that Muhammad had, at first, praised their intercession at the instance of Satan and later, at the instance of archangel Gabriel, retracted it, and replaced it by the following verse:

> Tell them, O Muhammad, that these
>   goddesses are nothing but names.
> They are the figments of imagination,
> Theirs and their fathers'.
> These goddesses cannot intercede.
> They draw no authority from God.
>
> (53:23)

An analysis of this episode has been given earlier, with particular reference to its historical perspective, exposing the hollowness of the charge against the Prophet. However, because of these 'Satanic Verses', this chapter has assumed a rather exaggerated and unusual importance in the hands of orientalists.

Though God's guidance has come through His messengers, unbelievers go by surmise and follow their fancies. They are concerned only with the present life. They do not follow what has been ordained in the scriptures given to Moses and Abraham, nor accept the fact of life and death and the final return of man to God. They see all His Signs and still persist in their unbelief. They are told of the terrible end that the tribes of Aad and Thamud met; about the drowning of Pharaoh and his forces; and of the rescuing of Noah and his followers from the onslaught of the flood. But the lessons of the past are lost on unbelievers. So those who believe in God must bestir themselves and bow before God and serve Him devotedly, knowing that they are in the right and will be favoured on the Day of Judgement.

SURAH LIII

19. Have you pondered over
     What Lat and Uzza are?

20. And the third goddess,
     Manat?

21.   For you, the sons,
       And for God, the daughters.

22.   The division itself
          shows a twisted mind.

23.   Tell them, O Muhammad, that these
          goddesses are nothing but names.
       They are the figments of imagination,
       Theirs and their fathers'.
       These goddesses cannot intercede.
       They draw no authority from God.

       To think otherwise
          is wishful thinking,
       Especially after the guidance
       That has come from God.

25.   Remember, to God alone
       Belongs the beginning
          and the end.

27.   Those who do not believe in the Hereafter
       Give female names to angels,

28.   But they possess no knowledge
       And only indulge in conjectures.
       But conjectures are no answer to truth.

29.   Hence avoid people who reject Our message,
       For they desire nothing but the pleasures of this world.

SURAH LIV: AL-QAMAR (THE MOON)
(55 verses)

This chapter begins with a description of the splitting of the moon, which Muslims regard as one of the miracles of the Prophet, brought about by the command of God; but even this was characterized by the pagans of Mecca as nothing but sorcery. God has, therefore, asked believers to pay no heed to them; the disbelievers would realize on the Day of Judgement how wrong they were, when they would be punished for their disbelief and brought out from their graves with faces downwards. They would then know the wrong that they had done to themselves. Their counterparts in the past had disbelieved Noah and called him mad; their chastisement was, therefore, certain. So was the case of Aad, whom a terrible wind plucked up and threw away like stumps of uprooted palm trees. The people of Thamud refused to listen to 'one from among them' and were reduced to something like the dry twigs used in enclosures of the building for cattle. Similarly, the people defied Lot and did not heed the divine call. They were obliterated. The same will be the end of those who refuse to believe the message of God as contained in the Quran; in the twinkling of an eye, God's will will be carried out and unbelievers will meet their miserable end.

SURAH LIV

17.   Indeed, We have made the Quran easy
        For everyone to understand.
        Why should you then not
        Receive its admonitions?

47.   Sinners are truly demented;
        They are, indeed, on the wrong path.

49.   Verily, God has created
        Everything in proper proportion
        And in right measure.

50.   His command is one;
         It is swift like the twinkling of an eye.

SURAH LV: AL-RAHMAN (THE MERCIFUL)
(78 verses)

This chapter is one of those most commonly recited by Muslims. It
extols the many benefits that God bestows on his creatures. After
every verse, creatures are asked, 'O which of your Lord's bounties
will you and you then deny?' Their rhythmic sequence uplifts both
the reciter and the listener. The eloquence with which the sun, the
moon and the stars are described is, indeed, enthralling; so is the
description of the variety of vegetation and all kinds of delicate
fruits and fragrant herbs. And then there is the reminder about
animate creation:

> Like a potter, God fashioned
> Out of clay, man, and
> Out of fire, Jinn.
> (55:14–15)

He is the ruler of 'the two Easts and the two Wests'. All that
exists on earth will perish; but God is eternal, ever resplendent:

> All those who inhabit the heavens and the earth
> Are doomed to die one day.
> It is your Lord alone who will abide for ever
> In all His power, glory and majesty.
> (55:22)

On the Day of Judgement, wrongdoers will be seized by the
forelock and pushed into burning hell. On the other hand, the
recompense for the righteous will be as 'pleasing as rubies, as
beautiful as coral'. They will be served by *houris* 'cloistered in
cool pavilions, untouched by human hands, reclining upon green

cushions covered with thick brocade.' Such will be the bounties of God, who always compensates godness with goodness. Who can then deny His benevolence?

SURAH LV

1. The most Gracious Lord!

2. Has bestowed the Quran on you.

3. And after creating man

4. Has taught him to express himself.

5. He has made the sun and the moon
   Follow their regular courses.

6. From the herbs to the trees
   Everything acknowledges His supremacy.

7. He has raised the firmament above
   To keep the right balance

8. So that none may transgress
   And upset the balance of creation.

9. Hence measure correctly
   And weigh justly.

16. How many of His favours will you deny?
    He is, indeed, the Lord of the East and West.

60. For the good the reward is good,
    That is the Law of God.

61. How many of His favours
    Can you then deny?

SURAH LVI: AL-WAQUIAH (THE EVENT)
(96 verses)

Once more, there is a graphic description of Doomsday, although every description differs from the other and has a characteristic of its own. In this chapter, God brings home to believers the scene of that occurrence, when terror will strike, the earth will rock and mountains will crumble and scatter like dust. Three classes of creatures will then emerge: one, the People of the Right; two, the People of the Left; and three, the 'Outstrippers', who were the earliest of the Companions, the helpers of the Prophet and the emigrants who left Mecca and settled in Medina. The People of the Right will be assigned paradise; the People of the Left, hell, while the Outstrippers, being the earliest of believers, will be put in gardens of delight, where the eternally youthful *houris* with beautiful, big and lustrous eyes will serve them goblets full of spring waters and delicious flesh of fowl: a recompense for the good they have done on earth.

Companions of the Right will live in the midst of thornless Lot trees and trees with long extended shade and a variety of fruits and flowers abounding, whose season is not limited, nor its supply forbidden. They shall have companions of equal age, virgin-pure and of special creation. The Companions of the Left will find themselves in the midst of fierce blazing fire, burning winds and boiling water. There will be nothing to refresh them nor please them. They have denied God and mocked at His revelations. They disbelieved the coming of Doomsday. They will now see for themselves the consequences of their disbelief. They will be made to eat from a bitter Zaqqum tree and to drink scalding water when they are, like a diseased camel, raging with thirst.

> Surely, this is the truth of which there is no doubt.
> Hence magnify the glory of Almighty God.
> And ask yourself who created you
> And your semen that procreates.
> Did you or your Lord?
> He is, indeed, the cause of your very creation.
>
> (56:57–9)

SURA LVI

57.   It is We who have created you.
Will you not accept the truth?

58.   Even the semen that procreates

59.   Has been created by Us, not you.

60.   We have made death the common
lot of all
And none has the power to undo it.

61.   We create and destroy
And again recreate
In forms of which no one knows.

62.   You know only the first form.

74.   Therefore celebrate the
glory of your Lord.

SURAH LVII: AL-HADID (THE IRON)
(29 verses)

This chapter celebrates the majesty of God, who is All-Wise. He gives life and takes it away. He is the All-Knowing, who controls everything. He is the First and the Last. He is the Outward and the Inward:

> Wherever you are He is with you.
> There is nothing hidden from Him,
> He knows even your innermost thoughts.
>
> (57:6)

To God belong the heavens and the earth. Those who fight for Him and spend in His cause before victory is achieved are better than those who do so after victory; rewards for the former will certainly be much higher than for the latter. Their contributions will be treated as a loan, which God will multiply for them. Hypocrites will suffer the worst plight on the Day of Judgement, when they will beg of believers to help them, reminding them that they were a part of them. There will, however, be a wall separating hypocrites from believers. They will ask hypocrites, 'Yes, apparently you were with us; but did you not succumb to temptation and go astray? Instead of remaining firm in your belief, were you not deluded by your own fancies?' They will have no answer. Therefore their refuge will be the fire of hell. God reiterates:

> Let all the people know
> That the life on this earth
> Is nothing but play and amusement.
> There is only show and boasting
> And rivalries galore,
> Also wealth and children.
> But it is the same as the growth
> Which the rain brings forth:
> The produce eventually withers
> And dries and becomes worthless.
>
> (57:20)

For a while people may have the joy of delusion; but eventually they have to return to God and be accountable to Him for their deeds and misdeeds. Hence believers are admonished to fear God and believe in His Messenger, so that He may grant them two-fold mercy: light to show the true path and assurance of forgiveness for their sins.

SURAH LVII

1. Everyone who is in the heavens
    and on this earth,
    Celebrates the might and glory of God,
    He is the most Exalted in Power
    He is Full of Wisdom.

2.   His is the Kingdom of the
            earth and the heavens.
         He is the giver and taker of life.
         He has power over everything.

3.   He is the First,
         He is the Last,
         He is the Transcendent,
         He is the Imminent.
         He is the Possessor of all knowledge.
         He is the Knower of all things.

20.   Let all the people know
         That the life on this earth
         Is nothing but play and amusement.
         There is only show and boasting
         And rivalries galore,
         Also wealth and children.
         But it is the same as the growth
         Which the rain brings forth:
         The produce eventually withers
         And dries and becomes worthless.
         In the Hereafter there is no withering;
         Both reward and punishment are permanent.
         Hence what is the life in this world?
         It is perishable like goods and chattels,
         Temporary, full of deception.

SURAH LVIII: AL-MUJADILAH (THE DISPUTANT)
(22 verses)

This chapter contains a warning against those men who, in anger, divorce their wives by declaring them to be their mothers; this is not only wrong but also unjust. Such husbands can be forgiven only if they set free slaves. Until they expiate their sin, they cannot touch their wives. And those of them who lack the means to do so must fast for two successive months; if they are unable to fulfil this condition, they must feed sixty poor people.

Whoever opposes Muhammad and denies the authority of God will be frustrated; God is aware of their designs even if planned in secrecy. As for believers, it is better that they come together, not in sin and enmity, but in piety and devotion to the Lord. To conspire secretly even in a good cause is not right; conspiracy is the work of Satan.

Believers should not take non-believers as friends. The latter are faithful to no one – not even themselves. Their oaths of fealty are false and they belong to Satan's party. They are full of distrust of one another. Believers, therefore, should never trust them, even if they be their fathers, brothers, sons or members of their clan. Believers belong to God's party; non-believers, to Satan's. The two cannot be together; they are, in fact, the enemies of one another, whatever be their filial affiliation.

SURAH LVIII

7.   Don't you realize that Allah knows
        What happens on earth and in the heavens?
        He has knowledge of all secret consultations.
        If it is between three,
        He is the fourth one,
        If between five, He is the sixth one.
        Whatever the number, big or small
        He is always there.
        On the Day of Judgement
        He will reveal everything,
        He has knowledge of all things.

9.   Believers, do not hold secret consultation
        For promoting hostility and inequity
        And for disobedience to God's Messenger,
        But hold consultation for righteousness
        And for exercising self-restraint;
        Everyone shall be brought before God.

14.   Do not listen to wrongdoers,
        Do not make them your friends.

They are the recipients of Allah's wrath,
They are faithful neither to you nor even to
   themselves,
They are faithful to falsehood, knowingly.

17.   Neither their wealth nor their sons
Will be of any use to them.
Their punishment is assured;
They will be the companions of fire.

SURAH LIX: AL–HASHR (EXILE)
(24 verses)

People are warned, in this chapter, not to commit a breach of trust of God and His messenger and to remember that whoever is guilty of the breach will receive a terrible chastisement. Further, whatever comes to the Prophet, wherever it came from, is his; as for the spoils of war, God has given authority to the Prophet to dispose of them as he thinks best. Hence believers should take whatever the Messenger gives ungrudgingly and hand over to him whatever he asks for. Orphans, the poor and the needy have a share in the spoils; so have soldiers and families of those who die fighting in the cause.

Emigrants, who left their homes and hearths to help the Messenger, are true believers, as are those who assisted them and accepted them as their own, 'even though poverty was their lot'. The Quran says, 'Whoever guards himself against his own avarice is the real prosperer.'

Believers should not trust hypocrites who lie and deceive. They are, in fact, allied with the People of the Book: the Christians and the Jews, who are no friends of believers. Hypocrites may show valour, but their hearts are really scattered; they are 'a people devoid of sense'. Punishment for them is inescapable.

SURAH LIX

22. God is the One
    Like whom there is none.
    He is the knower of all things,
    Of things known and unknown.
    He is the most gracious
    And full of mercy for all.

23. God is unique.
    He has no equal.
    There is no god but Him.
    He is the Mightiest,
    He is the Holiest,
    The source of all perfection.
    The guardian of faith,
    The preserver of peace,
    He is exalted in power,
    Irresistible and unequal,
    Above everyone.

24. He is the Creator.
    The maker of things,
    The fashioner of form.
    To Him belongs all that is
    In the heavens and on the earth.
    Sing his glory.
    He is Exalted in Power,
    He is Full of Wisdom.

SURAH LX: AL-MUMTAHANA (THE EXAMINED ONE)
(13 verses)

In this chapter believers are cautioned not to take enemies of God
and His prophet as friends; they should not secretly shower affection
on them even if they are their blood-relations, including their own
children. If they do so, they will incur the displeasure of God. For on
the Day of Judgement, none of them, whatever be their relationship,
will be of any help. God alone will be their protector. Abraham and
those who sided with him were discarded by their relations; Abraham
told even his own father, who did not respond to his call: 'I shall ask
God to forgive you for your inequity; but I will never follow you
and work against God.' In Abraham and the other prophets, believers
have 'a good example'. God knows what is best for everyone. It
might so happen, however, that He, in His wisdom, may bring
about love and friendship between the believers and the unbelievers.
God asks a believer to be kind and friendly to those unbelievers
who do not 'fight against your faith', especially those among them
who have not expelled the believers from their homes or fought
against them when they were propagating their religion. No believing woman, if she comes to a believer for succour or shelter, should
be sent away, but if a believer goes over to a non-believer, then
retaliation is permitted.

SURAH LX

1. O believers, do not take as friends
    Those who fight against Me
    Or who conspire against you.
    Show no kindness to them;
    They have rejected the true path.
    They drove the Prophet
    And also you from your homes.
    Only because you believe in Me.
    Hence you continue your struggle.
    But be not kind to those

Who hide their rejection of Me.
And remember I am aware of all that you do.
Hence do not go astray.

3. On the Day of Judgement,
Neither your children
Nor your relatives,
None of them will be of any use.
God will judge you by your deeds
For He sees everything you do.

7. God may make friends
Between you and your enemies.
He has the power to do anything.
He is Oft-Forgiving, Most Benevolent.

8. God forbids you to fight
Those who fight not your faith
And who do not drive you out.
Be just and kind to them
For God loves the just.
And fight against those
Who have driven you out from your homes
Or supported those who had done so.

12. O Prophet! When believing women come
To take the oath of fealty to you,
Assuring you that
They will worship only God
And neither steal nor commit adultery,
Nor kill their children
Nor slander anyone,
Nor utter any falsehood,
And that they will not disobey
In whatever is just,
Then do receive their fealty
And pray for their forgiveness
For God is Oft-Forgiving, Most Merciful.

SURAH LXI: AL-SAFF (THE FORMATIONS)
(14 verses)

This chapter emphasizes once again the supremacy of God and makes it clear that God loves those who fight in His way and hates those who do not. The people of Israel did not listen to Moses; God made 'their hearts to swerve'. Similarly, Jesus was rebuffed by the Jews, even when he confirmed the Torah. In the same way, when their scriptures gave the glad tidings that after Moses another prophet, by the name of Ahmad, would appear to guide them, they mocked at this reference and said that Muhammad was no prophet but a sorcerer:

> Unbelievers desire to put out the light of God
> But God will ever protect and brighten it.
>
> (61:8)

Believers are directed by God to have implicit faith in Him and His Messenger and to struggle in His way. They should be ever ready to sacrifice their lives and possessions for His sake. On the Day of Judgement, they are assured of dwelling places in the Garden of Eden.

SURAH LXI

11.   Believe in God and His Apostle
      And strive hard to advance My cause,
      Be it spiritual or material.
      That is best for you.
      If only you understand.

12.   God will then forgive your sins
      And admit you to gardens
          beneath which rivers flow
      And make you live in beautiful mansions.
      And grant you life eternal
      As your highest fulfilment.

14.   O Believers! Be helpers of God
             In the spirit of Jesus,
             Who asked his disciples
             To be helpers in God's cause.
             Some among the Children of Israel
             Listened to his call,
             But some of them did not.
             God gives power to those
             Who believe in Him,
             And it is they who prevail.

SURAH LXII: AL-JUM'AH (THE DAY OF CONGREGATION)
(11 verses)

Here there is specific reference to the 'unlettered' people of Arabia, for whose guidance a messenger has been sent by God 'from among themselves'. They are so ignorant of learning that, in the annals of Islam, the period preceding the prophethood of Muhammad is known as *Jahiliya* 'the Age of Ignorance'. The Quran refers repeatedly to the ignorance of these people; but it mocks at 'the learned Jews', who knowingly failed to respond to Muhammad's call. They have been compared to the donkey, which carries huge tomes but understands nothing of what these contain.

Believers are told to hasten earnestly to congregational prayers on Friday, the day that has a special place in Islam. On that day, in the afternoon, they should leave their business and pray together in a congregation. But there are some who prefer to stay away for 'some bargain or some amusement'. The Prophet is asked to tell them that the blessings of Allah are better than any amusement or bargain.

SURAH LXII

1.   The heavens and the earth
            Sing the Lord's praises
            Of His glory and sovereignty;

He is the Exalted in Power
Full of Wisdom.

2.   He has sent among the unlettered people
     A messenger, who is one of themselves,
     To reveal God's Signs
     And instruct them in His scriptures,
     To guide them through wisdom
     As they have been in error.

9.   Believers, when the call is given
     For prayers on Friday,
     Hasten in earnest
     To remember your God
     And leave your business.
     That is best for all.

10. And when prayers are over
     Then disperse quietly
     And seek Allah's bounty.
     Celebrate His praises
     So that you may prosper.

SURAH LXIII: AL-MUNAFIQUN (THE HYPOCRITES)
(11 verses)

Hypocrites pretend to be believers, but they are in fact unbelievers. They obstruct others from taking the right path and are truly 'evil in their deeds'. They look amiable and speak well; but they are enemies of the faith. When the Prophet asks them to pray to Allah for forgiveness, they turn away with arrogance. They are not appreciative even if he asks for forgiveness of the Lord on their behalf. How will God then forgive them their sins, for they are, indeed, 'transgressors' against His authority? They go about telling the people of Medina not to help those 'who are with Allah's Messenger'. They are certainly unbelievers in fact, if not in name.

Believers must be charitable and spend part of their wealth in God's way, aiding the poor and assisting the needy. They should not allow their riches or children to divert them from the true path; their salvation lies in seeking the pleasure of God.

SURAH LXIII

9.   O you believers!
Let not your riches or children
Make you forget your Lord.
If any one does so,
The loss is his own.

10.   And spend in charity out of what you have.
It is God who has bestowed it on you.
Remember, when death faces you
Then you will cry:
'O My Lord! Why did you not grant me
Respite for a little while,
So that I would have given more
And tried to excel in righteousness?'

11.   But no one will be given more respite
Than for his appointed time.
God knows all that everyone does.

SURAH LXIV: AL-TAGHABUN (DECEPTION)
(18 verses)

God has created both believers and unbelievers; unbelievers refuse to listen to messengers on the ground that they are 'mere human beings like ourselves'. How could they then direct their fellow humans on what and what not to do? They ask: 'How can mortals be our guides?' Hence they disbelieve the messengers and pay no heed. But, on the Day of Judgement, they will be consigned to hell and evil shall be their fate; in the past those who rejected the faith,

as propounded to them by God's messengers, suffered grievously.
Hence believers are told:

> So obey God and His Apostle.
> If you turn back on what is conveyed to you,
> Remember, it is your misfortune.
> The Apostle's duty is only to proclaim
> The message as given by the Lord.
>
> (64:12)

Those who believe in God and do what is right will be forgiven
their sins and will abide forever in gardens watered by running
streams.

SURAH LXIV

1. All those in heaven and on earth
   Celebrate the glory of God.
   To Him belongs the dominions
   And the praise of all.
   He has power over everything.

2. It is He who has created you,
   And among you are some
   Who choose to be unbelievers.
   God sees everything
   That everyone does.

3. God has created the heavens and the earth,
   Each in just proportions.
   And He has given to everyone
   A shape which is appropriate.
   To Him, all must finally return.

4. He knows all that is in heaven and on earth,
   What is open and what is concealed.
   Indeed God knows the secrets
   In every heart.

5.   Have you not heard
What happened to those
Who rejected Our Faith?
They paid for their evil conduct
A grievous penalty.

6.   Apostles came to people
With Our clear Signs.
But the unbelievers asked:
'Shall we be directed by mere humans?'
So they rejected the message
And turned away from Our messengers.
But to God it matters not.
He is free of all needs and wants.
And worthy of all our praises.

11.   No calamity takes place
Without the leave of God.
Only the believer is rightly guided;
And the unbeliever goes astray and suffers.
God knows and controls everything.

12.   So obey God and His Apostle.
If you turn back on what is conveyed to you,
Remember, it is your misfortune.
The Apostle's duty is only to proclaim
The message as given by the Lord.

16.   Fear God, listen to Him and obey.
Spend in charity for your good
So that you may be saved from covetousness.

17.   Any loan to God is beautiful.
He doubles it and credits it to you.
He forgives and rewards you.
For He is Most Forbearing.

18.   He is the Knower of all
That is known and unknown,
Seen and unseen.
He is Exalted in Power.
He is, indeed, All-Wise.

SURAH LXV: AL-TALAQ (DIVORCE)
(65 verses)

The Prophet is told that women who are divorced should observe the prescribed period of *iddat*, which is calculated as three menstrual months; in the case of pregnant women, this period should extend until after delivery, during which no intercourse should take place. They should not be turned out of their homes during this period unless they are guilty of 'open lewdness'. Otherwise, after they have completed their *iddat*, they may be taken back on 'equitable terms', or released on 'equitable terms'. Moreover, during *iddat*, women should be provided with the same style of living as before. Also they should be recompensed for suckling the new-born child:

> Let the husbands spend according to their means,
> And if their resources are limited,
> Let them spend according to what Allah has given them.
>
> (65:7)

In whatever they do, they should remember what the Prophet has taught them and God has commanded; for it is God's writ that runs everywhere and over everything.

SURAH LXV

11.   The Apostle has come to you
      To explain God's clear Signs.
      He will lead believers in God
      And doers of righteous deeds.
      He will take them out of darkness to light
      And God will admit them in the Hereafter
      To gardens with flowing rivers,
      To dwell therein for ever and ever;
      It will be an excellent habitation.

12.   It is God who has created
      The Seven Firmaments in the heavens

And a similar number on earth.
Everywhere God's writ runs,
For He has power over all.
He knows and understands everything.

SURAH LXVI: AL-TAHRIM (PROHIBITION)
(12 verses)

This chapter deals with 'a crisis of confidence' that had arisen between the Prophet and his wives. One of them had betrayed his trust by conveying a secret to two others. These two wives in consequence behaved towards the Prophet in a manner not befitting their status. They were warned that if they supported one another against the Prophet, he would be protected by Allah, who might give him better consorts. They were reminded of what happened to the wives of Noah and Lot; they were false to God's messengers and were, therefore, put into hell. On the other hand, the wife of Pharaoh was protected and rewarded for being faithful and true to God; likewise Mary, who was pious and chaste, was favoured by God, Who breathed into her His own spirit. She put her trust in God and was duly rewarded.

SURAH LXVI

8.   O you believers!
Always turn to God
In sincere repentance.
And pray to Him
To remove your ills.
In His benevolence,
He may admit you
To gardens beneath which rivers flow.
However, God will never permit
Anyone to humiliate the Prophet and the believers.
The light they have lighted
Will shine for ever and ever.

SURAH LXVII: AL-MULK (THE KINGDOM)
(30 verses)

After describing the infinite powers of God in creating the earth
and the skies, and in giving life and death to His creatures, there
is reference here to the lowest heaven, which has been adorned with
lamps. These lamps provide missiles against devils, who do not
believe in God. They will be asked: 'Did not a warner come to
you?' They will admit it, and say, 'Still we rejected him.' Had they
listened to His call, they would not burn in hell. For believers who
responded there would be a great reward:

> Whether one speaks loudly or in secret,
> God knows what goes on in man's breast.
>
> (67:13)

The truth is that it is God who has made the earth subservient to
man. He has provided various scources for his sustenance and comfort. And still man denies His authority, knowing full well that
those who did so in the past suffered terribly. Man must function
within limits and be thankful to his Creator, who has given him the
faculties of hearing, seeing, feeling and understanding. He has no
other helper except God, and without Him his life has no meaning
or purpose.

SURAH LXVII

3.   God has created the seven heavens,
        One above the other.
        How just are their proportions;
        Look at them once again,
        Can you find a flaw in them?

5.   God has adorned the lowest heaven
        With lamps endowed with missiles
        To drive away the evil ones,
        For whom the penalty is blazing fire.

12.   For those who fear the Lord,
        Though He is Unseen,
        They are, indeed, assured
        Of both forgiveness and reward.

15.   It is God who manages the earth
        And makes it possible for man to traverse
        Through its length and breadth
        And provides him the joys of sustenance
        Until the time of his resurrection.

22.   Who is better,
        The one who crawls, creeps and cringes
        Or the one who walks straight on the straight path?

26.   When people ask you, O Muhammad!
        'When will the Promised Day come?'
        Tell them, 'Its knowledge is only with God.
        I am sent only to give the warning.'

SURAH LXVIII: AL-QALAM (THE PEN)
(52 verses)

The Prophet is here reassured by God that he is neither mad nor
possessed. On the contrary, he is a man of sterling character. This
will soon become clear to his detractors. God knows who is on the
right path and who is straying from it. Muhammad is advised not
to listen to them or be concerned about what these despicable
creatures say or do. Nor should he bother about their slanders or
calumnies. They are deep in sin, despite their wealth and the pride of
their ancestry; their possessions will be destroyed by the Lord and they
will not be able to enjoy the fruits of their labour. Their punishment in
the Hereafter is inevitable. God will never treat People of Faith in the
same way as People of Sin. Therefore the Prophet should leave sinners
to God, who will punish them by the degree of the wrong committed
by each one of them. On his part, the Prophet should observe patience

in propagating his mission, for he has been sent by God for the good of the whole of mankind and not that of a particular group.

SURAH LXVIII

7.   The Lord has all the knowledge,
He knows who responds to His call
And who chooses to stray away
From His guidance and His path.

8.   So people should not hearken
To the call of those who reject the truth.

44.   Leave such persons to Me;
I shall punish them by degrees
In a way that they cannot perceive.

45.   I shall grant them a long respite
But My plan is truly powerful.

51.   Unbelievers may trip you, O Muhammad,
And call you a man possessed
When they hear My message from you.

52.   But in their ignorance they forget
That it is a message for all the worlds.

SURAH LXIX: AL-HAQQAH (THE TRUTH)
(52 verses)

Once again, a warning is given about the Day of Judgement, when everyone will know the truth. Thamud and Aad refused to accept it and were destroyed, one by a terrible storm and the other by a furious wind. Likewise, Pharaoh was punished and the flood drowned him and his army of supporters. The rebels cannot escape ruin and destruction; their fate will be sealed by God.

On that Day, when the Trumpet sounds the blast, the earth will shake, mountains will be crushed to dust and the sky will be rent. The Throne of the Lord will be borne by eight angels and He will judge what His creatures did; nothing will be hidden from Him. The righteous will be rewarded with a life of bliss; and wrongdoers will be seized and put into the blazing fire. They will find no friends or helpers; they will be consigned to hell.

The message given to the Prophet is divine; it is not the word of a poet or that of a soothsayer. If anyone were to invent a revelation from God, God would seize him and cut off the arteries of his heart. There are, no doubt, people who reject His message; but they will regret it grievously, for verily it is the truth.

SURAH LXIX

38. God calls upon people

39. To witness all that is around

40. And to respond to the message
    As conveyed by His Apostle.

41. What the Apostle says is not
    The word of a poet,

42. Nor that of a soothsayer,

43. But a true message from the Lord.

44. If the Prophet were to invent
    Any such thing in God's name,

45. God will certainly punish Him.

46. He may cut even the arteries of his heart.

47. Nor will anyone be able
    To save him from the wrath of God.

48.   What he has brought, therefore,
        Is, indeed, the Word of God.

51.   Verily, it is the truth

52.   From the Lord,
        Most High.

SURAH LXX: AL-MA'ARIJ (THE ASCENT)
(44 verses)

Unbelievers question the Day of Judgement; but it shall come and
will be a Day that compresses within it fifty thousand years. Those
who do not believe in its occurrence will realize how mistaken they
have been; it will turn the sky into molten brass and the mountains
into wool. Then they will wish to redeem themselves of their
unbelief and escape the punishment awaiting them. But none will
be able to save them; not even their wives, or their kith and kin.
They will be impatient to be rescued, but it will not happen. On
earth, they arrogantly indulged in boastful denial, mocking the Day
of Judgement. But on that Day, they will see the reality with their
own eyes; they will then be full of dejection and remorse, ashamed
of their inequity.

SURAH LXX

19.   Truly, man is impatient
        Since his very creation.

20.   He becomes fretful
        When in distress,

21.   He becomes niggardly
        When he has abundance.

22.   This is not so
        With those who pray

23.　　And are steadfast in their devotion.

24.　　Those who have wealth,

25.　　It is right for them
　　　　To provide for the needy
　　　　And for those who have nothing.
　　　　The latter a right in such wealth.
　　　　And those who believe in the Day of Judgement

27.　　And fear the displeasure of their Lord,

28.　　They must all so act as to please God
　　　　For His displeasure will result
　　　　In no peace or tranquillity for them.

SURAH LXXI: NUH (NOAH)
(28 verses)

In this chapter the story of Noah is repeated. He asked his people to believe in God, to fear and obey Him, but they rejected his call and persisted in their obstinate and arrogant behaviour. Noah pleaded with them publicly as well as privately, but they refused to follow him. The result was that they were all drowned in the flood; the small group of believers who stood by him and heeded the call were the only ones who survived. They were put on the ark and rescued. Noah turned to God:

> He pleaded with the Lord
> Not to spare a single unbeliever.
> For if God were to leave anyone unpunished
> That one would mislead the believers
> And breed more ungrateful wretches.

(71:26–7)

SURAH LXXI

1. Noah was sent by Us
    With the command to warn
    So that his people
    May not suffer
       a grievous penalty.

2. He told them
    That he had come
    As a warner to them,

3. That they should worship God;
    Fear and obey Him,

4. So that He may forgive them their sins
    And give them respite
       for life on this earth.
    For when death will come,
    No one will be able to put it off.

5. But the more Noah called his people,
    The more they fled from him.

7. Noah told them how mighty was the Lord
    And still how forgiving was He,
    But they remained deaf to his plea
    And arrogantly turned it down.

8. Noah shouted himself hoarse.

9. He spoke to them
    Publicly as well as in private.

10. Pleading with them
    To seek the Lord's forgiveness.

11. Reminding them as to how
    The Lord gives in abundance,

12.　　And increases people's wealth
　　　And provides them with sons
　　　And with gardens and rivers.

21.　　Noah told the Lord
　　　In pain and anguish
　　　That his people did not listen
　　　And continued to follow men
　　　Who could bring nothing but loss to them.

26.　　He pleaded with the Lord
　　　Not to spare a single unbeliever.

27.　　For if God were to leave anyone unpunished
　　　That one would mislead the believers
　　　And breed more ungrateful wretches.

SURAH LXXII: AL-JINN (THE JINN)
(28 verses)

The Prophet is informed in this chapter that a band of angels had listened to God's revelations and were wonder-struck by the sweep of God's power; but there were some among them who were defiant and rebellious. There were men on earth who similarly had come under Satan's influence. They were misled into believing that there would be no Day of Judgement. However, there were others – the righteous people – who accepted God's guidance. They proclaimed their faith in His justice. They invoked no other god but God and prayed to Him and worshipped Him.

SURAH LXXII

4.　　There are the unwise
　　　Who utter wanton lies
　　　Against their Lord.

5.   The wise, however, will not say
         Anything untrue against Him.

12.   Nor can anyone
         Frustrate the will of God
         Either by defiance of Him
         Or by fleeing from Him.

13.   As for those
         Who have accepted
         God's guidance
         And believe in Him,
         They need have no fear
         Of any kind of injustice.

20.   Tell the people, O Muhammad!
         'I do no more than invoke my Lord
         And refrain from associating anyone with Him.

21.   'I have no power to cause you harm
         Or to make you accept the right path.'

SURAH LXXIII: AL-MUZZAMMIL (THE MOUNTED ONE)
(20 verses)

The believers are extolled here to stay awake for about half the night to pray and recite the Quran in a slow, measured tone. This, indeed, is good for the soul. For the night is most suitable for contemplation and prayer when a serene calm and silence prevails: in the day, the mind is invariably distracted as a result of preoccupation with work.

During the day, man is indeed busy with ordinary duties; even so he must remember God at all times and while discharging his duties he should keep himself in His presence and devote himself whole-heartedly to Him, for his work may be on earth but his heart is in heaven. He must pray to Allah and give in charity to the poor and the needy. He must recite as much of the Quran as may be convenient, though ill-health, travel, or involvement in war may make it difficult for him to do so, but then that is understandable.

The Prophet should have patience with his detractors and deal with them with dignity. The unbelievers should realize that God has sent Muhammad as His Messenger to preach His message in the same way as He had sent Noah to guide Pharaoh and his supporters; they disobeyed him and suffered dire consequences. Likewise, unbelievers will suffer. The happenings of the past must serve as a warning to them.

SURAH LXXIII

9.   God is the Lord of the East and the West;
     There is no one like Him.
     Take him, therefore, O people!
     As the arbiter of your disputes.

11. It is for God, O believers!
     To deal with those who possess
     The good things of life
     And still deny His bounty.
     Bear with them for a while,
     Eventually, they have to return to God.

15. We have sent forth an apostle
     To testify to and admonish the people,
     As We had sent an apostle before
     To testify to and admonish Pharaoh.

19. Verily, therefore, this is Our admonition.
     Whosoever wants, let him take the right path.

SURAHL XXIV: AL-MUDDATHIR (THE ENWRAPPED)
(56 verses)

The Prophet is addressed here as one 'wrapped in a mantle'. He is asked to arise and glorify the Lord, and to keep his garments free from stains and to shun all abominations. He should remain constant and patient in pursuing God's cause. Until this revelation, the Prophet had carried out his mission privately, but this was the signal to start public preaching.

On the Day of Judgement, which will be the day of distress for unbelievers, God will deal firmly with those who, though created by Him and endowed with resources in abundance, persist in denying His message. They see His Signs but choose to ignore them. They will be visited by a mountain of calamities for having disbelieved and decried the call, given by the Prophet, as 'nothing but magic derived from of old'. Eventually their place is going to be in hell, of which they are already warned. On that Day, when they will be asked, 'What led you to hell-fire?', they will reply, 'We did not pray; we did not feed the indigent; on the other hand, we indulged in vain talk; and most of all, we denied the Day of Judgement.' Despite their admission, they will have no intercessors to help them, nor will they escape the consequences of their un-belief.

SURAH LXXIV

1. O you, Muhammad, wrapped in a mantle!

2. Arise and deliver the warning

3. And magnify the name of your Lord.

4. And keep your garments free of all stains.

5. And shun all abominations.

36.   This is a warning
         to all.

37.   That if anyone
         Goes forward
         Or lags behind
         On the true path,

38.   He will be accountable
         For whatever he has done.

SURAH LXXV: AL-QIYAMAH (THE RESURRECTION)
(40 verses)

On the day when man is dazed by what is happening, when the moon is covered in darkness and the sun and moon mingle and join together as one, he will in desperation ask, 'Where is the refuge for me?' But there will be no refuge; his wrongdoing will seal his doom. He may put forth excuses, but the evidence will be all against him.

For Muhammad, the Quran will be the guide, but he need not worry about the manner and timing of receiving the revelations:

> Do not make haste about the Quran:
> It is for Us to arrange
>   for its collection and recital.
> However, when We reveal,
> Follow Our words carefully.
> We shall explain their meaning.
>   (75:16–20)

But as soon as the Quran is revealed, stage by stage and part by part, it is the duty of believers to follow its precepts. They should not 'love this fleeting life', but, on the contrary, worry about the Hereafter. For on the Day of Judgement, 'some faces will beam with joy' and 'some will be sad'. Some will look to their Lord, and some will repent having denied Him. They will realize then that God has the power to give life to the dead, as He has the power to put life into a drop of sperm and fashion it into a male or female.

SURAH LXXV

3.   Does man doubt Our power
To assemble his bones?

4.   What of the bones
We can put together,
Even the tips of his fingers?

5.   But he wishes to wrong himself
In the little time available to him.

6.   He asks, in utter disbelief,
'When will the Day of Resurrection come?'

7.   The Day will come
When eyes will be dazzled
And the moon will be eclipsed.

8.   He will be called to produce
Evidence against himself.

9.   When the sun and the moon become one,

10.   That Day the wrongdoer will say:
'Where can I find the escape?'

11.   He shall, indeed, have no escape.

13.   That Day will man be told
All that he did from first to last.

14.   He will, in fact, bear
Witness against himself.

SURAH LXXVI: AL-INSAN, *OR* AL-DHAR (THE TIME)
(31 verses)

This chapter contains moving symbolism. For a long time man did not exist; then God created him out of 'a drop of mingled sperm' in order to test His ability to function on earth. He endowed him with the faculties of hearing and sight and the capacity to think and judge. He then guided him, through His messengers, as to what is right and what is wrong and informed him of the consequences, good or bad, that would follow. If man chose the wrong way, he would have nothing else in store but 'chains, yokes and blazing fire'; and if he took the right way he would enjoy *kafur*, or camphor, from the fountain of abundance, called *salsabil*, particularly if he loved God, avoided evil and fed the indigent, the orphan and the slave. He will then be shown the light of beauty and joy and be rewarded with silken garments and a garden of bliss, which will neither have the excessive heat of the sun nor the extreme cold of the moon. And he will be served with the choicest fruits, and vessels of silver and goblets of crystals will be passed round. He will be attended to by youths of perpetual freshness surrounding him like scattered pearls. Further, the Lord will provide him with a wine that will be pure and holy and will give him eternal ecstasy. That is the abode for the righteous, to which God will admit whomsoever He pleases out of His mercy. But for wrongdoers who love the fleeting, momentary life on this earth, doom will be in store.

SURAH LXXVI

1.   For a long, long time,
        Man was nothing,
        Not even known to anyone.

3.   God showed him the way.
        It is now up to him
        To be grateful or not
        To his own Maker and Creator.

24.   Hence have patience
        And obey Our command.
        Do not listen to the sinner
        Or the ingrate.

25.   And praise the Lord
        Every morning and evening.

26.   And worship Him even
            during a part of the night,
        Glorifying His power.

29.   Our admonition is clear:
        Whoever wishes well to himself,
        Let him take the straight path
        Reaching to the Lord.

SURAH LXXVII: AL-MURSALAT (THE EMISSARIES)
(50 verses)

God's warning of the Doomsday to come is not an empty one. Those who refuse to believe its coming will be shocked when it occurs. They will see the stars becoming dim, the heavens cleft asunder and mountains scattered all around as dust. It will also be the Day of Sorting Out. Rejectors of truth – unbelievers – will be consigned to a place with 'no shade of coolness' and no protection 'against the fierce blaze'. They shall not be able to speak, nor will it be open to them to put forth any plea for redemption. As to the righteous, they shall be covered by cool shades, with springs of water everywhere. They shall have all the fruits they desire and will be able to eat and drink to their hearts' content.

SURAH LXXVII

34.   The rejectors of truth
Will rue the Day

35.   When they will be struck dumb,

36.   And not be able
To put forth any plea
In their defence.

41.   As for the righteous,
They shall have on that Day
The best of amenities.

46.   Hence let the sinners enjoy
In the little time they have here.

SURAH LXXVIII: AL-NABA (ANNOUNCEMENT)
(40 verses)

This chapter describes, somewhat graphically, the scene on the Day of Judgement, when the Trumpet will sound and people of all ages and of both sexes will come forth and the heavens will be opened wide. The doubters will know the answer, much to their chagrin, and hell will be their destination. They will be subjected to the worst treatment. When thirsty they will be given 'a boiling, dark, murky fluid' to drink. But for the righteous there will be 'enclosed gardens', with 'companions of equal age'. They will speak no vanity nor untruth. Theirs will be a peaceful, harmonious existence. Even the angels will stand before them and none will argue with them.

SURAH LXXVIII

6.   Have we not made the earth
A wide expanse for Our creatures,

7.   And have We not made mountains
Pegs for their benefit?

8.   And have We not created them
In pairs for procreation

9.   And made sleep for rest,
And night as their covering,

10.   And day for their work
To provide subsistence,

12.   And have We not built
The seven firmaments for them,

13.   And placed in them
A light of shining splendour,

14.   And do We not pour down
Water in abundance for them
Through clouds in skies,

15.   And produce for them
Grains and vegetables

16.   And orchards of luxurious growth?

17.   And finally all will be
Accountable before God
For all that they did here.

18.   When the Trumpet will sound
And they shall come in
crowds before the Lord.

31.   For the righteous
There will be every comfort
To fulfil their hearts' desire.

35.   There will be no vain glorification
And no resorting to untruth.

SURAH LXXIX: AL-NAZIAT (THE SNATCHERS)
(46 verses)

In this chapter, apart from an explanation of the inevitability of the Hereafter and its awesome nature, there is a lucid exposition of pride and its inevitable fall, expressed through the story of Moses and Pharaoh. Moses called upon Pharaoh to cleanse himself of sin and to worship the Lord. God showed Moses the great Sign which He had granted him, but Pharaoh, in his arrogance, rejected it. He declared, 'I am the Lord, Most High.' He did not accept the supremacy of the God of Moses. The result was his death and destruction:

> Verily, in this is a warning
> For all those who do not fear Allah.
>
> (79:26)

Therefore, on the Day of Judgement, when the fire of hell shall be burning fiercely for all to see, those who have 'transgressed all bounds' and preferred the life on the earth to the Hereafter will find themselves in hell. But those who have restrained themselves from surrendering to 'lower desires' will have the promised paradise. As Sayyid Qutb, the Egyptian commentator has explained, 'Allah does not ask man to suppress his desires, because he knows that it is not possible for him to do so. He simply asks him to control his desires and not to let them control him.'[1]

SURAH LXXIX

35.   The day will come
When people will be accountable
For all that they did.

36.   They shall have the full view
        Of the fire of hell.

37.   For those who had transgressed all bounds

38.   And preferred the life of this world

39.   Their abode will be
        The fire of hell.

40.   But for those who had feared the Lord
        And were aware of their accountability to Him
        And who had restrained themselves
        From evil temptation or worldly desire

41.   Their abode will, indeed, be
        The garden in paradise.

SURAH LXXX: ABASA (HE FROWNED)
(42 verses)

This chapter contains an admonition to the Prophet not to be harsh
to a devotee and not to be indulgent to an unbeliever, however rich
or powerful. It refers to the incident when the Prophet was engaged
in explaining the message of God to a pagan leader belonging to the
tribe of Quraish. A blind man, keen to understand some verses of
the Quran, appeared and started interrupting him. The Prophet
was upset and sent him away. His behaviour was not approved of
by God, and at once this revelation came to Mohammad. Many
exegetists have characterized this revelation as a 'censure'.

There is also a reference to man's ingratitude to God in these
verses. He is reminded of his origin, the necessities and comforts
that are provided for him, and finally the death and resurrection
that await him. But what is man's response to it all? 'By no means
has man fulfilled His bidding.' He should not forget what would
happen to him in the face of the 'stunning blast', which will so grip

every being that no one shall think of anyone except himself, 'For each one of them will have enough preoccupations of his own.'

SURAH LXXX

1.   The Prophet, with a frown
            on his face,
        Turned the blind man away.

2.   He had come to him
        To understand the Book

3.   And perchance
            to grow spiritually

4.   Or to receive correct admonition,
        Which might have profited him.

5.   But one who was full of himself,

6.   You attended to, O Muhammad!

7.   However, the blame cannot be yours
        If he does not respond.

8.   But the blind man who
        Came earnestly to you
        And with fear in his heart,

9.   You were unresponsive to him

10.   This, by no means, should have happened.
        This is, indeed, Our admonition.

33.   And, at last, when the Day of Reckoning comes
        With its deafening noise,

34.   That Day, brother will flee from brother

35.   And son from his mother and father

36.   And husband from his wife
        And children from their parents.

37.   On that Day, each will be concerned
        With himself and no one else.

SURAH LXXXI: AL-TAKWIR (THE DARKENING)
(29 verses)

This chapter, like the previous ones, describes by means of a series of graphic images the end of the world and the reward and punishment that awaits believers and unbelievers on the Day of Judgement, when the world on high is unveiled and the scrolls are laid open. It will be preceded by a great upheaval in the universe, which will shake up everything, from the sun, the stars, the mountains and the seas, to the animals and humans. Each soul will be told what it has done.

Believers are cautioned to respect the world of 'the most honourable messenger', who is endowed with God's authority. He is not 'the one possessed'; nor is 'your friend mad'. In fact, God has granted him a 'clear vision', and those who do not see it should be asked, 'Wither then are you going?'

The message he has brought is not of 'an evil spirit', but one that is for the good of all. However, it is up to each individual to listen to it and choose the right path. God has given everyone the freedom to do so. The message given to man is for the good of all, indeed for all the worlds.

SURAH LXXXI

1.   When the sun
        will no longer shine

2. And the stars
   will fade away

3. The mountains will disappear

4. And pregnant she-camels
   will be left unattended,

5. And the wild beasts will
   Meekly come together.

7. Then the souls of people,
   These will be sorted out.

8. The infant girl will be asked:

9. Why was she buried alive?

10. Then the scrolls will be opened

11. And the heavens will be unveiled.

12. The blazing fire will burn
    to fierce heat.

13. And the garden of paradise
    will bloom.

14. Each soul will then realize
    What its records are.

SURAH LXXXII: AL-INFITAR (CLEAVING)
(19 verses)

Man is questioned here as to why, despite being the recipient of abundant grace from his Lord, he shows no gratitude to Him. He should not forget the Day of Reckoning, when the sky will be cleft asunder, the stars will be scattered, the oceans will burst and the graves will be opened up. He must remember the angels guarding over him who record everything that he does. Hence no one can escape reward or punishment; the righteous will be in bliss and the wicked in hell.

SURAH LXXXII

6.   O Man! What has kept you away
   From your Lord, the most beneficent?

7.   He, who has created you, and
   Fashioned you in right proportion,

8.   Then gave you in His benevolence
   The form as He liked.

9.   And yet you deny, O Man!
   His authority and judgement.

10.   Verily, God has provided
   Guardian angels to protect you.

11.   They are illustrious
   And sympathetic to you.

12.   They will write down whatever you do.

13.   On their evidence
   The righteous will go to the heavens,

14.   And the wicked assuredly to hell.

SURAH LXXXIII: AL-MUTAFFIFIN (THE CHEATERS)
(36 verses)

Believers are told that it is best to be honest in business dealings. There should be no fraud, either in weight or measure, nor any misappropriation. Do people think that they will not be called to account for any cheating or defrauding on their part? If so, they are mistaken. The record of every wrongdoer is being preserved in a register called *Sijjin*. The Quran says, 'Would that you knew what *Sijjin* is! It is a sealed book.' The wrongdoers will be put in the same category as those who mock at the Messenger. Why? Because both reject the truth and adopt falsehood and follow wrong beliefs and practices. Their own deeds cast a veil over their hearts. They cannot, therefore, escape the consequences of the wrong that they do. They will enter the fire of hell. The record of the righteous, on the other hand, will be preserved in a register called *Illiyum*; it is also 'a sealed book, witnessed by those who are closest to Allah.' They will be blessed with a 'beaming brightness of bliss', and will have pure wine to quench their thirst and water which will be 'mixed with the water of Tasneem, a fountain in paradise, from which only the favoured ones can drink'. On earth, unbelievers mocked at believers for having gone astray; but in the heavens, believers will laugh at unbelievers, and theirs will be the last laugh.

SURAH LXXXIII

1.   Those who deal in fraud
           Shall ever be in distress.

2.   They exact full measure
           While taking from others

3.   But give short measure or weight
        While giving to others.

4.   They think they will
        not have to account

5.   On the Day of Judgement,

6.   When all mankind
        will be on trial
     Before the Lord of
     all the worlds.

SURAH LXXXIV: AL-INSHIQAQ (THE RENDING)
(25 verses)

Man is reminded in these verses that, whatever he may do on this earth, he has ultimately to return to His Creator. He has, therefore, to labour hard to obtain His pleasure. He lived among his people joyfully; he never thought that he would be returning to his Lord, who was watching over him.

Two kinds of people will appear before the Lord on the Day of Judgement. Those whose record is in their right hand will rejoice; and those whose record is behind their backs will cry, fearing perdition. No one will listen to them, no one will come to their rescue when they are thrown into hell. They were so arrogant, indulgent and full of themselves on earth that they were not prepared to face God. In fact, when the Quran was read to them they refused to listen to it and did not prostrate themselves before their Lord. Their punishment will be heavy. But for those who believed in God and did righteous deeds, reward for them is assured in heaven.

SURAH LXXXIV

6.　　O Man! Verily you must struggle
　　　In the cause of your Lord
　　　Until you meet Him.

7.　　Then the one who is given the ledger
　　　In his right hand,

8.　　He will have an easy reckoning

9.　　And return to his people, full of joy.

10.　　But the one who is given
　　　The ledger from the back

11.　　Will cry, fearing perdition.

12.　　He will, indeed, enter
　　　The blazing fire of hell.

SURAH LXXXV: AL-BURUJ (THE CONSTELLATIONS)
(22 verses)

This chapter deals with the essentials of faith; this is illustrated by the 'pit [of fire] incident' which occurred much before the advent of Islam, when a group of believers were subjected to torture by the enemies of God. When they failed to dissuade the believers from the chosen path, they dug a pit and lit it with a blazing fire and cast the believers into it. A large crowd watched the gruesome sight. The Quran reveals that they did so for no other reason than that the faithful believed in Allah; the Quran declares, 'Those who persecute the believers, men and women, and do not repent, shall suffer the chastisement of hell.'

Unbelievers must surely have heard the story of the fall of Pharaoh and the plight of the people of Thamud? Why do they then deny the might of God? In doing so, they alone will be the sufferers. They will assuredly burn in hell. But for believers who do good, there will be gardens of paradise with rivers of sparkling waters. There is no doubting the vengeance of the Lord, but He is also Most-Forgiving, Ever-Benevolent.

SURAH LXXXV

10.   Those who persecute believers,
Whether men or women,
And do not repent,
Their punishment is
The burning fire of hell.

11.   For those who believe in God
And do the righteous deeds,
Their abode will be
In the garden of paradise,
With rivers flowing by.

12.   Strong is the grip of your Lord,

13.   Who creates, destroys
And then recreates.

14.   He is the Oft-Forgiving, the Most Kind.

15.   The Lord of the Throne of Glory.

16.   He does what He intends.

SURAH LXXXVI: AL-TARIQ (THE NIGHT VISITOR)
(17 verses)

For every man there is a guardian who watches over his acts, a night visitor in the form of a star of piercing brightness. It can penetrate every dark corner with its rays. Hence on the Day of Judgement, everything, including all that is secret, will be brought out, and good will be distinguished from bad. Unlike the world below, the heavens above are not for mere amusement. Let unbelievers realize that their scheming against God will not stand them in good stead. For if they scheme against God, God will scheme against them. They will be helpless before Him and no one will succour them.

SURAH LXXXVI

5.   Let man ponder his birth,

6.   How he was created
    Out of a drop emitted

7.   From between the backbone and the ribs.

8.   God has the power
    To bring him back
    To life after death.

9.   On that Day
    All his secrets
    Will be known.

10.   He will stand hopelessly
    With no one to help him.

SURAH LXXXVII: AL-ALA (THE MOST HIGH)
(19 verses)

God tells Muhammad that he will be taught to read what is being revealed to him so that he will not forget. By this process, his way will be made easy and he will be able to give the warning to those who are on the wrong path. Those who listen and purify themselves will be prosperous. But those who refuse, and prefer the joys of the present life, shall be cast into the burning fire, in which they will neither live nor die.

What is told here by Allah to Muhammad is nothing new; it will be found in the earlier scriptures of Abraham and Moses as well.

SURAH LXXXVII

6. By degrees, O Muhammad!
    We shall deliver Our message
    So that you may not forget,

7. Except what We will,
    For We know what is manifest
    And what is hidden.

8. And We will make it easy
    For you to follow the right path.

9. So remind the people
    Of what is good for them.

10. Those who fear the Lord
        will receive it.

11. But the wretched will turn away.

12. They will burn in the
        terrible fire.

13.   They will neither live nor die.

14.   But those who grow in goodness
         They will surely prosper.

SURAH LXXXVIII: AL-GHASHIYAH (THE EVENT)
(26 verses)

On the Day of Judgement — 'the event', as the Quran refers to it here — many people's faces will be downcast and weary; their bodies will be burning in the scorching fires. They will be given no wholesome food, and will have to drink scalding water. They will be the wrongdoers. But there will be others — the righteous ones — who will be granted the bliss of life; their abode will be in paradise, where they will stroll in a lofty garden, with running streams of crystal clear water. They will have luxurious cushions to rest on and rich carpets to walk upon.

The Prophet's duty is to admonish people. He is not to manage their affairs, nor to oversee their activities nor to force them to the right path. They must know what to do with themselves. If they go astray and reject the truth, God will punish them; if they choose the true way, God will reward them. To God they shall return; He will call them to account for what they have done on the earth.

SURAH LXXXVIII

17.   Do these people not wonder
         How the camels are born?

18.   And how the heavens above
         Are so high

19.   And the mountains so fixed

20.   And the earth so spread out?

21.   Remind them, O Muhammad!
       Of what is what,
       For surely you are sent by Us
       As a reminder to them,

22.   And not as a guardian over them.

SURAH LXXXIX: AL-FAJR (THE DAWN)
(30 verses)

Here, man is once again reminded of what God did to those who defied His authority. For instance, the people of Aad, who were as tall as pillars and of Thalmud, who specialized in rock-cutting, as also Pharaoh and his chiefs, who terrorized people and indulged in corrupt and immoral practices, were all given with 'the scourge of His punishment'.

Man is a strange creature: when his Lord bestows favours and gifts on him, he feels honoured; but when He restricts his resources, he feels humiliated. He forgets the wrongs he has committed, such as the neglect of orphans and the poor, and how he has devoured the inheritance of others and loved his wealth. He would be called to account for all these wrongs on the Day of Judgement; but of what avail would his repentance then be? Only the righteous are God's true devotees. He is pleased only with them. They shall have their reward and enter paradise.

SURAH LXXXIX

17.   O Man, you do not
       Respect orphans,

18.   Nor feed the poor nor
       encourage others to do so.

19.   On the contrary,
       You devour others' inheritance

20.   And cherish wealth
           with all your heart.

21.   Surely, On the Day when
           The earth will be reduced to dust

22.   And your Lord will appear,
           with angels in rows,

23.   Then hell will break loose.
           And man will remember what he did.
           But of what use then
           Will his repentance be?

SURAH XC: AL-BALAD (THE CITY)
(20 verses)

This chapter opens with a reference to the city in which the Prophet
was born – Mecca – and of which he is a free citizen. Man is asked
why he forgets that he has been created by God in toil and struggle;
indeed, his life is a process of continued hardship, which can never
end. He should, therefore, reflect on his responsibilities. Does he
think that the One who has created him has no power over him?
Man is shown two highways – one of virtue and the other of evil.
The good one is steep; to climb it man must do righteous deeds,
namely freeing a slave, feeding the hungry, looking after orphans
and taking care of the poor in distress, being kind to others and
urging them to be kind to one another. They are the righteous ones,
who belong to the right hand; they will be favoured by their Lord.
But the sinners, who deny God's revelations, belong to the left
hand. They will burn in hell.

SURAH XC

4.   Man has been created
     To go through toil and trouble.

5.   Does he think that no one
     Has power over him?

6.   He may boast of
     The abundance of his wealth.

7.   Does he think that no one sees
     What he does?

8.   God gave him eyes to see,

9.   A tongue and a pair of lips,

10. And showed him two highways:
     – one good, the other evil.

12. The good is of steep ascent.

13. It consists of freeing the slaves.

14. Of feeding the deprived.

16. Of being kind to orphans.

17. And to do so with patience and compassion.

18. It is the people of the right hand
     Who will succeed before the Lord.

19. But the people of the left hand
     Who reject the Signs of God,

20. They will be denizens of fire,
     Which will scorch them all around.

SURAH XCI: AL-SHAMS (THE SUN)
(15 verses)

Does man know that if he keeps his life pure, he will be successful, and if he becomes corrupt, it will be ruined? That is the law of nature. What happened to the people of Thamud? In their perversity they denied God. Salih, the apostle, told them: 'Let my she-camel, which is the symbol of God's benevolence, drink the water.' They refused; instead, in their insolence, they killed her. Their action resulted in their obliteration. Such is the retribution of God!

SURAH XCI

1.   By the sun,
           which shines in splendour.

2.   By the moon,
           which follows in its wake.

3.   And the day,
           which brightens

4.   And the night
           which darkens.

5.   The heavens and their
           magnificent structure

6.   The earth,
           with its wide expanse

7.   By the soul
           and its integration

8.   And the enlightenment
           which determines
       What is right and
           what is wrong.

9.   Truly the one who succeeds
Is the one who purifies himself.

10.   And the one who fails
Is the one who corrupts himself.

SURAH XCII: AL-LAYL (THE NIGHT)
(21 verses)

God assures believers that whoever among them fears Him, and gives in charity from his wealth, will be favoured by Him. The path of salvation will be made easy for him. But for one who is not righteous and does not give charity, the path will be full of adversity. His wealth will be of no avail. He is bound to fall headlong into the abyss of hell. The more a person gives to others of his wealth, the more he will grow in virtue. He needs no favour from anyone; on the contrary the Lord will be with him and he will be content.

SURAH XCII

1.   By the night as it darkens

2.   And the day as it brightens.

3.   By the mystery of creation
Of the male and the female.

4.   Verily you are headed
For diverse ends.

5.   For him who gives in charity
And fears His Lord,

6.   And affirms goodness,

7.   For him
       We will ease
       The path of bliss.

8.   But for the one
       Who is a miser
       And full of himself

9.   And who rejects goodness,

10.   For him
       We will smooth
       The path of misery.

11.   His wealth will prove
       Of no avail to him.

12.   Verily We show each one the way.

13.   To Us belongs
       The end and the beginning.

SURAH XCIII: AL-DUHA (THE FORENOON)
(11 verses)

This chapter was revealed during one of the darkest periods in the Prophet's life; it came down after a long lapse, which distressed him greatly for he felt forsaken by the Lord. It is full of tenderness and compassion for him; it gives him hope and reassurance. God informs the Prophet that He will protect him as always, just as He did not forsake him when he was an orphan. Hence, whatever the difficulties, he would be looked after and given whatever he seeks. Nothing should therefore deter him from pursuing the right path. The Hereafter would assuredly be better than this world.

SURAH XCIII

1. By the glorious
    Hours of the dawn

2. And the still darkness
    Of the night.

3. Your Lord has neither forsaken you,
    Nor is He displeased with you.

4. Verily, what is to come
    In the future
    Is better for you
    Than what has already happened.

5. For Your Lord will give you
    Whatever will please you.

6. Did He not find you an orphan
    And provide shelter for you?

7. Did He not find you confused
    And show you clear direction?

8. You were poor and
    He blessed you with riches.

9. Hence do not ill-treat an orphan,

10. Nor turn away a beggar.

11. Proclaim the favours of your Lord
    And recite His praises.

SURAH XCIV: AL-SHARH *OR* AL-INSHIRAH (THE SOLACE)
(8 verses)

Here the Prophet is reminded that God has opened a whole treasure-house of knowledge for him and removed the obstacles in his way and exalted his name. He must bear in mind that after every hardship, there will be relief. Hence he must work hard, continue with his mission, and 'seek your Lord with all fervour'.

SURAH XCIV

1. Have we not expanded your breast

2. And eased your burden

3. And raised your hope

4. And given you honour?

5. Remember after hardship

6. Comes the relief.

7. Therefore,
    Work hard.

8. And turn to your Lord
    With all your heart.

SURAH XCV: AL-TIN (THE FIG)
(8 verses)

Man has been created by God in the best mould; he is endowed with an upright nature. But because of his misdeeds, God has to bring him down to the lowest level. That is man's nature, unless he endows himself with faith in God and performs righteous deeds. His reward in the Hereafter is then assured, for God is, indeed, the most judicious of all judges.

SURAH XCV

1. By the fig
    And the olive

2. And the Mount Sinai

3. And by this wondrous city,
    Safe and secure

4. We created man
    In the best form

5. And then abased him
    To the lowest level,

6. Except those among men
    Who do righteous deeds.
    For them, there is unfailing reward.

7. Who dare then deny
    The judgement to come?

8. Is not your Lord
    The most judicious of all judges?

SURAH XCVI: AL-ALAQ (THE CLOT) *OR* AL-IQRA
(19 verses)

The first five verses of this chapter were the earliest to be revealed to the Prophet on Mount Hira; they gave the signal for his prophetic mission. They are, therefore, of utmost significance. Here, Allah ordains Muhammad to take over the mantle as His Messenger. The emphasis here is on the pen, which teaches man what he does not know; but once he knows, he becomes rebellious and thinks he knows all. He begins to defy His Creator. He forgets that God alone knows everything. He will drag him by the forelock and none will be able to help him. Therefore, he must draw closer to God, for therein alone lies his salvation.

SURAH XCVI

1. Proclaim the name of your Lord
Who is the Creator and
Cherisher of all.

2. He created man
Out of a clot of blood.

3. Proclaim the glory of your Lord
Who is the most bountiful.

4. He taught man
The use of the pen.

5. Taught him
What he did not know.

6. And yet he is rebellious

7. And is full of himself.

8. Surely, all have to return
To the Lord of Creation.

SURAH XCVII: AL-QADR (POWER)
(5 verses)

This is one of the shortest chapters, and by the force of its rhythm and words it extols the virtues of the Night of Power, in which the Quran was revealed. This night is, therefore, better than a thousand months. On that night, angels descended, bringing the dispensation from the Lord and heralding peace till the dawn.

SURAH XCVII

1. On the night of power

2. Our revelations have been sent to you.

3. How to explain to you
   This night of power?
   It is better than
   One thousand months.

4. On this night, angels descend
   Bringing the blessings of the Lord

5. And heralding peace until the dawn.

SURAH XCVIII: AL-BAYYINAH (THE CLEAR PROOF)
(8 verses)

Here believers are acquainted with the general attitude of the People of the Book – Christians and Jews, who despite clear evidence in their scriptures about the advent of the Prophet refuse to heed him. For the polytheists, it opens the door for their reformation.

The message that Muhammad has brought from the Lord only rehearses what was revealed earlier; it contains laws and decrees for the good of mankind, it distinguishes between right and wrong. Unfortunately, both the People of the Book and the polytheists have rejected the faith, brought by Muhammad, and shall suffer grievously, for they are the worst of creatures.

SURAH XCVIII

6.   The unbelievers, whether among People of the Book
      Or the idolators,
      Are the worst of creatures.
      They shall abide in hell.

7.   But those who believe in God
      And do righteous deeds,
      They are the best of creatures.

8.   Their recompense is with the Lord.
      They will reside in the Garden of Eden
      With rivers flowing by.

SURAH XCIX: AL–ZALZALAH (THE EARTHQUAKE)
(8 verses)

This chapter graphically describes the day when the earth will be in utmost convulsion and everything will be uprooted. Everyone will be shown the register of his deeds and misdeeds: the righteous will see it, and so will the sinner. They will all face the consequences of their deeds and misdeeds respectively; the process of reward and punishment will take its own course.

SURAH XCIX

1. When the earth is
    in convulsion,

2. Throwing out
    its burden,

3. Man will cry out:
    'What is the matter?'

4. On that day
    He will know
    What is what.

5. Inspired by the Lord.

6. Men will then proceed in broken bands
    And be shown separately their records.

7. Whoever has done
    An atom's weight of good
    Will see it himself.

8. And whoever has done
    An atom's weight of evil
    Will see it himself.

SURAH C: AL-ADIYAT (THE CHARGERS)
(11 verses)

With a force and rapidity of expression that is unique, this chapter bemoans the lot of man, who is so ungrateful to his Lord. He fails to realize that neither his present position nor his wealth will be of any avail. On the Day that he is raised from his grave and brought before the Lord, he will know the reality.

SURAH C

6.   Truly man is ungrateful to his Creator,

7.   Though he is himself a witness
        To his own acts.

8.   He is so involved
        In his love for worldly goods

9.   That he is oblivious
        To his condition in the grave,

10.   And to the secrets in his heart
        Which will be brought out.

11.   Surely the Lord is aware
        Of all that he has done.

SURAH CI: AL-QARIAH (THE DISASTER)
(11 verses)

Here the clamour and noise of Doomsday is described with such power that the hearts of those who hear or read it will tremble with fear. It foretells how men and women shall be scattered like moths. Their deeds will be weighed in the scales of justice. Those whose good deeds weigh more will be granted the pleasures of paradise; and those whose evil deeds weigh more will be consigned to hell.

SURAH CI

1. On the Day of
   noise and clamour:

2. But what, indeed, is
   the Day of noise and clamour?

3. How, indeed, to explain
   That Day to you?

4. It is a Day
   When men will be scattered
   like moths.

5. And the mountains will become
   tufts of carded wool.

6. Then he whose deeds are good
   Shall weigh heavy in the balance,

7. And will be assured a blissful life.

8. But he whose deeds weigh light,

9. He will have his home
   In the scorching fire.

SURAH CII: AL–TAKATHUR (THE LURE OF WEALTH)
(8 verses)

In their lust for the pleasures, joys and comforts of this life, people remain neglectful of their obligations to God until they are consigned to the grave. Realization dawns on them only after they are raised and brought before the Lord on the Day of Judgement. Then they see the fires of hell waiting for them. But of what use is this realization? It is too late for any redemption.

SURAH CII

1. Let mutual rivalry
   For a mass of material goods
   Not divert you
   From the right path.

2. Remember, on the Day of Judgement
   You shall be questioned
   About the pleasures
   That you indulged in.

SURAH CIII: AL–ASR (THE TIME)
(3 verses)

Through the ages, it can be seen that man has been the loser whenever he has chosen the wrong path. Eventually, he has gained only through implicit faith in God, performing righteous deeds and helping his followers to take the right path.

SURAH CIII

1. Time is the witness

2. That man is ever at a loss,

3.   Except those among men
         who believe in God and
         do righteous deeds
      And help each other
      To the right path,
      Counselling patience
         and fortitude.

SURAH CIV: AL-HUMAZAH (THE SLANDERER)
(9 verses)

This chapter rebukes slanderers, backbiters and those who boast of their wealth: their sorry end is certain. The wrath of God will destroy them and the fires of hell devour them.

SURAH CIV

1.   Curse be on every slanderer and backbiter

2.   And those who amass and horde wealth.

3.   Do they think that their wealth
      Will last them for ever?

4.   Each of them will certainly be crushed to pieces

5.   By the crusher; but what is that crusher?

6.   It is the fire kindled by God,

7.   Which will roar over the hearts of wrongdoers.

8.   It will vault them over

9.   In columns outstretched.

SURAH CV: AL-FIL (THE ELEPHANT)
(5 verses)

There is a reference here to the attack on the Kaaba by the hordes of King Abraha. His forces were led by a mighty elephant, considered invincible. However, God knows well how to foil the worst onslaught. Thus when the Meccans became helpless and were unable to protect the House of the Lord, a flock of birds converged over the attackers and pelted them with stones which they carried in their beaks. Then came the scourge of small-pox, which afflicted not only Abraha's soldiers and officers but also the King himself; one by one, everyone died, including the King. The Kaaba was thus saved.

SURAH CV

1.   Have you not known
   what the Lord did
   To the people of the
   Elephant?

2.   Did he not
   frustrate
   Their evil plan

3.   By letting loose on them
   Flocks of birds,

4.   Who hurled on them
   Stones of baked clay

5.   And turned them into
   Stalks and straws,
   All eaten up?

SURAH CVI: QURAISH
(4 verses)

This chapter directly concerns the tribe of Quraish, who had mounted a virulent campaign of calumny against the Prophet. God asks them who has given them security on their journeys through thick and thin, through winter and summer. It is the same Lord of the House of Kaaba who provides them food and protects their caravans of trade and commerce. And yet they remain ungrateful to their protector and refuse to worship Him.

SURAH CVI

1.   Who has united and protected
      The Quraish

2.   And formed caravans for them
      To journey through winter and summer?

3.   Let them thank their Protector
      And out of gratitude
      Worship Him,
      The Lord of this House.

4.   He gives them food
      And also security.

SURAH CVII: AL-MAUN (THE ALMS)
(7 verses)

Believers are admonished not to repulse the orphans. They should also encourage the feeding of the indigent. They should not neglect their prayers and should worship God with devotion. This should be done sincerely and not just for appearance. They should also look after the needs of their neighbours.

SURAH CVII

1. Who are those
   Who deny the judgement to come?

2. They are the ones
   Who drive away the orphan

3. And restrain people from
   Feeding the needy.

4. Curse be on such worshippers,

5. Who neglect their spiritual duties

6. And are heedless of the moral spirit,

7. And refuse to supply
   The needs of even their neighbours.

SURAH CVIII: AL-KAWTHAR (THE ABUNDANCE)
(3 verses)

There is a reference here to the Fount of Abundance, which will quench the spiritual thirst of believers. Muhammad is assured by God of happier prospects in his struggle and is told that those who hate him have no future.

SURAH CVIII

1. You have been
   blessed with
   abundance

2. So serve your
   Lord with

                    devotion
                 And sacrifice
                    in His cause.

SURAH CIX: AL-KAFIRUN (THE DISBELIEVERS)
(6 verses)

In these verses, the Prophet is advised as to what his attitude should
be towards the followers of other faiths; it is a testimony to Islam's
tolerance of non-Muslims and a guarantee of freedom of worship. It
states clearly that non-believers are free to practise their religions as
believers are entitled to practise theirs. There should be no confusion
on this point; as Sayyid Qutb has said, 'to cut short all arguments
and to distinguish firmly between one form of worship and the
other, between one doctrine and concept and the other, this chapter
was revealed in such a decisive, assertive tone.'[2]

SURAH CIX

1.   Tell the
            disbelievers:

2.   'I do not worship
            What you worship,

3.   'Nor do you worship
            What I worship.

4.   'I will not worship
            What you worship.

5.   'Nor will you worship
            What I worship.

6.   'To you, your religion
            And to me, mine.'

SURAH CX: AL-NASR (HELP)
(3 verses)

Here, the Prophet is told of the coming victory of Islam over the pagans of Mecca, which in turn will bring people in large numbers to accept the true faith. It calls upon Muhammad to celebrate God's praises and to seek His forgiveness.

SURAH CX

1. When, with God's help, victory comes,

2. And you see men in hordes
   Accepting His way,

3. Then glorify the Lord
   And ask for His forgiveness
   And proclaim
   His grace and mercy.

SURAH CXI: AL-MASAD *OR* AL-LAHAB (THE FLAME)
(5 verses)

In the verses of this chapter there is the condemnation of an uncle of the Prophet, Abu Lahab. He and his wife, Arwa, were the most vicious and unbending foes of the Prophet. The Quran describes Abu Lahab as 'the Father of the Flame' for his intemperate nature. He and his wife carried on a relentless campaign against Muhammad: they humiliated and harassed him; they persecuted and killed his followers. God assures believers that neither Abu Lahab's position as chief of his tribe nor his wealth will save him from the scourge of hell. Nor will his wife escape the twisted rope around her neck.

SURAH CXI

1. The hands of
   the Father of the Flame
   Will be
   reduced to ashes
   And he will perish.

2. Neither his wealth
   nor his position
   Will be of any avail.

3. He will be consumed
   by the fire.

4. And so will be
   his wife,

5. Burnt as wood
   with a twist of rope
   Round her neck.

SURAH CXII: AL-IKHLAS (PURITY OF FAITH)
(4 verses)

These verses are repeated most often in the prayers of the faithful. It is a confirmation of the oneness of Allah and an excellent exposition, in a few words, of His incomparable power. Stress is laid here on the fact that He is unique: He has been begotten by none nor has He begotten anyone. There is a tradition in the *Sahih* of Bukhari that the Prophet regarded this chapter as 'equivalent to one-third of the Quran'.

SURAH CXII

1. Proclaim to all:
   God is One.
   He is the only one.

2.   He is the Eternal
      He is the Absolute.

3.   He has begotten none
      And of none has He
          been begotten.

4.   There is, indeed, none
      To compare with Him.

SURAH CXIII: AL-FALAQ (THE DAYBREAK)
(5 verses)

This is a prayer to the Creator to grant the faithful refuge from the mischief of evil-doers — hidden or visible, known or unknown. It also asks for protection from the conjuring witches, and from the evil that comes from the jealous ones. According to Aisha, his youngest wife, Muhammad would recite these verses every night before going to bed; he found them most soothing.

SURAH CXIII

1.   Say: I seek refuge
      With the Lord of the Dawn

2.   From the mischiefs of created things

3.   And from the darkness that spreads

4.   And from the evil designs of those
      Who indulge in sorcery,

5.   And from the envy of the envier.

SURAH CXIV: AL–NAS (MANKIND)
(6 verses)

This is the last chapter in the traditional order of the arrangement of the Quran; it calls upon believers to trust God and to seek His protection from the mischief of the slinking prompters, who poison the hearts of men. The Prophet is reported to have told his uncle Ibn Abbas: 'Satan besieges man's heart; he fails whenever man sincerely remembers God, but succeeds whenever man forgets Him.'

SURAH CXIV

1. Say: I take refuge
    With the Lord
      of the people,

2. The King of mankind,

3. The Arbiter
      of the Universe,

4. From the evil of those
    Who put temptations

5. Into the minds
      and hearts

6. Of man and
      jinn.

SURAH CXIV AL-NAS (MANKIND)
(6 verses)

This is the last chapter in the traditional order of the arrangement of the Quran. It calls upon believers to trust God and to seek His protection from the mischief of the slinking prompters, who poison the hearts of men. The Prophet is reported to have told his uncle Ibn Abbas: 'Satan besieges man's heart; he fails whenever man sincerely remembers God, but succeeds whenever man forgets Him.'

SURAH CXIV

1. Say: I take refuge
    With the Lord
    of the people.

2. The King of mankind.

3. The Arbiter
    of the Universe.

4. From the evil of those
    Who put temptations

5. Into the minds
    and hearts

6. Of man and
    jinn.

PART III
QURANIC STORIES

You have been sent,
O Muhammad, as a mercy
to all mankind

THE QURANIC STORIES
OF THE
PROPHETS FROM ADAM TO JESUS

The stories of the prophets who had preceded Muhammad account for almost a quarter of the Quran; they number twenty-eight in all, fourteen are referred to only casually. The list of twenty-eight is, however, by no means exhaustive. According to a tradition attributed to Muhammad, God had sent as many as 1,24,000 messengers to different parts of the world. Allah tells the Prophet that there had been messengers before Muhammad: 'Some We have mentioned to you, and others We have not' (40:78). The Quran contains another verse to the effect that there was no land to which God had not sent His messengers. These messengers had revealed the truth to their people in their respective languages. Their accounts form part of the Quran; these are meant to 'put firm resolve in people's hearts' and to convey God's admonitions to all believers (11:120–23).

Allah's first messenger was Adam. The account of his creation, his life with Eve in paradise and their lapse at the instigation of Satan, their fall from God's grace and their forgiveness by Him, their being sent down to earth as a measure of their rehabilitation and finally Adam's appointment as His viceregent, are recounted in several places in the Quran. The point to note is that, after his fall, Adam is not only forgiven by God but is made His deputy on earth. Thus Islam does not endorse the Christian concept of the original sin, to atone for which on behalf of the human race Jesus had to be crucified. In Islam, man is not born in sin; he does not need to be redeemed. He is, on the contrary, assured of happiness on earth and of paradise hereafter if he follows the path shown by Allah and does not go astray.

Linked with Adam's story is that of his two sons, Cain and Abel.

The Quran takes the severest possible view of Cain's assassination of Abel and helps bring out forcefully the Islamic view that taking of life without a just cause is a heinous, almost unforgivable, sin, so much so that the loss of one innocent life is reckoned equal to the loss of all mankind.

Noah's struggle to propagate the oneness of God is told in several surahs. The moral is simple: whoever defies God's authority is doomed, and no one can destroy those whom the Lord protects.

The Quran regards Abraham as the spiritual progenitor of Muhammad; his story, therefore, occupies a special place in it and in the hearts of the faithful. He is the builder of the Kaaba, or the House of God, and the first to destroy idols of false gods. His unequivocal devotion to God, demonstrated by his willingness to sacrifice even his son Ishmael, has inspired believers through successive generations, and is celebrated as the Festival of Sacrifice, known as *Id al-duha*, when an animal is symbolically sacrificed in the name of God.

The stories of the Prophets Lot, Hud, Salih and Shuyab bring out the supremacy of virtue over vice, right conduct over wrong, and fair-dealing over unfair practices.

The Quran devotes an entire surah to the story of Joseph, and emphasizes through it the significance of love and compassion and man's ability to overcome, with God's help, all pain and anguish which he may have to suffer in establishing his innocence.

Of all prophets, Moses occupies the largest space in the Quran; his encounters with Pharaoh are referred to in different surahs. Several instances are quoted from his life which throw light on his prophetic mission and on the way he pursued the path of truth amid hostility from his enemies and detractors and betrayal by his own followers. Several lessons are highlighted in this narration of the life of Moses, notably (1) that falsehood can never triumph over truth; (2) that oppression cannot last for ever; (3) that the mightiest, too, are mortal; (4) that he whom God blesses is bound to succeed finally; and (5) that there is no power mightier than God.

The Quran contains graphic accounts of the rise of David, particularly of Saul's fight with Goliath and Goliath's death at the hands of David. His story reveals that justice is an essential part of faith and, further, that God loves the just and abhors the unjust.

David's son Solomon was a wise king; his efforts to first subdue the powerful Queen of Sheba and later to persuade her to take the right path also find a place in the Quran. Similarly, the story of Zachariah and his son Yahya, or John, and their unbounded faith in God and His Mercy, shows that faith can conquer mountains. Job is presented as an embodiment of patience, which, it is emphasized, is necessary for the pursuit of faith. Impatience is not the way of God.

There are several references in the Quran to Jesus and his mission. His story, as narrated in the Quran, differs somewhat from that in the Bible. The broad outlines are similar, but the Quran does not accept that he was crucified, or that he is the son of God. He was God's messenger, as were Abraham and Moses; to make him a partner with God is, according to the Quran, *shirk*, or heresy. In the Quran, Jesus himself disowns this attribute and chides his followers for embarking on the wrong path.

References to the prophets are interspersed throughout various surahs (except for Joseph's story, which is narrated in one chapter). In the following pages I have put the pieces together to provide coherent biographical material in each case, while remaining scrupulously faithful to Quranic representation. One question that disturbs the followers of other faiths is why have *their* prophets not been mentioned in the Quran. The answer is simple: the immediate audience that Allah addressed in the Quran were Arabs. Hence they were given examples of messengers whose words and deeds they were familiar with, so that the message could be properly comprehended. The Arabs had never heard of India, China, South-East Asia, Africa, and the other far-away places; to cite the examples of the prophets in those lands would, therefore, have been of little avail to the Arabs. However, it was made clear to them that there was no land to which God had not sent messengers who spoke in the language of their own people; that is why the Quran states that 'about some of Our messengers We have mentioned to you and of others We have not.' This is so categorical a statement, that it should leave no doubt in anyone's mind that the Quran recognizes the prophets in other lands, despite their accounts not appearing in its pages. If the work of each of them had been recounted, the

Quran would have been a record of world history and not a document of precepts, admonitions and injunctions for the material benefit and spiritual enlightenment of the faithful.

In this chapter the names of the prophets are given in their biblical form. The following table shows their Quranic equivalents.

BIBLICAL NAMES	QURANIC EQUIVALENTS
Adam	Adam
Noah	Nuh
Hud	Hud
Salih	Salih
Abraham	Ibrahim
Lot	Lut
Shuyab	Shuyab
Jacob	Yaqub
Joseph	Yusuf
Moses	Musa
Jonah	Yunus
Job	Ayub
David	Dawood
Solomon	Sulaiman
Zachariah	Zakariya
John	Yahya
Jesus	Isa

THE STORY OF ADAM

The creation of man is referred to in the Quran in many places. Adam was the first man God created. Then he created Eve, and they lived together in heaven.

God regarded man as his noblest creation. He sent him as his viceregent on earth. Before creating Adam, He told the angels in the heavens that He was creating 'man from clay, moulding him from earthly substance', and asked them to 'fall down before him in prostration, when I have given him form and breathed into him My spirit'. The angels were aghast:

> They asked:
> 'Pray, will you put man there
> Who will do mischief and shed blood?
> Why not send us instead
> Who worship and glorify You?'

(2:30)

They prayed to the Lord not to humiliate them. Allah told them to obey His command, for, he said, 'You know not what I know.'

The Quran states:

> So each one of them obeyed except Satan.
> God asked him: 'Why did you not prostrate?'
> Satan replied: 'Because I am worthier, my Lord, than Adam.
> Of fire You have created me,
> From clay you have created him.'

(7:12)

God thundered:

> Begone from my presence!
> There is no place for you here.
> Your arrogance makes you
> The meanest of My creatures.

(7:13)

Satan bowed before the Lord, and made one plea:

> Grant me, My Lord, a reprieve
> Until the day man is raised again.

(7:14)

God granted Satan the reprieve. Satan then said:

> Since you have thrown me out,
> I shall now waylay man
> On the straight path you have laid
> And make him commit sin,
> From the right hand to the left,

From before him and behind him;
You will not find in Adam and in most of his progeny,
Gratitude for your bounties.

(7:16–17)

God told Satan that he was disgraced, and banished him from paradise:

Those of My creatures who follow you
They shall be consigned to hell with you.

(20:123–4)

Turning to Adam, God said:

You and Eve can reside
In the garden of paradise.
Eat fruits from any tree you like,
But there is one to which you shall not go
Nor shall you eat its fruits.
For, indeed, it will be a transgression.

(2:35)

Adam and Eve began to live blissfully in paradise, but Satan would tempt them so as to swerve them from the right path. He whispered into their ears that they should enjoy their bare bodies, which until then they had not perceived. He told them that their Lord had asked them to keep away from the prohibited tree because He did not wish them to become angels and thus immortal. He asked them to swear that they would not betray his trust and then urged them to eat the forbidden fruit. He assured them that he was their 'true friend'. He used all his guile to entice them. Eventually, Adam and Eve succumbed to his incitements and tasted the forbidden fruit. They covered themselves with leaves in order to conceal their shame.

On seeing this transformation, their Lord asked them:

Did I not forbid you to go near that tree?
Did I not warn you that Satan is your enemy?

(7:20–22)

Adam and Eve realized their mistake and begged forgiveness of their Lord:

> O Lord, we have sinned grievously.
> Please grant us Your forgiveness
> Or else we shall be lost forever.
>
> (7:23)

The Lord in His mercy forgave them, but cast them down to live on earth. He told them that there shall be eternal enmity and feuding between them and Satan.

The Lord reminded Adam and Eve, and their progeny who followed them, that clothing might cover their shame, but what was more important for them was to cover themselves with the 'garment of true piety':

> O Children of Adam!
> Let Satan not be your guide
> As he has been of your parents.
> He misled them and drove them out,
> Stripping them of their nakedness.
>
> (7:27)

Satan made Adam and Eve commit indecency. Thus they disobeyed the command of their Lord. They were warned of Satan's designs; they were asked to tell Satan:

> Our Lord commands us to do what is right and just.
> He is to be worshipped in every place
> And prayed to with all the sincerity of faith.
> It is He who has brought us to life,
> And it is He who will raise us again.
> After we die we shall return to Him.
> Some of us have been guided right
> But some have taken to Satan's ways.
> They are, indeed, in the wrong.
>
> (7:29–30)

Referring to Cain and Abel, the two sons of Adam, the Quran says that each of them made an offering to God; the offering of Abel was accepted and that of Cain was rejected:

> Cain said to his brother: 'I will kill you.'
> But his brother replied: 'Only from those

Who truly fear the Lord does God accept an offering.
If you try to kill me, I will not do the same to you.
For I fear my Lord, who is the Lord of all beings.
If you kill me, the sin will be on your head
And you will be consigned of hell.'

(5:27–29)

Abel's words had no effect on Cain. He murdered his brother without any cause and 'took his place among the lost'. God sent a raven who dug the ground to cover the corpse of Abel. Seeing this, Cain felt most remorseful and cried, 'Woe to me. I am worse than this raven, for I cannot hide the evil that I have done to my brother.'

The Quran admonishes:

O Children of Israel! If anyone
Kills another without a just cause,
Except in retaliation for a murder
Or for causing corruption in the land,
It is as if he has killed the whole of mankind.
And whosoever saves a life,
It is as if he has saved the whole of mankind.

(5:32)

THE STORY OF NOAH

Allah sent Noah to His people and asked him to tell them to worship none but the One, who was the Creator of all. He was also told to warn them that 'stern retribution will overtake them' if they did not heed his call. The nobles among them refused to believe him. They said:

You are just a human being like us;
Why should we follow you?
Except the vulgar who may thoughtlessly
Hasten to listen to you,
You have no superiority over us;
In fact, you are nothing but an imposter.

(11:27)

Noah beseeched them not to misunderstand him:

> I have a clear message from the Lord
> Who in His mercy has granted me this task.
> I ask you not to be deaf
> To what I have to say.
> I am not coercing you
> Nor am I asking you for wealth.
> My reward is with my Lord.
> I will not turn away believers.
> Only pause and think of your future.
> I do not claim to possess God's treasures
> Nor have I the knowledge of the unseen;
> I am also no angel.
> But do not be scornful of those
> Who believe in God or talk ill of them.
>
> (11:28–31)

These people, however, remained adamant in their opposition and told Noah bluntly:

> You have raised a dispute between us;
> We have heard your contentions
> And also the warnings of dire consequences.
> Bring upon us the calamity that you threaten;
> Let us see what your God can do to us.
>
> (11:32)

Noah warned them that if God so willed, He would do what he wanted and nothing could frustrate it. He pleaded with them again to come out of their 'persistent delusion'. But they refused to listen to him. In desperation, Noah told the Lord:

> O my Lord, night and day I
>   have pleaded with my people,
> But instead of listening to me
> They have fled away from me.
> Each time I have asked them
> To seek your forgiveness,
> They have put their fingers in their ears
> And wrapped their heads with garments;

> They have persisted in their arrogance.
> Even so, I pleaded with them,
> Privately as well as publicly,
> In all earnestness, entreating them
> To seek Your forgiveness
> And to remember your bounties
> And your Awesome Majesty.
> But they have said 'no' to me.
> On the contrary, they have asked people
> Not to abandon the worship of their gods.
>
> (71:5–23)

God then asked Noah not to be distressed and to construct an ark 'under Our eyes and by Our inspiration'. As he began the work, the chiefs of his people mocked him. He told them that soon they would realize who was in for 'lasting doom'.

And so it happened; under a decree from the Lord, the waters gushed forth and flooded the earth. Noah was commanded by the Lord to take into the ark two creatures of each species, a male and a female, members of his family, except the wrongdoers among them, and all the believers who numbered just a handful. Noah's son refused to board. The father pleaded with him, but he said, 'No, I will climb the mountain and take shelter there and protect myself.'

Noah cried out:

> This day there shall be no protection
> From the wrath of Allah,
> Save for those who will receive His mercy.
>
> (11:43)

The waves came gushing forth in torrents and swept off Noah's son and all unbelievers; when Noah saw his son drowning, in a moment of weakness he asked God to forgive his son and to save him. The Lord said, 'He was not a true son of yours; what he did was wrong. Do not ask for something which is wrong and of which you have no comprehension. Otherwise, you may be counted among the ignorant and the wilful.' Noah realized his folly and was repentant. He asked for God's forgiveness, and the blessings came:

> Noah! Take to the way of peace;
> Our blessings are upon you
> And upon people descending from you.
> We will give satisfaction to believers
> And retribution to unbelievers.
> The future is only know to Us;
> Neither you nor your people have an inkling,
> Hence be patient and fear your Lord.
>
> (11:48)

As the floods overwhelmed the unbelievers and took them to their doom, Noah prayed to the Lord:

> O my Lord! Forgive me and all believers
> Who have taken shelter under my roof,
> But do not leave on earth a single unbeliever.
> For if You spare any one of them,
> He will lead Your servants astray
> And also their off-spring
> And make them faithless wrongdoers.
>
> (71:26–8)

Noah and his companions in the ark were safely conveyed to the shore. God kept them steadily under His grace and granted them His bounties.

THE STORY OF HUD

To the industrious and hard-working people belonging to the tribe of Aad, God sent Hud as His messenger. He told them:

> O my people, worship God.
> There is no one other than Him.
> The other notions you have are all false.
> He is the only true God.
> I ask you to worship Him.
> I ask nothing for myself.
> My reward is with Him who has fashioned me.
> Will you not understand this?
> Seek His forgiveness and remember His bounties,
> And do not revert to your evil ways.
>
> (11:50–52)

The elders of the tribes rebuked Hud:

> We think you are a simpleton.
> Nay, worse, a liar.
>
> (7:66)

Hud assured them:

> I am not a simpleton; I am God's apostle.
> I bring His message to you.
> A faithful mentor I am to you,
> Hence, heed the warning I give,
> For you are Noah's people.
> If you have God's blessings,
> Everything will go well with you.
>
> (7:67–9)

But they persisted in their unbelief and told Hud:

> You have brought us no clear Signs
> Save what you are telling us.
> How can we abandon our gods?
> It seems some of our gods
> Have smitten you with evil
> So that you go on the wrong path.
>
> (11:53–4)

Hud answered them thus:

> I swear by my Lord that I am
> Not guilty of your charge.
> I believe only in my Lord;
> To me no one else matters
> And none can delude me
> And make me go against Him.
> Nothing moves without His will;
> His path alone is the right path.
> If you do not respond to my call
> And turn away from the Lord
> The loss will be yours, not His.
> In your place, He will bring others,

> For He has control over all things,
> He watches over all that happens.
> (11:54–7)

Hud reminded the elders of the tribe of how God gave them tenure of the land upon which they built their castles and homes. They had forgotten all His bounties and resorted to corrupt dealings and evil ways. Eventually, they had to pay the price of their unbelief: they were overwhelmed by a raging tempest. The fury lasted for seven nights and eight days; the people of Aad perished and their castles and dwellings became like 'stumps of hollow palm-trees'.

THE STORY OF SALIH

For the good of the people of Thamud, God sent Salih as His messenger. He asked them to believe in the Oneness of God and to worship none but Him. He told them that God had sent a Sign to the arrogant oppressors of the poor in the form of a she-camel. Water was scarce at the time, and the privileged class tried to prevent the poor and their cattle having access to the springs and pastures. The she-camel was made a test case to see if the haughty, rich people would come to see reason. Salih wanted them to allow the she-camel to graze without any let or hindrance. He warned them that they should have no evil intention towards her, or the wrath of God would fall upon them. He reminded them that the Lord had been kind to them in the past and had made them successors to the people of Aad, who were destroyed for their evil deeds. They had been given land, so as to build palaces and castles on the plains and homes in the mountains. Salih beseeched them not to spread disorder in the world, to remain ever-conscious of God's power and to be grateful for His kindness.

But the chiefs of the tribes jeered at him; they asked the people not to believe in what Salih said. Some did not listen to them and heeded Salih's call, but many followed the advice of their chiefs. And as a mark of their defiance, they hamstrung the she-camel and killed her, challenging Salih to bring upon them the calamity which he had threatened them with.

Salih grieved for his people, for he knew what lay in store for them. He therefore left Thamud with his followers, and soon thereafter there was a dreadful earthquake, which destroyed the inhabitants of Thamud, burying them along with their castles and palaces.

THE STORY OF ABRAHAM

After Noah, Abraham was selected by God to be His prophet. Abraham first preached in his own country, now known as Iraq. Then he moved to Syria, Palestine and Egypt. Finally, he settled down in Arabia. In carrying on with his mission, he was assisted by other messengers appointed from his own family by God: Lot, his nephew, who lived in the midst of the people of Jordan, and Abraham's two sons, the elder son Ishmael (or Ismail), and the younger Isaac (or Ishaq). Isaac preached in Syria and Palestine. Ishmael assisted his father in Arabia and is credited with having helped him in building the Kaaba, which is now the religious centre of the Islamic world. Ishmael and Isaac founded two sects, the Ismailites and the Israelites respectively. The tribe of Quraish, to which Muhammad belonged, is said to be Ismailite in origin, while the Jews and the Christians are said to be descendants of Jacob, whose other name was Israel, the son of Isaac and the grandson of Abraham. Hence Abraham is regarded as the father of all Semitic peoples; from him were born not only Jews and Christians but also Muslims. He is the common bond who links them all. After him, God transferred the leadership to Isaac and Jacob, and their descendants are collectively described in the Quran as 'the Children of Israel'.

As soon as Abraham received the commission from the Lord to propagate the Oneness of God and preach His worship among the people, he called upon the Lord to preserve the Kaaba that he had built to eradicate the worship of idols, which had led many people astray. Abraham asked them, 'What is it that you worship?'

They replied:

> We worship the idols, as did our fathers.
> And in devotion to them we shall remain steadfast.
>
> (26:72,74)

Abraham asked them:

> Do they hear you when you call them?
> Have they the power to do anything,
> Either good or bad for you?
>
> (26:73)

He reminded them that there was only one God, the Lord of all creation, who controlled life, death and resurrection. He told his own father, Azar, to desist from worshipping idols. He said he had learnt from his own experience that God alone was worthy of worship. He was shown by God 'the Kingdom of the heavens and the earth so that he might be convinced of the faith' in his Creator. The Quran narrates:

> When the night was dark, Abraham saw a star;
> He said to himself, 'This must be the Lord.'
> But soon the star set and his faith was shaken.
> Then he saw the moon rising in the sky.
> 'This is the Lord,' he said.
> However, when it waned, he lost faith in it.
> Likewise, when the sun rose, brighter than everything,
> He was convinced that it was the Lord.
> But the sun also set, and Abraham cried:
> 'I set my face against all these.
> I repudiate every other kind of worship
> Except the worship of God,
> Creator of all that is in the heavens
>   and on the earth.'
>
> (6:76–9)

The people jeered at Abraham and remonstrated with him; they cautioned him, and even stoned him; they tried to frighten him into believing that their idols would destroy him and his God would not be able to save him. But Abraham responded:

Will you dispute with me
About Allah who has guided me?
I have no fear of the idols you worship.
Unless my Lord wills nothing can happen.

(6:80–81)

Turning to his father, Abraham asked what the images were to which he and his people were devoted. Azar replied that they worshipped what their fathers had worshipped. Abraham said: 'Then assuredly, you and your fathers are clearly in error.' Earlier, he had told Nimrod, the King of Iraq, not to forget that it was God who gave him the Kingdom and power and glory; but the King, in his arrogance, had denied it and had declared that he determined the life and death of his subjects. Abraham had then asked him: 'Allah makes the sun rise from the east; can you make it rise from the west?' The King had no answer. He sentenced Abraham to be burnt alive.

Abraham bore all hardships but remained firm and steadfast in his loyalty to God. One day he broke all the idols in the Kaaba, one by one, except the largest. As soon as the people heard of the destruction, they rushed to the temple and, seething with rage, cried:

Who has done this to our idols?
This is, indeed, an outrage.

(21:59)

They were told that young Abraham was the culprit. 'Fetch him,' they demanded. 'And let everyone witness what we do to him.' When Abraham was brought before them, they asked him: 'Who has done this to our idols?'

'Not I; it is that big idol over there. Why don't you question him?'

They replied that idols did not speak. Abraham said,

Isn't it strange that you should worship
These idols which can neither speak nor do anything.
They can neither help nor harm anyone.

> Shame on you and on your idol worship.
> How foolish of you to worship them.
>
> (21:66)

They were fashioned, he reminded them, by their own hands. He beseeched them to worship the One God who created and fashioned everything. They were so angered by his words that they decided to throw him into a pyre of blazing fire. They could not succeed, however, because God 'made them bite the dust'.

Abraham prayed to the Lord to grant him an heir, who 'will be numbered among the righteous'. So God gave him a gentle boy, Ishmael. But Abraham had pledged to God in a dream that if he had a son, he would offer him in sacrifice to the Lord. Abraham told his son of his dream and his pledge. 'Then, Father,' said Ishmael, 'you should honour your commitment and surrender me to the will of God.'

So Abraham laid him down, and as he was about to slay him, he heard the Voice commanding him:

> Enough, Abraham!
> You have kept your word with Us.
> You have already fulfilled the vision.
>
> (37:105)

The Lord had intended merely to test Abraham; He now declared that he had fulfilled his commitment:

> We redeem Abraham's son with a great sacrifice
> And we give Our benediction to him
> And bless him through generations to come
> And shower Our peace upon him.
>
> (37:107-9)

Thus God rewarded the righteous and His 'believing servants'.

In Isaac, Abraham's other and younger son, the Lord gave to the world 'one of the best of prophets'. Among their descendants some did good deeds, but those who did bad, 'were blatant evil-doers, who sinned against themselves' (37:110-13).

The Quran clarifies:

> Abraham was neither a Jew nor a Christian.
> He was a *hanif*, a man of pure worship,
> He was not an idolater but a believer in one God;
> Only those who follow him
> Are entitled to claim relationship with him.
> Muhammad and his followers
> Are nearer to him.
> Allah is the protector of all believers.
>
> (3:67–8)

Referring to the House at Mecca, 'the place of sanctuary and serenity for the people', Allah asked Muhammad to 'make it your House of prayers'. Thus God's covenant given to Abraham and Ishmael was fulfilled and the Kaaba became for the believers 'the pilgrim circuit' for worship and for prostration. Abraham and Isaac had prayed to Allah to 'send among our people after us a messenger of our own kin who recites to the people Your revelations, teaches them the Book and the wisdom it contains and purges them of all evil' (2:129). Allah admonishes:

> Tell the people, O Muhammad!
> That to be rightly guided
> One need not be a Jew or a Christian.
> The righteous belong to the community of Abraham,
> Who was pure in his worship of God.
> So were Ishmael, Jacob and the tribes,
> And Moses, Jesus and the rest.
> They are all Our messengers;
> We make no distinction between them.
>
> (2:135–6)

THE STORY OF LOT

Lot lived among a people who practised naked lewdness; they went lustfully after men instead of women. God chose him as His messenger to tell them to give up their perversity and fear Him. He told them:

> My people, ask forgiveness of your Lord
> And repent for your evil ways.
>
> (27:55)

But instead of listening to him, they jeered at him, calling him and his family 'these despicable, puritan folks'. They hounded them out of the town. God rescued all of them except Lot's wife, who turned back and decided to be with the unbelievers. Suddenly a rain of fire and stones fell on the inhabitants of the place and they were destroyed. The Quran reminds:

> In your travels either by morning light
> Or the faint glimmer of the fall of night
> You can see their ruins as you pass by.
>
> (37:136–8)

THE STORY OF SHUYAB

Shuyab was sent as a messenger by God to the people of Madyan, who were mostly merchants. They lived in an area surrounded by thick forests. He told them:

> I beseech you, my people, to worship God
> And fear the coming of the Last Day.
> Do not take to perverse habits
> And generate corruption in the land.
>
> (29:36)

Instead of heeding his call, they called him a liar; he reminded them that they should fear the Lord, who had sent him as His faithful apostle. He asked them to give up their practice of cheating in business:

> Fear the One who has created you
> And listen to what I have to say.
> Pay in full measure and do not defraud
> By stinting and giving short measure and weight.
> Use the right balance,
> And be honest and cease to be perverse.
>
> (26:179,181–3)

The people scolded Shuyab and called him 'bewitched'; they told him:

> How can we forsake what our fathers taught us
> And abandon the methods which have come down to us?
>
> (11:87)

They praised his gentle nature and asked him to follow his forebears and give up his new fangled ideas.

Shuyab told them he did not wish to cross swords with the people of Madyan, but he could not do what they were asking him to do. He explained:

> My mission is to set things right
> And to fulfil God's will.
> My trust in Him is implicit.
> I always turn to Him in need.
> I beseech you not to disobey His call
> Lest the same fate befalls you
> As befell the detractors of Noah, Hud and Salih.
> The people of Lot, who lived near by,
> Also suffered because of their unbelief.
>
> (11:89)

The people of Madyan were deaf to his plea:

> You are weak in the head;
> But for your family, we would stone you.
>
> (11:91)

Shuyab answered them resolutely:

> My people, do what you like;
> I hold on to my belief.
> You will know who is a liar
> When God's punishment comes to you.
>
> (11:93)

The elders of the tribe warned Shuyab:

> We will expel you from our city
> And all those who follow you.
>
> (7:88)

Shuyab replied that his Lord controlled everything. The people jeered at him:

> If you are speaking the truth
> Let pieces from the sky fall on us.
>
> (26:187)

Shuyab told them:

> Watch me then;
> And I am also watching you.
>
> (11:93)

Soon thereafter, Shuyab left the city with his followers. One night, a blast struck the inhabitants of Madyan and by next morning they lay lifeless, as if they had never lived.

THE STORY OF JOSEPH

Joseph was the eleventh of the twelve sons of Jacob. One day, he told his father that in a dream he had seen eleven stars, the sun and the moon prostrating before him. Jacob realized that Joseph, who had always impressed him as a noble and gentle soul, was blessed by God. Sensing the greatness that lay ahead of his son, Jacob became more protective of him and asked him not to narrate his dream to his brothers, who, out of jealousy, might try to harm him. He told his son:

> The Lord has chosen you, O Joseph,
> For a much loftier purpose;
> He has given you the power
> To interpret dreams and foretell events;
> He has blessed you with His grace,
> As He had likewise blessed your forebears
> From Abraham to Isaac,
> For He is All-Knowing
> And full of wisdom.
>
> (12:6)

The other sons were aware of their father's extreme fondness for

Joseph and were resentful of it. They decided that they would either have to 'kill Joseph or cast him out to some unknown land in order to win Jacob's favour'. One of the brothers pleaded with the others not to kill Joseph; instead he suggested that they should find a pit or well and leave him there for some passing caravan to take him away. The others agreed. They asked Jacob to let Joseph go out and play with them, assuring him that Joseph would be taken good care of. Jacob was not happy at the suggestion; he told them that he feared they might not attend to him, and a wild animal such as a wolf might devour the young Joseph. But the brothers told their father not to worry, for they were so many of them that even if a wolf were to attack them, it would have to devour them first before it could do harm to their little brother.

So they took Joseph along with them, far away from home, threw him into a well and returned home weeping. They told Jacob that while they were away, racing with one another, a wolf, as the father had feared, had seized Joseph and devoured him. 'We searched for him but in vain; all we could find was his blood-stained shirt.' This they showed to Jacob, who refused to believe their story. In his distress he turned to God; he had a strong feeling within him that no harm could have come to Joseph, for God was sure to protect him.

Meanwhile, a caravan passed by the well into which Joseph had been cast. Halting to draw a bucket of water, a water-carrier saw the handsome young boy struggling to get out of the well. He dragged the boy out, took him along with him and hid him in his merchandise. When he reached Egypt, he sold Joseph for a few dirhams to an Egyptian nobleman of high rank, an officer in the royal court. He took Joseph home and told his wife, Zuleikha, a lady of great beauty and charm, to take good care of him. As they had no children, he told her that they could adopt him as a son. And so Joseph was brought up in happy surroundings. He was given the best of training in the affairs of the world. The Almighty was working out His objective – of which no one was aware – of equipping Joseph with worldly wisdom and spiritual knowledge, with a view to making him His messenger.

Zuleikha felt deeply and passionately attracted to Joseph, but he maintained his distance and did not respond to her overtures. One occasion, when her husband was out, Zuleikha called Joseph to her room. As soon as he entered, she locked the door and said, 'Now come to me, my dear one.' Taken aback by this advance, Joseph told her: 'God forbid. My master has been generous to me; I cannot betray his trust. Those who do evil can never prosper.' So saying, he rushed towards the door and tried to unlock it. Zuleikha caught hold of his tunic from behind and, in the tussle, it was torn. Joseph managed to unlock the door, but only to find his master outside. Zuleikha cried:

> What is the fitting punishment, my master!
> Against one who has evil design
> Against your wife, but prison and chastisement?
>
> (12:25)

Joseph denied the charge and said that it was Zuleikha who had sought to seduce him. An adviser from the household, a lady of reputation, was asked to settle the dispute. If Joseph's tunic was torn from the front, she said, then he was guilty; but if it was torn from the back, then Zuleikha should be held accountable. The husband saw that the tunic was torn from the back; he told his wife that she had been at fault. He asked her to seek forgiveness, for truly it was she who had sinned.

The news of the incident spread through the city like wildfire, and women in particular began to gossip about Zuleikha having gone astray. When she heard of their malicious talk she was furious. She invited all the noble ladies to a banquet at the palace; when they sat down for the feast she gave each of them a knife to hold in their hands, and then ordered Joseph to present himself. The women were so struck by the extraordinarily good-looking young man that they could not take their eyes off him; in the excitement they cut their fingers with their knives in their hands. They exclaimed:

> O God preserve our chastity.
> He is not a man!
> He looks an angel.
>
> (12:31)

Zuleikha retorted:

> This is the man about whom
> You noble ladies blamed me.
> It is true I tried to seduce him,
> Though he resisted me
> And remained guiltless.
> Even now I shall not give him up.
> If he does not respond,
> He shall be cast into prison
> And He will be with the vilest.
>
> (12:32)

Joseph prayed to God:

> Help me, O my Lord!
> Prison will be better
> Than what I am asked to do.
> Do not desert me.
> The snare is such
> That in my youth
> I may succumb to temptation.
>
> (12:33)

Joseph was all the same jailed, since the master could not displease his wife. In prison, Joseph had two young men as his companions, who became friendly with him. One day, one of them told Joseph that he had dreamt that he was pressing grapes to make wine. The other prisoner narrated his dream, in which he saw himself carrying bread on his head while a flock of birds were pecking at it. Joseph interpreted these dreams for his companions. He told the first that he would pour wine for his master, while the other would be beheaded and birds would peck at his head. That was what the future held for them. Joseph asked the one who was to serve wine not to forget him when he took service in the royal court. But after his release, when he became a cup-bearer to the King, the young man forgot to mention Joseph, and so he continued to languish in jail.

One day, the King told his counsellors that he had had a strange dream. He saw seven lean cows devour seven fat cows, and he saw seven green corns being replaced by seven dry, withered ones. He asked the wise men to tell him what this dream foretold. The counsellors tried, but had to admit that they did not have the knowledge to interpret dreams. At that time the cup-bearer informed the King of his erstwhile friend Joseph and his uncanny ability to interpret dreams. The King sent the cup-bearer to the prison with orders that Joseph should be freed at once. The King asked for Joseph to be brought before him, but Joseph refused, saying that unless the false charge of seducing Zuleikha was investigated and he was exonerated, he would not appear at the royal court. The King agreed and ordered an investigation into the matter. The charge was found to be false, and Zuleikha admitted that she had tried to seduce Joseph and that Joseph was innocent. The King acquitted Joseph with honour. Joseph was happy that his innocence had been proved and that everyone now knew that he had not betrayed his master. He cautioned the people, however: 'I do not want to justify myself or boast about my innocence. For any man can succumb to temptation and give in to evil; it is by the mercy of God that I was able to resist it and remain pure.' In his case, he said, the Lord was more than merciful to him.

Joseph then appeared before the King, who was so impressed by his honesty and candour that he declared that thenceforth he would be his most trusted minister. Joseph asked the King to put him in unfettered charge of the storehouses of the kingdom, so that he could look after the needs of people. The news of Joseph's appointment spread far and wide, and people from every part came to him for grain. His brothers were among those who came in search of food. They did not know of Joseph's real identity, but Joseph recognized them and asked them to bring their youngest brother, Benjamin, who was Joseph's only real brother. He would then, he said, give them the full measure of their requirements, warning them at the same time that if they failed to bring Benjamin, they would get no supplies. They promised to bring Benjamin with them on the assurance that Joseph accepted their money and kept it as a deposit against future sales of grain.

The brothers returned home and told their father what had happened. They begged him to send Benjamin with them, for otherwise they might all have to starve and die of hunger. They promised to take good care of him.

'No', said Jacob angrily. 'How can I trust him with you, knowing what you did to his brother Joseph?' The brothers persisted, pleading with their father to let Benjamin go with them, so that 'we can secure what we need to keep our families alive'. Jacob reluctantly relented, but on one condition: that they would take a solemn oath before God that they would bring Benjamin back unless some dire calamity overtook each one of them. The brothers readily took the oath. Jacob advised them 'not to go to the city through the same gate; each one of you should enter from a different gate.' So they entered the city through different gates and went straight to Joseph.

Joseph was happy to see Benjamin; he called his younger brother aside and informed him that he was his long-lost and only brother; the others were his step-brothers. He told Benjamin that he was deliberately putting the King's drinking-cup into his saddle-bag so that Benjamin could stay back with him. Joseph then directed the attendants to search every visitor since the King's cup was missing. Before doing so a reward was announced: whoever brought the cup back would get a camel-load of corn. The brothers were upset; they told the attendants that they were no thieves, nor had they come to do any wrong. They agreed that whoever was found guilty should be punished.

Everyone was searched, and of course the cup was discovered in the saddle-bag of Benjamin; the brothers told the minister that they were not surprised, as his brother Joseph was also a thief. Little did they realize that the person they were addressing, the King's minister, was none other than Joseph himself. But they were worried about how they would face their father, who had made them take a solemn pledge that they would bring back Benjamin. They pleaded that Benjamin be freed:

> O, powerful minister!
> We have a father
> Old and venerable;
> He will grieve for him.

> Please take one of us
> In his place as a surety.
> Grant us this request,
> For you are most gracious.
>
> (12:78)

But Joseph refused. He told them:

> God forbid that we take
> Someone other than the one
> With whom our property was found.
> That would be against the law,
> And we cannot act wrongfully.
>
> (12:79)

The brothers returned with the grain but without Benjamin. They told their father what their youngest brother had done, but he refused to believe them, saying that it was the evil in their hearts that was the real cause of the trouble. They had done the same with Joseph as they had now done with Benjamin. He scolded them for their lapse but said that he would also bear this loss with fortitude, for he knew the Lord would bring both his sons back and thus unite the family. But he wept so bitterly that his eyes grew weak and weary. He told his sons that God had endowed Joseph with knowledge of which they were not aware. 'Hence,' Jacob said, 'go and search for Joseph and Benjamin. God's spirit is protecting them.'

So the brothers were back in the city once again. They told the King's minister of their father's state of health. 'He is heartbroken; he cried so much that he has lost his eyesight.'

Joseph then revealed his true identity and the reason for keeping Benjamin with him. The brothers felt ashamed of their past conduct and their evil ways. They begged Joseph's forgiveness. Joseph embraced them and said:

> This day let us forget the past
> And let me not reproach you.
> God will forgive you for what you did
> For He is, indeed, Most Merciful.
>
> (12:92)

Joseph asked them not to worry about the condition of their father. 'Take this shirt of mine,' he said, 'place it on his eyes, and he will recover his eyesight. Then all of you — our parents and you, my brothers — come to me, and we will once again be one family and live together.'

The brothers went back and brought their parents to Egypt, where Joseph embraced and welcomed them. He asked them to live with him in safety. He brought his father and mother on to the royal dais, and all of them prostrated before the Lord in gratitude. Joseph reminded his father of his dream, long long ago, and told how it had come true. Then, raising his hands in supplication to God, he prayed, 'O my Lord, you have given me power and taught me to interpret events. I beseech you to guide me to the right path so that I may die in peace and be among the righteous.' He was well aware that all he encountered in life was in fulfilment of God's plan. He told his father:

> God has indeed been
> Good to me all along;
> Even when I was in prison
> It was He who took me out.
> Again He has brought
> All of us back together here.
> Though Satan had sown enmity
> Between me and my brothers,
> God wiped out everything
> And united us in one family.
> Verily, He understands
> The worst of our miseries
> And arranges to remove them,
> For He is Wise and All-Knowing.
>
> (12:100)

THE STORY OF MOSES

A hundred years after the passing away of the Prophet Joseph, the rulers of Egypt passed a decree that a son born to an Israelite parent would be put to death; only daughters would be spared to serve the Copts, the followers of Pharaoh. This was 'a dreadful torment' inflicted on Israelites. During this dreaded era, Moses was born; his mother was, however, commanded by God 'not to cast the child into the river on birth, but to suckle it' till such time as she felt that there was real danger to his life. For about three months she reared him and then she put him in a box and lay it on the river. God promised her that her child would be safe, that he would soon be restored to her, and that he would be made 'one of our apostles'.

The box was carried by the river Nile to the banks close to the palace of Pharaoh. A servant of Pharaoh who was passing by picked up the box and took the child to the Queen. Pharaoh was informed, and he ordered that the child be put to death. But the Queen, who was childless, was enchanted by the baby, for, she said, God had made him 'such a lovely child that the beholder could not but love him'. She beseeched Pharaoh to spare his life.

'Let us adopt him. He will be raised in our palace and would never know that he was an Israelite. He will be one of us and will, in fact, be useful in our fight against the Israelites.'

Pharaoh relented. The Queen took to Moses as a mother would to her own new-born son. But the baby was restless and cried incessantly; no nurse was able to feed him.

Moses' mother, who felt utterly bereft without her child, had asked her ten-year-old daughter to follow the course of her brother's journey in the box, and to keep a watch on him. The little girl did as she was told. She entered the palace after the baby was taken there and managed to get close to the Queen, eventually gaining her confidence. As the child became weak through lack of nourishment, she talked to the Queen of a 'particular' nurse who might be able to suckle the child, to feed him with great affection and to bring him up. 'Thus,' says Allah in the Quran, 'We restored Moses to his mother, so that her eyes might be cooled and she would cease to grieve and would know that Allah's promise was fulfilled.'

Moses grew up in Pharaoh's household under the benevolent care of the Queen. When he reached manhood, Allah 'gave him the power of knowledge and judgement'. Once, while on a visit to the city, he saw two men fighting; one was an Israelite, the other a Copt. The Israelite asked Moses for help, so Moses came to the rescue and struck the Copt forcefully. The Copt collapsed and died instantly. Moses was most perturbed and asked God for forgiveness, saying, 'I shall never come to the help of those committing wrong.' The next morning, the man he had helped again called out for assistance. Moses realized that he was a quarrelsome person and rushed to lay his hands on him.

'Do you intend to kill me as you had killed the man yesterday?' the man shouted. 'Do you wish to become a tyrant in the land?'

Moses prayed to the Lord. 'Oh my Lord, save me from such people who are given to wrongdoing.' Then a man came running and informed Moses that Pharaoh's chiefs were planning to hang Moses and advised him to run away.

So Moses left Egypt in the direction of Madyan, praying to the Lord to guide him to the right path. On reaching the waters of Madyan, he saw a number of men drawing water for their animals, while two women stood by quietly, holding back their animals. Moses asked them why were they waiting. They replied, 'We cannot water our animals until the men have left; that is our misfortune. Our father could not come to draw water for our animals as he is too old.' Moses drew water for both of them, and the women were grateful for his help. One of them went home and informed her father of what Moses had done. The father asked her to fetch Moses so that he might pay him the wages for the work. Moses told the old man the circumstances under which he had had to leave Egypt.

'Have no fear any more,' he assured Moses, 'It is good you have escaped from those wicked people.' He was impressed by Moses and offered one of his daughters in marriage, provided Moses promised to live with them for eight years, or even longer if he so wished. Moses agreed and started his life in Madyan.

After eight years, Moses left with his wife and family. On their journey he saw a fire in the direction of Mount Tur. He made his family halt there, while he ran towards the fire hoping to obtain some information about the neighbourhood, or at least get a burning firebrand to keep his family warm. When Moses reached the spot he heard a voice from above the trees on the right side of the sacred valley.

'What have you in your right hand?' the voice asked.

Bewildered, Moses, replied: 'It is my staff, with which I bring down the leaves for my sheep and do many other things.'

The voice spoke again:

> O Moses, I am the Lord of the Universe.
> Cast down your staff and listen to me.
>
> (20:19)

Moses threw it down, and there before his eyes it became a writhing serpent. The Lord spoke again:

> Draw near it and fear not:
> Now seize the serpent
> And do not be afraid.
> It will become a staff again.
>
> (20:21)

Moses did as he was told. God then asked him to place his right hand into his bosom and to bring it out again; it was shining white and without any stain. God then blessed him with supreme revelations and commanded him to go to Pharaoh and his people and to preach to them the Oneness of God and the glory of righteous conduct.

Moses prayed to God:

> Oh my Lord, enlarge my heart
> And strengthen me by curing my speech
> So that people may understand what I say.
> Also lighten my burden by assigning
> Aaron, my brother, to assist me.
>
> (20:25–32)

The Lord granted his prayer and asked him to proceed with His Signs:

> Go, you, O Moses and your brother,
> With Our Signs to Pharaoh.
> Speak gently to him but make him
> See the truth and fear Us.
>
> (20:43–4)

Moses and Aaron told the Lord that Pharaoh might subject them
to violence, as Moses was wanted by his chiefs for killing one of
their men. The Lord assured them not to have any fear in their
hearts:

> I am with you; I hear and see everything.
> Tell Pharaoh that you are My messengers.
> Ask him to let the Israelites be with you,
> And to torture them no more.
>
> (20:46–7)

Armed with the divine mission and the Book that was sent down
to him which was to be the 'means of enlightenment to the people
and a guidance and mercy to mankind', Moses left for Egypt with
Aaron. They first went to the people and asked them to worship
the true God. Moses showed them His Signs, but the people
dismissed these as 'nothing but false magic' and laughed at him. He
asked them to sacrifice a cow as an offering to God.

'What sort of cow?' they asked him in jest. Moses told them that
God wanted a cow which was neither old nor young but of middle
age.

'What about its colour?' they asked. Moses said it should be deep and
bright yellow. There were several cows of this colour, they told Moses.
He clarified that it should be a cow that was neither yoked nor had
ploughed any field; further, it was to be of sound mind and wholesome body. The people then realized what Moses meant; he wanted
them to kill the golden cow that they and their forefathers had been
worshipping. They asked Moses to first approach Pharaoh, their
King, and if he agreed, they too would follow him. Moses
approached Pharaoh and appealed to him to give up his arrogant and
high and mighty ways and to bow before the Lord, who was
indeed the ruler of the world.

> Purify yourself, O Pharaoh, so that
> I may guide you to the right path.
>
> (29:18)

Pharaoh was furious and asked Moses who was this God of his,
whose messenger he claimed to be. Moses replied:

Our Lord is the one who creates all things;
He gives them form and then guides them.
(20:50)

Pharaoh enquired about the generations that had passed away. Knowledge of them, Moses said, was with God alone. He then asked Pharaoh to look around and see the variety of God's creations – the rain, the wind, the cattle and the plants, all were the signs of His supremacy. Pharaoh asked Moses whether he had any proof of his prophethood; Moses threw down his staff and it became a live serpent. He then drew his hand out of the pocket of his cloak, and it shone with dazzling brightness.

Pharaoh's chiefs said Moses was no more than a magician; they told Pharaoh: 'Call the best of magicians from our cities to counter his magic.' Moses agreed to face them, and the Festival Day was fixed for the event. Two of the best magicians confronted Moses. They threw their ropes and staves at Moses, which turned into serpents and coiled round him. Moses prayed to his Lord for help. The Lord told him not to lose nerve, and commanded:

Throw your staff down and
It will swallow everything
Which they have faked here;
Theirs are only magic-tricks,
What you have is real.
No magician ever thrives,
Whatever he may do
Or wherever he may go.
(20:69)

Moses threw his staff on the ground and it turned into a bigger serpent which swallowed all the other serpents. The magicians were wonderstruck and at once prostrated themselves, declaring that they believed in the God of Moses and Aaron. Pharaoh thundered with rage. 'How dare you do so without my leave?' He warned them that he would cut off their hands and feet on alternate sides and crucify them on the trunks of palm trees if they did not desist from following Moses. The magicians showed no fear and told Pharaoh that he could do what he liked with them but they would not retract from the clear path shown by Moses.

They believed that his God was superior to Pharaoh. They asked for the forgiveness of the Lord for the sins of sorcery that Pharaoh had compelled them to commit.

Pharaoh grew more furious, and decided to wipe out every trace of the teachings of Moses. He issued a proclamation:

> O my people, I am the sovereign of Egypt;
> Even rivers flow beneath my feet.
> Are you to listen to a man
> Who cannot even speak properly?
> If he is really the Almighty's messenger,
> Why is he not loaded with gold
> Or attended upon by angels?
>
> (43:51–3)

Moses warned him that, if he disobeyed his call, 'we have been told by Allah that a grievous punishment awaits you.' But Pharaoh and his men paid no heed to Moses' warning. Thus they were struck by the plague and other diseases; they begged Moses to save them from the scourge. But no sooner were they cured than they went back to the worship of Pharaoh. Two of Pharaoh's chiefs, Qaran and Haman, behaved particularly abominably; greed for wealth and lust for power blinded their vision.

With the passage of time, the attitude of Pharaoh towards Moses worsened: he denounced him publicly and tortured his followers. He declared that there was no other God except he. He told Haman: 'Build me a high tower, so that I may go to the top and find out who this God of Moses was.' He ordered his chiefs to show no mercy to Israelites; they should be driven out of Egypt. A reign of terror was unleashed. As a result, many of Moses' people left him, while only a few remained as his followers. But Moses was not dismayed: he remained steadfast in the pursuit of his faith.

Then God came to Moses' rescue. He was told to gather his followers and take them through the midst of the seas, on a path that would be specially carved for them by God. Pharaoh and his men, fully armed, attempted to pursue them along the same path. As soon as Pharaoh and his men set foot on the path, however, it vanished, and they were drowned in the raging seas.

Israelites then settled in a secure habitation provided with all amenities and comforts. After some time, Moses, accompanied by seventy of his followers, ascended to the heavens to see God, leaving his people in the charge of his brother, Aaron. He bade Aaron to have no dealings with evil-doers and to perform his task with 'an honest heart'. Moses had what the Quran describes as 'a communion with God for thirty nights'. Subsequently, ten more nights were added, to make forty nights in all, which was the appointed time of communication with the Lord.

> When Moses came
> To the appointed place,
> The Lord blessed him.
> Moses prayed: 'O my Lord,
> Let me look at You.'
> The Lord said, 'You cannot see Me
> When I manifest My glory.
> But look upon the mountain;
> If it stays firm in its place,
> Then you shall see Me.
> Now turn towards it.'
> And in an instant
> The mountain crumbled and became dust.
> Seeing this, Moses fell down in a swoon.
>
> (7:143)

When Moses recovered, God enquired: 'Why have you come in such haste to Us?'

'My people have taken to the path shown by You, my Lord,' he replied. 'I have come to seek Your blessings.'

'In your absence your people have gone astray,' God told him. 'They have been misled by a person called al-Samiri.'

Moses was grief-stricken. He begged God to forgive his followers and not to destroy them for their betrayal. God granted his wish and gave him tablets of stone bearing precepts that his people were to follow in order to achieve the best, both on earth and in the hereafter.

Moses returned to earth with a heavy heart and found that, under the guidance of al-Samiri, his followers had begun to worship the image of a calf made out of their ornaments. More in sorrow than in anger, he chided them and asked why they had broken their pledge to him. They said that al-Samiri had asked them to throw their ornaments into a fire, out of which had appeared the effigy of a golden calf which made a lowing sound. They were misled by this and began to worship the calf, believing that it was the God of Moses. Moses asked them if they were so naïve as to think that the calf had life? It could neither hear nor speak, nor do any good or harm to them. Aaron had warned them of the wrong they were doing, but they had insisted that until Moses returned they would continue to worship the calf.

Moses threw down the tablets, telling his people that they were not worthy of them. He dragged Aaron by the hair and asked him why he had flouted his command and not prevented his people from being misled. Aaron replied that the people had become so rebellious that they would have killed him had he tried to restrain them. Besides, he did not want to create a division in their ranks.

Moses asked God to forgive Aaron, and then turned to al-Samiri.

'Begone,' said Moses. 'You will remain an untouchable all your life, and hell shall be your destination.'

Taking the effigy of the calf in his hands, Moses consigned it to the fire, which soon reduced it to ashes. He told the Israelites that he had been chosen as the messenger; God had said to him:

> O Moses! I have chosen you
> In preference to others,
> And entrusted you with the mission
> To convey My words
> As contained in My revelations
> To all the people around,
> And to join the ranks
> Of these who are grateful to Me.
>
> (7:144)

God imparted knowledge to Moses for the good of Israelites, and inscribed on the tablets 'detailed precepts' of faith in His oneness and the code of righteous conduct.

> In the tablets We have ordained
> Laws concerning all matters,

> And We command you
> To hold to them firmly
> And be among those who are faithful
> To the best of the precepts they contain.

> (7:145)

Moses warned his people that those who repudiated God's Signs and the judgement to come were bound to meet their doom; no one would be able to save them then. He also asked them to remember the grace of God, because of which prophets were raised among them and were made rulers. No other people in the world had had such benevolence from the Lord. God had assigned Palestine to them, and so Moses called on his followers to enter this holy land. They hesitated and told Moses: 'How can we? The land is inhabited by mighty people. Until they leave, we cannot possibly enter it.' However, two men among them, who were brave and God-fearing, volunteered. Moses asked God for His direction. He answered:

> To those who have defied your command, O Moses!
> This land is proscribed for forty years.
> They will wander around the world
> But will have no home of their own.
> You need not sorrow over them,
> For that is the fate of rebellious people.

> (5:29)

The Israelites were divided into twelve tribes:

> The Lord commanded Moses
> To strike the rock with his staff.
> No sooner was this done
> Than twelve springs gushed forth.
> Each group then took
> Its own spring to drink,
> And to each the Lord gave
> Shades of clouds as cover
> And manna and quails to eat,
> And all other good things.
> But the unbelievers rebelled

And did not follow the command;
They only harmed themselves.
The Lord is, indeed, above all harm.

(7:160)

THE STORY OF JONAH

Jonah was a simple man who lived in a large town on the shores of
the sea. He was appointed by God to be His messenger and to
preach faith in His unity and virtuous conduct. But the people
jeered at him and paid no heed to his call. Jonah became angry and
lost patience; he was so disgusted with the attitude of his people
that he decided to leave his town and take to the sea. When his ship
was in deep waters, it was rocked by a storm and Jonah was
thrown overboard and swallowed by a big fish. As he lay in the
belly of the fish, Jonah wondered why he was being punished when
God had chosen him to be His messenger; where had he gone
wrong? He then realized that he should not have acted in anger,
because God wished that he be patient and more persuasive. He
prayed for forgiveness and for another opportunity to prove
himself.

Thus did his Lord
Choose him and make him
Of the company
Of the Righteous.

(68:50)

God listened to his prayers and miraculously took him out of the
belly of the fish and cast him, albeit in a sickly condition, upon a
deserted shore. Having recovered in the shadow of a gourd-tree, he
went to the nearby town, where he pursued his mission, this time
with greater persuasion and forbearance and despite all the jeers of
the people, continuing with his work to bring them to the right
path.

God told Jonah:

Had your Lord so wished,
All people everywhere

> Would have been believers.
> But that is not His way,
> Hence do not force anyone
> To take to Our path
> Unless they do so willingly.
> No one can believe
> Except by the will of God;
> Only those who are sceptics
> Do not understand His message.
>
> (10:99–100)

THE STORY OF JOB

Job was the epitome of suffering. He was made a messenger by God not only to preach the true faith revolving around the oneness and supremacy of God, but also to demonstrate how a believer should never lose faith despite all the tribulations he might have to go through in its pursuit. He was asked to take in his hand 'a bundle of rushes to strike with' and under no circumstances 'to go back on the oath' he had taken. He remained steadfast and firm in his commitment to his Creator. He was afflicted with a great deal of pain but he never wavered in his faith in God. Finally, the Lord relieved him and his family of their suffering; they were dying of thirst, when God asked Job to strike the ground and cool water gushed from the earth.

THE STORY OF DAVID

David was a shepherd whom God chose to be not only His messenger but also the King of his people. This came about in a strange way.

After Moses passed away the chiefs of the Israelites approached the aged Prophet Samuel and asked him to appoint a king who would lead them in their fight for the cause of their Lord. Samuel told them he was not convinced they would want to fight Goliath, their powerful enemy. 'How can we not fight him,' they replied, 'when he has driven our people out of their homes and separated parents from their children?'

Samuel, under God's command, appointed Saul as king. The chiefs were not happy with the appointment, but Samuel said that Saul would get them back the Ark which contained the sacred relics of the house of Moses and Aaron and fragments from the divine tablets given to Moses. The chiefs were satisfied and joined the army of Saul.

Saul warned his army that God had commanded them not to drink the water of the river when they halted by it; one could at best take a sip of it. But despite the warning, most of them drank to their fill to quench their thirst. With their bellies full and bloated, they were unable to fight Goliath and his army.

Saul was left with just a few believers who decided to put up a fight against Goliath. David, then a young man with hardly any experience of fighting, was one of those who stood by Saul. He challenged Goliath, who laughed at his audacity. But in the encounter, David slayed Goliath and his men were routed. As a reward for his bravery, David was made the King of the Israelites.

David's rule was just and good; the mountains praised him at sunrise and sunset and the birds sang his praises while in flight. His Kingdom prospered and became strong because of his wisdom and vision. He was given *Zabur*, or the Psalms, and he was in particular charged by God to keep the scales of justice even. As the Quran says:

> O David! God made you
> A viceregent on earth
> So that you may judge properly
> Between men and men
> And not be misled
> By lust within your heart.
> Remember, those who stray
> From the right path
> Will suffer grievous penalty
> When accounts are taken.
>
> (38:26)

Two intruders broke into David's private sanctuary one day, climbing the high walls surrounding it. He was taken aback, but before he could apprehend them, they pleaded with him, for they had come to him, they said, only to get justice. A quarrel had taken place between the two brothers and one had injured the other. They wanted David to decide who was at fault. One of the brothers had ninety-nine ewes, and the other had only one. The former demanded that the latter hand over his ewe; when his brother refused, he overpowered and assaulted him.

David told the injured one that he had been wronged, but life is like that: the strong always oppressed the weak. The oppressors were no doubt in the wrong, and they would be punished by God. He explained that only believers were on the right path, for they feared the wrath of God and thus acted justly.

On another occasion, a herd of sheep belonging to one person had wandered at night into somebody else's field and eaten up the crops. The owner of the field approached David for justice. David's son, Solomon, was with him at that time. David decreed that, as compensation, the owner of the sheep must hand over the sheep to the person who had lost his crops. Solomon disagreed with his father; he said the compensation was not fair. For the loss of just one year's crops, it would not be just for the whole herd of sheep to be handed over. The owner should get back the sheep as soon as the owner of the field had recovered the loss of his harvest. David upheld Solomon's view, because it was, as the Quran points out, based on 'fuller understanding of the matter'.

THE STORY OF SOLOMON

Solomon was the youngest son of David; he succeeded his father, according to some historians, in 965 B.C., almost a thousand years before the birth of Jesus. Like his father before him, Solomon was chosen as God's messenger. The Lord granted him knowledge of the speech of birds and many other bounties, as well as an 'abundance of wealth'. He could harness the winds at his bidding; he could summon up demons and those fettered in chains. His army consisted of men, jinn and birds. As he told his people:

> We have been taught the speech of birds
> And on us God has bestowed knowledge

Of all things in this world.
Indeed, He has been most gracious to us.

(27:16)

One day, while Solomon was passing through the Valley of
Ants, one of the ants, seeing Solomon and his army, cried: 'Get into
your anthills, all you ants, lest you may be crushed unwittingly.' As
Solomon knew their language, he smiled and prayed to God that he
might be guided right, as were his parents. He should be prevented
from committing any wrong and be ever mindful of doing good,
so that God might be pleased with him and take him into the ranks
of 'His righteous servants'.

While inspecting his army of birds once, Solomon found the
hoopoe missing. He was upset and said he would punish the hoopoe
unless it gave good reason for its absence. The hoopoe did not take
long to return. On arrival, it informed Solomon that it had seen a
prosperous kingdom called Sheba, which was ruled by a powerful
queen who possessed a magnificent throne. But neither she nor her
people were rightly guided: they worshipped the sun and not God,
the Lord of the universe.

Solomon promptly despatched the hoopoe with a letter, calling
upon the Queen to take to the true faith and to give up the worship
of everything else except the Creator of all beings. On receiving the
letter, the Queen consulted her council of advisors. She asked
them to give their considered view so that she might take a correct
decision. They told her she was powerful enough not to bow before
anyone, and further that they were prepared at her behest to fight
against Solomon. She pondered for a while: wars, she said, only
resulted in destruction. She would therefore resort to a peaceful
method: she would send a precious gift to the King as a gesture of
goodwill and await his reaction.

Her envoys took the gift to Solomon, who was very angry.

'Do you want to bribe me with this wealth?' he asked. 'God has
given me much more than what your Queen possesses. She will
now have to face our armies and her people will suffer an ignoble
defeat.'

Solomon asked his nobles which of them would be the first to bring the Queen's throne to him. One from among the jinn assured Solomon that before he rose from his seat, the throne would be at his feet. And within the twinkling of an eye, the throne was brought and placed before him. Solomon bowed his head in gratitude to God for the esoteric power with which he was blessed.

Meanwhile, the Queen decided to see Solomon personally. When she came, Solomon asked her whether the throne that she saw in his palace was hers. The queen was dumbfounded, for it did indeed look like hers. Solomon then asked her to enter the palace. At the entrance, there seemed to be a lake. The queen lifted her skirt and bared her legs in an attempt to cross it. But Solomon stopped her, saying that it was no lake: the way was paved with glass, and hence what looked like something was really not. It was a mere reflection in the glass.

Likewise, there was only one reality and that was God. Everything else was an illusion. Hence the Queen should give up the worship of the sun and worship the One who created everything. She understood the significance of Solomon's message and at once embraced the new faith. Such was Solomon's power of persuasion:

> He enjoyed a nearness to God,
> For which he has been granted
> A beautiful abode in the Hereafter.
>
> (38:40)

THE STORY OF ZACHARIAH

Zachariah was very old when God made him His messenger. His wife, who had borne him no children, had also reached an advanced age, and it was no longer possible for her to bear a child.

One day, while praying in the Kaaba, Zachariah beseeched the Lord: 'Please hear my prayer, My Lord! Grant me an offspring. I am a feeble old man. My hair has become snow-white. My wife is forlorn without a child. Both of us yearn for an heir. I am afraid my kinsfolk will harm the cause I have served all my life if I die without an heir.'

When Zachariah finished his supplication, angels descended from above and told him: 'O Zachariah! God has granted your prayer.

You will soon be blessed with a son. He will be called John [Yahya]; he will be a prince among men, chaste and virtuous, and he will be a messenger of God.'

Zachariah prostrated himself before Allah and thanked Him for granting a son to an old man and his barren wife. He declared, 'God does what He wills and so it shall be.' Zachariah then asked the Lord: 'What should I do now?'

'Do not speak to anyone for three days,' the voice replied. 'Convey whatever you have to only by gestures.'

Zachariah followed the instructions faithfully and waited for the happy event. As ordained by God, a lovely son was born to his wife. Zachariah and his wife doted on John. He brought great happiness to his aged parents. When he was still a child, God blessed him with the Book and asked him to hold it 'with all your strength'. John grew up to be straightforward, humble and gentle-mannered. He was loving, caring and compassionate to all creatures; he was especially kind to animals. The Quran refers to him fondly:

> Allah's blessings were upon him
> From the day John was born
> To the day he passed away
> And His blessings will be upon him,
> The day he is raised again.

> (19:15)

THE STORY OF JESUS

When the wife of Imran gave birth to a daughter, she had already vowed to God that her then unborn child would be offered to Him. She was disappointed not to have a male, but the Lord told her, 'We have named her Mary and entrusted her to your care and her seed after her.' From then on, the Lord made Mary grow in purity and beauty, and He assigned her to the care of Zachariah. Whenever Zachariah went to her chambers, he found her well provided with food.

'Who provides you with all this?' asked Zachariah.

'The Lord Almighty,' replied Mary. 'He gives in plenty to whom He pleases.' The angels told her:

> O Mary! God has purified you
> And chosen you above all women.
> Hence worship Him with devotion
> And prostrate yourself before Him.
>
> (3:42–3)

Apart from the fact that Mary had all her needs taken care of, she also had angels attending to her. They informed her that she was the purest of the pure; she had been placed above every woman in the world. One day, they told her that she was to give birth to a son:

> The Lord gives you glad tidings
> That you shall be blessed with the Word.
> His name will be Jesus.
> He will be honoured by Him
> In this world and in the Hereafter
> And he will have his place
> Among the nearest to His Lord.
>
> (3:45)

Mary was taken aback. 'O my Lord,' she asked in bewilderment, 'how shall I bear a son when no man has touched me?'

'It is God's will,' came the reply. 'He creates as He wishes. When he decrees something, He has only to say "Be" and it is done.'

But how would she face the world? The Voice declared, 'Your son is Our responsibility. We will teach him the Scripture, the Torah, the Gospel and the Wisdom, and he shall be Our messenger.' He would be, Mary was assured, 'a sign to humanity and a token of Our mercy'.

As Mary's pregnancy became more evident, she withdrew to a remote spot. When she suffered the pains of labour she cried out to the Lord in anguish. She heard a Voice that came from above a palm tree.

'Be not depressed. We have provided a stream beneath you and fresh ripe dates on the palm tree. Look around and enjoy Our bounties. If anyone accuses you of anything, tell them that you are under an oath to Us and that you will not converse with anyone.'

After the birth of her son, who was named Jesus (Isa), she took him to her family.

'Mary! What have you done?' they rebuked her. 'You are the sister of prophet Aaron. Your father was not a man of evil, nor your mother an unchaste woman.'

The child, from the cradle, spoke to them:

> I am the slave of God.
> The Lord has given me the Book
> And made me His messenger.
> I am blessed by Him wherever I be.
> He has commanded me to worship Him
> And show compassion to all.
> It is my duty to serve my mother
> And not be overbearing or miserable.
> I am blessed now, at my birth,
> And I shall be blessed on my death
> And on my resurrection.
>
> (19:30–33)

On achieving manhood, Jesus went forth among the people and told them:

> Verily, I have come to you
> To show you the path of wisdom
> And make clear to you things
> Which may cause you confusion.
> So listen to me and fear the Lord.
> Fear Him, for He is my Lord and yours;
> Worship Him and be steadfast in your belief.
>
> (43:63–4)

In order to convince them about the truth of his mission, Jesus was endowed by the Lord with powers of life and death; he was asked to tell them:

> I have come to you
> With my Lord's blessings.
> Out of clay, I will shape for you
> The form of a bird;
> And as I breathe on it,
> It will become a bird
> By God's will.
> I will heal the blind

> And the lepers, and bring
> The dead to life
> By God's authority.
>
> (3:49)

Jesus showed in practice what the Lord had endowed him with: he cured the ailing and brought many people to life. He gave eyesight to the blind. He made birds out of clay and breathed life into them. Despite these signs, the people of Israel mocked him and accused him of sorcery. His disciples asked him whether his Lord could send down a table from the heavens so that they could have a feast and thus be assured of a good life ahead; such was their scepticism and their love of hedonism. Jesus warned them to fear the Lord and not be enamoured with the pleasures of this world. The disciples protested that they had asked for the table so that their minds might rest in the knowledge that Jesus had spoken the truth and that they might themselves be witness to the miracle. Jesus then prayed to the Lord:

> O Lord, send us from Above
> A Table spread with food
> So that we may have
> A solemn celebration.
> Provide amply for our sustenance,
> As You are the Supreme Provider for all.
>
> (5:115)

And the Lord granted Jesus his prayer. At the same time He warned that whoever resisted faith in Him would suffer the severest retribution. Jesus told his people:

> O People of the Book!
> Do not indulge in excesses;
> Remain steadfast in truth.
> Resist vain desires
> And do not follow
> People who were in the wrong
> And who strayed from the even path.
>
> (5:80)

Among the disciples of Jesus, only one group stood by him; the rest betrayed him. So God helped the former and made them victorious, while the non-believers suffered chastisement.

The Quran does not endorse the concept of Trinity: Jesus himself repudiates it in one of its verses. He asks Christians to stop associating anyone with God. Allah describes Jesus as 'the son of Mary' and 'Our messenger and Our Word – which We imparted to Mary – and Our Spirit'. The Quran states:

> Proclaim to all:
> God is One.
> He is the only one.
> He is the Eternal.
> He is the Absolute.
> He has begotten none
> And of none has He
>   been begotten.
> There is, indeed, none
> To compare with Him.
>
> (112:1–4)

The Quran also does not accept the Christian belief that Jesus was killed on the cross. It states that he was neither killed nor crucified:

> There are people who boast
> That they killed Jesus Christ,
> The son of Mary and apostle of God;
> But that is not really so
> Though it was made to appear so.
> The truth is that God lifted him up
> And brought him closest to Himself.
> God is, indeed, wise and exalted in power.
>
> (4:157–8)

THE ARRANGEMENT OF THE QURAN

The Quran was revealed to Muhammad piece by piece, depending on the occasion; he then recited these revelations to his followers who learnt them by heart and conveyed them to others. The first revelation came to the Prophet in 610, when he was past forty. It was followed by a series of revelations that were sent down after intervals that were sometimes short and sometimes long. Muhammad continued to receive the revelations until his death in 632. These constitute the whole Quran, which is broadly divided into two parts: (1) the earlier revelations, sent down in Mecca; and (2) the later revelations, which came to the Prophet after his migration to Medina. According to tradition, the Prophet himself divided the revelations into separate surahs, or chapters, of which there are 114. Some are of three to five verses, while some contain more than 200. They are arranged, by and large, in order of decreasing length, the main exception being the first surah, which is of seven verses in the form of a common prayer. The second surah is the longest; from here on, the decreasing order is more or less followed to the end.

The authenticity of this arrangement is borne out by the fact that the Prophet used to recite the whole of the Quran in Ramadan, the month of fasting, during the special night prayer known as *taraveeh*. For this purpose, the Quran was divided into thirty parts, or *juz*, of more or less equal length, so that each part could be recited on one night; the thirty *juz* could thus be completed by the end of Ramadan. Since the faithful recited it loudly together, there could have been no tampering with the text. This arrangement of the Quran has been handed down to successive generations, and so its authenticity is clear.

Each of the 114 surahs contains a certain number of *ayat*, or verses; these are numbered for the sake of reference. Eighty-eight of the surahs were revealed at Mecca and twenty-six in Medina. In the traditional arrangement, the name or title of the surah is given first, then the number of verses it contains, and finally the period of its revelation; no exact date is mentioned, only whether it is Meccan, which means from 610 to 622, or Medinian, which means between 622 and 632. Commentators are, however, of the view that several surahs are composite, containing revelations received at Mecca and at Medina. But most of the surahs were received in full at one place. Accordingly, the following surahs are said to have been received at Mecca:

1, 6, 7, 10, 11, 12, 13, 14, 15, 16, 17, 18, 19, 20, 21, 23, 25, 26, 27, 28, 29, 30, 31, 32, 34, 35, 36, 37, 38, 39, 40, 41, 42, 43, 44, 45, 46, 50, 51, 52, 53, 54, 55, 56, 67, 68, 69, 70, 71, 72, 73, 74, 75, 76, 77, 78, 79, 80, 81, 82, 83, 84, 85, 86, 87, 88, 89, 90, 91, 92, 93, 94, 95, 96, 97, 99, 100, 101, 102, 103, 104, 105, 106, 107, 108, 109, 111 and 112.

And the following were received at Medina:

2, 3, 4, 5, 8, 9, 22, 24, 33, 47, 48, 49, 57, 58, 59, 60, 61, 62, 63, 64, 65, 66, 98, 110, 113 and 114.

Each surah begins with the words (*Bismillah ar-Rehman ar-Rahim* ('In the name of God, the Compassionate, the Merciful'). The only exception is surah 9. Each surah contains a number of verses and each verse is marked by a rhythm or resonance, though there is no fixed meter, either of syllables or stresses. A surah does not deal with a particular subject; it refers to a variety of topics and is a varied combination of parables, stories, injunctions, commandments and invocations. That is the reason why the title of the chapter has hardly any bearing on the contents of the surah. For instance, the surah entitled 'The Bee' has just a passing reference to the bee in verses 68–70. Again, the longest surah, 'The Cow', which deals with a variety of subjects, has little to say about the animal; and 'The Poets' does not refer to them except at the very end, in verse 24. In some cases, two titles are given to one surah – for instance surahs 9, 40 and 41. Thus, the title is not indicative of its contents. The mystery surrounding the titles remains unsolved, even though scholars have advanced various theories. The common perception among Muslims is that they are mystical symbols pregnant with spiritual benediction.

Some critics have attacked the apparently disjointed form in which the surahs are arranged and have criticized what they consider, the 'odd headings', which give no clue to the contents of the surahs. However, a close scrutiny shows that there is a system behind the arrangement. The first surah, called *al-Fatiha*, is in the nature of an invocation; the second surah, commentators agree, is a sort of summary of the teachings and commandments elaborated in the Quran. In subsequent chapters, the themes are expounded with parables and actual current happenings, to fully acquaint the believer with his duties and responsibilities.

The verses are of various kinds. The simplest are the didactic ones; they number about 250 and are found in a number of surahs. In some cases, these are answers to questions, in others they are counter-arguments, and on other occasions they are explanations or clarifications of the fundamentals of the faith. Many a verse begins with the word 'say', for the revelation is a direction to Muhammad to relate to people what God has told him.

Two of the most moving surahs in the Quran are *Ya sin* and *Rahman* (surahs 36 and 55), which convey Allah's merciful and benevolent attributes. But the emphasis throughout the Quran is more on two other qualities of Allah: *tawhid*, or oneness, and *zikr*, or remembrance. These are repeated frequently, and are, indeed, the bedrock of the faith. Next in importance is the theme of the Hereafter, with picturesque descriptions of the pleasures of heaven and the tortures of hell. Other subjects dealt with are man's vice-regency of God on earth, his social, economic, political and administrative problems, matrimonial and other family affairs, and rites and rituals. Stories of the prophets who preceded Muhammad are in different surahs, some of which are named after them. The Quran states 'There is in the stories of our apostles a lesson for men of understanding' (12:111).

The arrangement of the subjects is such that verses on a specific issue are dispersed over various surahs; as shown in the previous chapter, even events from the lives of other prophets are found, as and when necessary, throughout the Quran. They have to be pieced together to obtain a correct and complete picture, whether in respect of the morals to be drawn or the social or legal rules to be obtained.

An eminent commentator, Jalaluddin Sayuti (1445–1505), made an attempt to rearrange the surahs chronologically, but there was no acceptance of it among Muslims. Then, Theodor Noldeke and other orientalists applied a scientific method and tried to put them in chronological order. But their efforts also did not find much favour among the faithful. The traditional order has, therefore, continued to prevail. Some orientalists now accept that trifling with it will create confusion. Thus, the Quranic arrangement, as it has come down from the time of Uthman, has received universal acceptance.

According to the chronological order, the first revelation should have been verses 2–6 of chapter 96 of the traditional order; the last chapter should have been chapter 110 of the traditional order. Surah al-Fatiha, which is the first chapter, should be chapter 7, says Noldeke, while chapter 2, according to Sayuti, should be 86. The comparative table of the chronological and traditional order of the chapters can be found in several translations of the Quran, and also in Richard Bell's classic *Introduction to the Quran*, as revised and enlarged by W. Montgomery Watt.

Some critics have argued that the traditional order is arbitrary and was adopted by Zaid bin Thabit after the death of the Prophet. But as Maududi explains,

Zaid had frequently acted as an amanuensis to the Holy Prophet and was one of those Companions who had learnt the Quran directly from him. Moreover, he was also present on the occasion when the Holy Prophet recited the whole of the completed Quran to angel Gabriel. Arrangements were, therefore, made to collect and gather all the written pieces of the Quran left by the Holy Prophet, and those in the possession of his Companions. Then, with the cooperation of those Companions who had committed the whole or any part of the Quran to memory, word for word, all the written pieces were compared with each other for verification.

Hadrat Zaid would not take down anything in his manuscript unless all the three sources tallied with one another. Thus was compiled one correct, authenticated and complete copy.[1]

As regards the sequence of the surahs, it is well established that Zaid followed the same order as he had learnt from the Prophet. There are a number of well authenticated traditions that show how Muhammad indicated to his Companions where to place a particular verse, which verses were to make up a surah, and how it was to be completed. Detailed instructions were given by the Prophet, which were scrupulously followed. These surahs were then memorized by the Companions and repeated in prayers and during other rituals. Thus the Quran, during the Prophet's lifetime, came to be arranged in a more or less systematic manner and in the order prescribed by him. Hundreds of Muslims memorized these surahs as a religious obligation, and these were passed on from generation to generation. The oral Quran was, therefore, the greatest proof of its authenticity, and it has remained so ever since. Even today, if anyone were to make a mistake in the recitation, other Muslims, hearing him, would instantly correct him.

The reasons for the non-chronological order are given by Maududi:

Though it was to be the Book for all times, it had to be revealed piecemeal in twenty-three years according to the needs and requirements of the different stages through which the Islamic movement was passing. It is obvious that the sequence of the revelations that suited the gradual evolution of the movement could not in any way be suitable after the completion of the Quran. Then, another order, suited to the changed conditions, was needed. In the early stages of the movement, the Quran addressed those people who were totally ignorant of Islam and, therefore, naturally it had first of all to teach them the basic articles of Faith. But after its completion the Quran was primarily concerned with those who had accepted Islam and formed a community for carrying on the work entrusted to it by the Holy Prophet. Obviously, the order of the complete Book had to be different from the chronological order to suit the requirements of the Muslim community for all times. The Quran had, first of all, to acquaint the Muslims thoroughly with their duties concerning the regulation of their lives. It had to prepare them for carrying its message to the outer world which was ignorant of Islam. It had also to warn them of the mischiefs and evils that appeared among the followers of the former Prophets so that they should be on their guard against them. Hence *al-Baqarah* and similar Medinian surahs, and not *al-'Alaq* and similar Meccan surahs, had to be placed in the beginning of the Quran.[2]

It should also be borne in mind that it did not suit the purpose of the Quran that all the surahs dealing with common subjects should be put together. Hence it became essential that the Meccan surahs should be mixed with Medinian surahs; similarly, the earliest Meccan surahs should be placed between those revealed in the later Medinian period, so that the composite picture of Islam emerges.

The shorter Meccan surahs, which come at the end of the Book and have been highly praised by orientalists for their eloquence and spiritual significance, are, in reality, an introduction to the values the Quran preaches. Their emphasis is more on the fundamentals of the faith than the specifics. Consequently, these verses are short and rhythmic, ethereal and poetic; they contain picturesque imagery and cast a spell of serenity and calm on the reader. The Medinian surahs, on the other hand, deal with hard realities of life and are full of injunctions, commandments and admonitions for the observance of laws and regulations by the faithful. Their language is naturally more prosaic and assertive; the mode of speech also changes with varying subjects. In the narration of historical anecdotes it becomes more vigorous as the story develops, with a view to emphasizing the morals that are drawn from it.

As regards the style of the Quran it would be best to quote George Sale's objective description:

The style of the Koran is generally beautiful and fluent, especially where it imitates the prophetic manner and scripture phrases. It is concise and often obscure, adorned with bold figures after the eastern taste, enlivened with florid and sententious expressions, and in many places, especially where the majesty and attributes of God are described, sublime and magnificent.[3]

THE LIFE OF MUHAMMAD:
A CHRONOLOGICAL SURVEY

Muhammad was born on an August Monday, in the year 570, to 570 the Banu Hashim family, which belonged to the tribe of Quraish in Mecca. Banu Hashim were custodians of the Kaaba, the most sacred shrine of the Arabs in the pre-Islamic period. Muhammad's father, Abdullah, died two months before his birth; his grandfather Abdul Muttalib then took care of him. Muttalib was the chief of Banu Hashim and was highly respected, since he had restored and cleaned the ancient spring of *Zam Zam*. Tradition has it that the spring dates back to the time of Abraham.

In accordance with an Arab custom, Muhammad was reared by a Bedouin nurse, Halima, in the desert, and was thus exposed from his infancy to the harsh rigours of nature and the life of the common people.

Muhammad was barely six when his mother, Aminah, died. As 576 the Quran says, he grew up as an orphan 'in miserable circumstances'.

When Muhammad was eight, Abdul Muttalib passed away at the 578 age of eighty-two. Young Muhammad was then taken charge of by his uncle Abu Talib. There was fierce rivalry between the two leading families of the tribe of Quraish, Banu Hashim and Banu Ummaya, with the former enjoying the dominant position. But on the death of Abdul Muttalib, Banu Ummaya gained supremacy over Banu Hashim.

Muhammad received no formal education. As a boy, he tended a 578–
582 flock of sheep and herded cattle.

When he was twelve, Muhammad began accompanying his uncle on trade journeys outside Mecca, particularly to Syria. During one of these trips, he stopped at Busrah, where he met a Nestorian monk, Buhairah, who was the first to notice signs of an enlightened soul in Muhammad.

Muhammad was scrupulously honest in his business dealings. He came to be known as Al-Amin, or the trustworthy. His reputation for integrity brought him an offer to run the business of a rich twice-widowed woman named Khadijah. She offered to marry him. He was then twenty-five and she forty. She bore him four daughters and two sons, but the sons died in their infancy.

One of the important developments in Muhammad's life was his alignment with the Quraish in the latter's fight against another tribe, Qais, which harassed pilgrims at the annual fair at a place called Ukaz on the outskirts of Mecca. The fight between the two tribes, known as the Battle of Fijar, continued year after year, with considerable loss of life and poverty. Eventually, the Quraish won, and at the instance of Zubair, an uncle of Muhammad, an agreement called *Hilf al-Fudul* was reached to prevent further wars. The Quraish then formed a league to safeguard peace in future, to aid victims of oppression and to protect pilgrims from harassment. Muhammad took an active interest in all its activities, although he was not involved in the actual fighting.

A dispute arose between the various Quraish clans over who should place the sacred black stone in the reconstructed Kaaba. Muhammad was asked to intervene. He placed the stone on a sheet of cloth and asked each tribal chief to hold one corner of it and lift the sheet. Together they then carried the stone to the Kaaba. This is an early demonstration of his skill in conciliation.

Muhammad continued to travel extensively to Syria, Yemen and Bahrain for business. But already his interest had begun to shift to the life of the spirit. Often, he would retreat to Mount Hira and meditate, pondering over the mysteries of nature, of life and death, of good and evil. As the Quran later revealed: 'Here in the cave, he often remained for nights, plunged in profoundest thought, deep in communion with the unseen yet all-prevailing God of the Universe.'

One day, in the month of Ramadan, while meditating on Mount Hira, Muhammad received his first revelation from God, communicated by archangel Gabriel. He was utterly shaken. On his return home, however, Khadijah assured him that he had been chosen to serve as the Messenger and declared herself to be his first disciple. She was soon followed by his cousin, Ali, though he was still a teenager, then by Zaid, his freed slave, and then Abu Bakr, his closest friend. They were the first Muslims. Slowly, the message began to spread. It was at that time conveyed in secrecy and privacy, and Muhammad could gather only thirty followers in three years. The Quraish, under the leadership of Abu Sufiyan, who were the custodians of the Kaaba where the idols were placed, were positively hostile to Muhammad and his message. They ridiculed him and his claim to prophethood. They were particularly angered by his denunciation of their idols and his insistence that there was only one God.

610–613

After a lapse of three years, Allah called upon Muhammad to intensify his work: 'O you, Muhammad, wrapped in a mantle! Arise and deliver the warning, and magnify the name of your Lord. And keep your garments free of all stains. And shun all abominations.' He was told clearly to 'Call unto the way of your Lord with wisdom and fair exhortation, and reason with the disbeliever in the best way.' Thus began Muhammad's public preaching of his faith. The Quraish, meanwhile, became increasingly hostile, persecuting the Prophet and his followers. They assaulted him physically, and one of his early disciples, Haris, was killed trying to protect him. They prevented Muhammad from worshipping in the Kaaba, strewed thorns in his path and threw rubbish at him. Street urchins were engaged to harass and abuse his followers. Some of them were brutally beaten up, others were made to lie on burning sand, while some were mercilessly tortured by having heavy boulders and rocks placed on them or a noose put around their necks. Many succumbed to the injuries.

613

Unable to bear the hardships, a group of fifteen Muslims, on the advice of Muhammad, migrated to Abyssinia, where a benign Christian ruler, King Nagus, gave them shelter. This is the first migration (*Hijra*), which is commended in Islam.

613–615

Two years after the first migration, a second group of about a hundred of the persecuted Muslims, led by Jafar, brother of Ali, left for Abyssinia. The Quraish sent a powerful deputation to King Nagus requesting him to deport the emigrants to Mecca. Jafer pleaded:

O King, we were plunged into the depth of ignorance and barbarism; we adored idols; we lived in debauchery; we ate dead animals and we spoke abominations; we disregarded every feeling of humanity, abhorred hospitality and ill-treated our neighbours; we knew no law but that of the strong. Then God raised among us a man whose birth, truthfulness, honesty and purity everyone vouched for. He asked us to believe in the unity of God, and taught us not to associate anyone with Him. He forbade us the worship of idols and enjoined us to speak the truth, to be faithful and merciful, and to respect the rights of our neighbours. He forbade us to speak evil of women, or to defraud the properties of orphans. He ordered us to abstain from evil, to offer prayers, to render alms, to observe fast. We have believed in Him, we have accepted His teachings and injunctions. For this reason, our people have risen against us, persecuted us and asked us to forgo the worship of God and to return to the worship of idols of wood and stone and other abominations. They have tortured us and injured us, until, finding no safety among them, we have come to your country; we hope you will protect us from their oppression.

King Nagus was moved by the plea and declined to deport them. In spite of the persecution of Muslims and the exodus of many of them out of Mecca, Muhammad's mission did not collapse: gradually, it gathered strength. It received an impetus with the conversion of Hamza, an uncle of the Prophet, whose valour was renowned, and that of the powerful Umar, who later became the second caliph. Muhammad gained a number of other important adherents not only from the Quraish but also from neighbouring tribes.

These developments caused great anxiety to the Quraish, who tried to arrive at a compromise with Muhammad, under which they would stop persecuting his followers provided he accepted their three goddesses al-Lat, al-Uzza and Manat as intercessors with Allah. Muhammad refused, and it was then that the 'Satanic Verses' incident occurred, which the pagans took as a gesture of reconciliation. Later, they found that there was no basis for their assumption, and their attitude towards Muslims hardened. They decided to ostracize Abu Talib and his family, who had to take refuge in a valley and suffer considerable hardships. Their women and children had to live for months on leaves and dirty water.

Meanwhile, Khadijah died, followed by Abu Talib. Their loss was a great blow for Muhammad, who felt forlorn and forsaken. The years that followed were the worst for him. His enemies became even more belligerent, and they demanded his head. He repaired to Taif (the biggest town in Arabia after Mecca), to pursue his mission. But its people also scoffed at him, stoned him and drove him out. He returned to Mecca undeterred and carried on with his mission. He gave up preaching to Meccans and concentrated on travellers and pilgrims who came to Mecca.

During the annual pilgrimage, twelve men from Yathrib, belonging to the tribes of Aas and Khazraj, came to Muhammad and became Muslims; they were persuaded by some of their friends who had been converted earlier by the Prophet during their journey to Mecca. The twelve men took a pledge known as the 'First Pledge at Akaba', a place near Mecca. They assured the Prophet that they would accept his teachings unreservedly, that they would adhere to them sincerely and that they would also propagate them among his people. They promised to stand by the Prophet against all odds. Muhammad accepted their pledge and sent some of his Companions to Yathrib to instruct them in the new faith. At this time, God assured Muhammad of His protection, and lifted him, as in a dream, to His presence in the heavens. The Quran refers to Muhammad's *meraj*, or ascension, in mystical terms; according to some commentators it took place a year and a half before his migration to Yathrib.

A year after the first pledge, another seventy persons came to Muhammad and took the pledge, the 'Second Pledge at Akaba', swearing allegiance to him and inviting him to come to Yathrib and pursue his mission unhindered. They told him that they would protect him as they protected their women. The sincere and spontaneous pledges induced the Prophet to despatch some more Companions to Yathrib and to prepare the ground for his migration.

When the Meccans came to know of the move, they were perturbed, and their hostility took a more virulent form. Some of their chiefs, like Abu Jahl, Abu Lahab and Abu Sufiyan, decided to thwart Muhammad's movement by capturing him or assassinating him. They sent word to Abdullah ibn Ubayy in Yathrib that Muhammad and his followers should be thrown out. To carry out their design, the tribal chiefs met at *Darul Nadwah* (the Council Chamber) and agreed to provide one man from each tribe to assault and, if necessary, kill the Prophet while he was asleep. Muhammad learnt of the plot well in time and was able to frustrate it. Accompanied by Abu Bakr, he went secretly to Mount Thaur. Meccans scoured the whole area, but to no avail. Muhammad and Abu Bakr hid in a cave for a few days and then proceeded on a long, tiring journey to a place called Quba, arriving on 20 September. There they built the first mosque of Islam. Muhammad and his followers entered Yathrib on 24 September. From this date, the Islamic calendar, known as the *Hijra* calendar, commences.

Many of the Prophet's Companions had already preceded him, and many more followed him. At last, they felt a sense of relief. After suffering at the hands of the Quraish in Mecca for thirteen long years, they were finally able to live as free men among friendly people. The event, therefore, has great significance in Muslim annals. The word Hijra does not mean 'flight', though it is often translated as such; it means departure, or separation from one's dwelling.

On his arrival in Yathrib, Muhammad told the people: 'I am neither desirious of riches nor ambitious of dignity or dominion; I am sent by God, who has ordained me to announce glad tidings unto you. I bring you the Word of my Lord: I admonish you. If you accept the message, God will be favourable to you, both in this world and in the next; if you reject my admonitions, I shall be patient, and leave God to judge between you and me.' As a result, they gave up their licentious ways, their drunken orgies and their life of fraud and deception.

Muhammad imposed upon them discipline in the shape of prayers, fasting, alms-giving and continence, and called upon them to refrain from avarice, slander, falsehood, indecency and other vices which had permeated their society. A spirit of brotherhood was inculcated among Meccan emigrants and natives who were new converts to Islam. The religious bond proved more powerful than tribal affiliations: ancient rivalry between the tribes of Aas and Khazraj was eliminated, the two groups uniting under the banner of Islam. They were given the honorific name of *ansar* (helpers). The emigrants, forty-five in number, were called *muhajirun* (emigrants). They lived and worked together; they helped one another. In the building of the mosque at Yathrib, each one contributed, and even the Prophet himself laid bricks. It was a simple, unostentatious structure, built with unbaked bricks and erected on trunks of palm trees with a thatch of palm leaves serving as the roof. A few rooms were constructed adjoining the mosque, in which the Prophet and his wives lived. His followers, both *muhajirun* and *ansar*, gratefully changed the name of the city to Medinatun Nabi (City of the Prophet), or simply Medina.

Soon after settling in Medina, Muhammad called upon Jews and pagans to join him and his followers in establishing a welfare state, where everyone would be equal before the law and enjoy equal rights, provided everyone carried out his obligations to defend the city. He incorporated these assurances in a document that came to be known as the 'Constitution of Medina'. It knit Muslims, Jews and pagans into one state and a single community, with Muhammad as the sole judge or arbitrator of their disputes. Though Jews and pagans were party to it, they did not honour its terms. They joined hands with the Quraish in its attacks on the Prophet and the Muslims. They also worked with *munafiqun*, the hypocrites and pagans who pretended to be Muslims. Their leader, Abdullah ibn Ubayy, committed acts of treachery against Muslims. He was very close to Jews, whose interests he often protected. However, despite the pact, Jews and hypocrites started harassing Muslims. They did not like the rise of Muhammad as the undisputed leader.

One of the most powerful chiefs of the Jews, Karz bin Jabir Fahri, organized raids on the outskirts of Medina, and destroyed fruit-bearing trees and stole flocks of sheep belonging to Muslims. Subsequently, Jews and hypocrites established contacts with Meccans, and assured them of their help in the case of an attack on Muslims. Already, the Quraish had warned Abdullah ibn Ubayy, 'You have given shelter to our man. You should either kill him, or turn him out of Medina, or we swear that we will attack you, kill all the males, and capture and enjoy your women.' Ubayy assured them that he was no friend of Muhammad. The Prophet, therefore, sent reconnoitring parties to keep a watch on enemy movements. One such party of twelve people, led by Abdullah, was despatched to Nakhla, a spot between Taif and Mecca, with orders in a sealed envelope to be opened two days after they reached Nakhla.

But Abdullah spotted a group of Meccans whom he suspected of being spies; without waiting for the expiry of the two days he killed one of them. In doing so, he had disregarded the Prophet's instruction; Muhammad was annoyed. Soon after, Abu Sufiyan passed through Nakhla with his caravan. He heard of the incident, which had already been reported to Abu Jahl in Mecca. The latter proceded towards Medina with a thousand armed men to avenge the death of their comrade. On learning of their arrival, Muhammad organized a defence force that consisted of barely 313 ill-equipped men, with two horses and seventy camels.

Under his instructions, these men camped at Badr, a place about eighty miles from Medina. The two sides fought a pitched battle. The Prophet prayed for God's help: 'O Lord, if this little band were to perish, there will be none to offer unto you pure worship.' The Muslims succeeded against heavy odds and drove back the Meccans, killing seventy of their men, who included Abu Jahl and other notable chiefs. The Muslims lost only fourteen men and took a number of Meccans as prisoners, including the Prophet's son-in-law Abdul Asa, his uncle Abbas, Ali's brother Aqil, Abu Bakr's son and Umar's uncle.

Sir William Muir, one of the most hostile biographers of the Prophet, observes, 'In pursuance of Mahomet's command, the citizens of Medina and such of the refugees as possessed houses received the prisoners and treated them with much consideration.' He quoted a prisoner who vouched that 'the men of Medina made us ride, while they themselves walked, they gave us wheaten bread to eat when there was little of it, contenting themselves with dates.' The more affluent of the prisoners paid ransom and were set free. The others were asked to teach ten children each and this was treated as their ransom.

Shortly after the battle, Ali married Muhammad's youngest daughter, Fatimah. From this union there were two sons, Hasan and Husain. This filial connection later led to the birth of a separate sect in Islam, whose adherents came to be known as Shias, as against the rest, who are called Sunnis.

Despite their pact with the Prophet, Jews did not support Muslims in the defence of Medina; Banu Qaynuqa, their most powerful tribe, 'attempted sedition during the Battle of Badr', according to the historian Ibn Saad. Their relationship was further worsened by an incident that occurred there. A Jewish shopkeeper tried to molest a veiled Muslim woman, who cried for help. A Muslim youth rushed to her rescue, and in the altercation the Jew was killed. The Jews standing nearby killed the Muslim. The Prophet, when informed about it, remonstrated with the leaders of Banu Qaynuqa, to whom these Jews belonged, but to no avail. The two sides fought. The Muslims laid siege to the Jewish fortress and did not allow any provisions to reach them. After fifteen days, the Jews surrendered and sued for peace; Muhammad ordered Banu Qaynuqa to leave Medina with their possessions.

624

Hardly had the Prophet subdued the Jewish insurgency than he learnt that the Quraish, with three thousand fully armed men, were marching towards Medina. They camped at a vantage point in the hills of Uhud, a short distance to the north of Medina. Muhammad asked other Jewish tribes for help, but they refused. Their sympathies were with Abu Sufiyan and the Meccans. Likewise, the chief of the *munafiqun*, Abdullah ibn Ubayy, who had at first provided Muhammad with 300 men, withdrew them at the last moment. The Prophet could enlist only 700 men. Of them, only a hundred wore mail. He could obtain only two horses.

625

Muhammad had to contend with trouble within his own ranks as well. He had to resolve acute differences between his Companions and the younger followers in regard to military strategy. Then there was the betrayal by Jews and *munafiqun*, who acted as a fifth column for the Quraish. His force was also only one third of that of the enemy. Nevertheless, his exemplary leadership kept up the spirit of his men. He ordered them to take up positions below the hill, and put them in different formations. Fifty archers were posted, under Abdullah ibn Jabir, at a pass on the hill to watch the movement of forces from the rear. In the fight, the Meccans paid a heavy toll; stiff resistance by the Muslims resulted in disorder in their ranks.

At this stage, instead of consolidating their gains, some Muslims started gathering booty. Seeing this, the fifty archers also left their post and joined in the division of spoils. Khalid bin Walid, a great general on the Meccan side, seized the opportunity and launched an attack from the rear. The Muslims were taken aback. Consternation broke out among them, and the Meccan forces forged ahead. A cry was heard that the Prophet had been killed, causing further confusion and dismay among Muslims. Omar threw away his sword and cried that it was useless to continue fighting when the Prophet was no more. Though the report was false – Muhammad was only injured – the damage to the morale of his men had been done. The Quraish pushed forward from all sides, and although the Muslims put up strong resistance, they lost the battle.

The Meccans were, however, too exhausted to invade Medina. They returned to Mecca, declaring that they would be back the following year to take over Medina.

626   Encouraged by the Meccans' victory at Uhud and the treachery of Abdullah ibn Ubayy, the Jewish tribe of Banu Nadir plotted to kill the Prophet. They were determined to avenge the banishment of their sister tribe, Banu Qaynuqa. The Muslims learnt about the plot and laid siege to their fortress. It was lifted after seven days when the Jews surrendered. Like Banu Qaynuqa, they were also exiled by Muhammad but, except for weapons of war, they were allowed to take away all their possessions. They left Medina and took refuge in Khaibar.

627   The tales of woe of Banu Nadir provided their co-religionists with enough provocation to prepare for the final onslaught on the Muslims. They contacted the Meccans and sent emissaries to a

number of neighbouring tribes. Banu Ghaftan and Banu Asad responded readily. A strong coalition of all these people was formed, and a force of ten thousand soldiers encircled Medina under the command of the Quraish chief Abu Sufiyan. The Muslims were, however, fully prepared to thwart the attempts of the enemy, referred to in the Quran as *al-Ahzab*, or 'the confederates'. The Muslims had dug deep trenches to the north, on the sloping, open approach to the city. This was suggested by one of the Companions, Salman Farsi, the Persian, who had studied the strategy adopted by Sassanid rulers. It completely nonplussed the Meccans; they could not use the other sides as these were strewn with blocks of lava. After some skirmishes, the Meccans retreated and the 'War of the Trenches' came to an end. With this, Muhammad's position became stronger than ever before.

In view of the overt and covert help that Banu Qurayzah had given to the invading forces, the Muslims were furious with them. So, as soon as the threat to their city was dealt with, the Muslims attacked the fortress in which Banu Qurayzah lived. The Jews fought back but finally surrendered. They pleaded that their fate be decided by Sa'ad ibn Maa'z, chief of Aas, who was their close associate. The Prophet accepted their plea. Sa'ad gave his verdict on the basis of a directive in the Old Testament that all traitors should be put to death. The Muslims, it is said, carried out the verdict, although this has been disputed by several historians.

Having won some respite from wars, the Prophet decided to perform the pilgrimage to the Kaaba; due to the hostility of the Meccans, he and his followers had long been prevented from doing so. He gathered 1400 of his followers, directing them not to carry any arms other than their swords. He put on the *ahram*, a pilgrim's ceremonial robe. A number of camels were also taken for sacrifice. Muhammad then sent an envoy to the leaders of the Quraish to obtain their permission. They refused, and instead they organized a force to prevent the Muslims from entering Mecca. The Muslims set forth on their journey regardless, and set up camp at Hudaibiyah, a few miles from Mecca. Muhammad then sent another envoy to Mecca to assure their chiefs that he and his followers had not come

628

to fight but to perform the pilgrimage. After some hesitation, the Meccans agreed to negotiate with Muhammad and signed a treaty which came to be known as the 'Treaty of Hudaibiyah'. Its terms were:

1. that the Muslims would return to Medina that year without performing the pilgrimage to the Kaaba;
2. that the pagans would, however, allow them to do so the next year, provided their stay in Mecca did not exceed three days;
3. that Muslims would not bring any arms with them;
4. that no Muslim residing in Mecca would migrate to Medina, but if any migrant in Medina wished to return to Mecca, he would not be prevented;
5. that pagans visiting Medina would be permitted to return to Mecca, but Muslims visiting Mecca would not be allowed to return;
6. that tribes were at liberty to join any of the two contracting parties.

Many of the Companions were unhappy about the terms. They felt that they had almost surrendered to the pagans. The most humiliating part was the loss of face, as pilgrims had to return without performing the rites. But the Prophet advised caution. He saw in the treaty the flowering of Islam, and subsequent events proved him right. It also gave him the much needed peace to pursue his mission. On his return to Medina, he sent his envoys with letters to a number of rulers, notably Hercules, Emperor of Greece, Khusru Parviz of Persia, the kings of Egypt and Abyssinia and the chiefs of Yamama and Syria, inviting them to join the fold of Islam.

629　　One of the minor rulers to whom such a letter was sent was Sharhbil, a satrap of the Byzantine emperor. Instead of replying to it, Sharhbil tortured and killed the envoy. The Prophet was shocked to hear the news, and his Companions prevailed upon him to avenge the dishonour. A force of 3000 was therefore despatched under the command of Zayd bin Harith. It included many other notable warriors, like Ali's brother, Jafar, and Khalid bin Walid.

They encountered the much bigger and better equipped Byzantine force at a village called Muta, having travelled through Syria on a long and arduous journey. Zayd and Jafar were fatally wounded. Eventually, Khalid bin Walid took command, and by adopting a clever strategy brought about a ceasefire. The Byzantine soldiers were also tired; they did not press further and Khalid was able to retreat. The return of the beleaguered force created much disappointment in Medina; many Companions nicknamed the returning fighters 'runaways', but Muhammad hailed them, saying they were the 'real battlers'.

Meanwhile, many of the Jewish tribes, who had become openly hostile to Muslims and had settled at Khaibar, eight miles from Medina, began to conspire against Muhammad. They contacted neighbouring tribes and with their support decided to invade the city. Their chief, Usir bin Razam, incited the excitable Ghatfan; they went out and killed a herdsman and twenty camels, which belonged to the Prophet. Worse still, they took his wife as a prisoner. This served as a signal for the Battle of Khaibar. The battle raged for days, with the Muslims finally inflicting a decisive blow on the Jews and their allies. A treaty was then signed under which the Muslims allowed the Jews to keep their lands and possessions but asked them to give up their weapons. They were, however, required to pay a tax equivalent to half the produce of their lands. Later, after a lapse of a few months, in accordance with the Treaty of Hudaibiyah, the Prophet, accompanied by over 2000 Muslims, left for Mecca to perform the pilgrimage. The Quraish did not want any contact with them. They left their homes and watched the Muslims from camps pitched on the heights of the surrounding hills. Muhammad and his followers carried out their religious rites, and after a three day sojourn returned to Medina.

Banu Khuza'a, aligned with Muslims under the Treaty of Hudaibiyah, were attacked without any provocation by Banu Bakr, who were aligned with the Quraish. Banu Khuza'a demanded protection from the Prophet. He sent an emissary to the Quraish and asked them to agree to any of the following terms:

1. reparations to be paid for the massacred people of Banu Khuza'a; or
2. the Quraish break their alliance with the Banu Bakr; or
3. abrogation of the Treaty of Hudaibiyah.

The Quraish abrogated the treaty; this was a signal for war. The Prophet marched with 10,000 fully armed men and camped at a short distance from Mecca. The Meccans sent a few scouts, including Abu Sufiyan, to find out the real strength of the Muslim army. Abu Sufiyan was caught, but the Prophet freed him. He returned and advised surrender; the Meccans laid down their arms and the Prophet entered Mecca as a victor.

Clearing the Kaaba of idols, Muhammad declared: 'There is no god but God. He has no partners. He has fulfilled His promise and helped His slave and defeated all coalitions against Him. His is the final authority. There will be no revenge and no blood reparations. The guardianship of the Kaaba is secured; arrangements for supply of water to pilgrims will be free.'

Then, addressing the Quraish, he advised them to give up the arrogance of their heathen days and the pride of their ancestry. He reminded them that mankind descended from Adam and Adam was made of clay.

'Descendants of Quraish,' he then asked, 'how do you think I should act towards you?'

'With kindness and pity, gracious brother and nephew,' they beseeched.

The Prophet replied, 'I shall speak to you as Joseph spoke unto his brothers: "I shall not reproach you today; God will forgive you." He is the Most Merciful and the Most Compassionate.'

In his hour of supreme triumph, Muhammad did not allow a house to be plundered or a woman to be molested. He told the Muslims that everyone who joined their fold, irrespective of the past, was a brother. He issued a general amnesty and, except for four people guilty of treason, all were pardoned.

However, Muhammad's troubles were still not over; the tribes of Hawazin and Thakif rebelled and attacked the Muslims at Hunain, about ten miles from Mecca. The Muslims fought back and routed the rebels. With this, the last nail in the coffin of paganism had been struck, and the whole of Arabia embraced Islam.

Outside, there was some trouble, when the Roman Emperor suddenly decided to send a large force to invade Arabia. To counter it,
the Prophet hastily collected 30,000 volunteers with 10,000 horses.
In spite of severe famine in the provinces of Najd and Hijaz, he
marched to Tabouk, a place midway between Medina and Damas-
cus. The Roman forces, however, turned back, perhaps exhausted
by the heat. Muhammad waited at Tabouk for almost a month and
then returned to Medina. As a result, the Prophet's prestige was
much enhanced, and a large number of deputations representing
tribes from Yemen and other far-away regions came to Medina,
paid homage to Muhammad and accepted Islam.

The Prophet had a premonition of his approaching end; he
therefore decided to go on a pilgrimage to the Kaaba, described in
Muslim annals as the 'Farewell Pilgrimage'.

More than 100,000 Muslims accompanied him. After completing
the rites, he addressed the assembled gathering from the top of a
hill, Jabal-ul-Arafat, on 7 March 632, and emphasized the egalitarian
character of the brotherhood. He then informed Muslims of the
revelation that proved to be the last. It proclaimed to the faithful:
'This day, O Believers! I have perfected for you your religion and
completed My favour unto you, and have chosen for you Islam as
your religion.'

The Prophet then left for Medina. On the way, he halted at a place
called Khum, where he told his Companions: 'All praise to God, O
people! I am a human being. It may be that the angel of death may
visit me soon and death may overtake me. I leave in your midst,
however, two things – the Revelation of God in which is light and
guidance; you hold to it tightly. And the other is my family.'

Muhammad spent the remaining months of his life in Medina.
Though tired and exhausted, he worked ceaselessly to organize
the community, to settle the affairs of state, to sort out problems
between various tribes and groups, and to put the state on a
sound footing. He paid special attention to the young, to the
teaching of the Quran to them and to other aspects of their
education. He often visited the public graveyard to invoke God's
blessings and forgiveness for all those who died in the cause of
Islam. One day, while returning from one of these visits, he fell ill.

He did not rest and continued with his work, leading prayers in the mosque.

As his condition deteriorated, he had to be confined to bed. His youngest wife, Aisha, was in attendance; she tended him with great care. He told her to distribute among the poor the few gold coins that were lying in the house.

The end came at noon on Monday, 8 June 632.

NOTES

PART I

Introduction: The Prophet's Mission

1. Gibb, H. A. R., *Islam*, London, 1975, p. 25.
2. Iqbal, Muhammad, *The Reconstruction of Religious Thought in Islam*, Lahore, 1971, p. 126.
3. Wells, H. G., *The Outline of History*, London, 1956, pp. 613–14.
4. Smith, Wilfred Cantwell, *Modern Islam in India*, Lahore, 1947, p. 24.
5. Muslim, Abul Husain, *Sahih Muslim* (rendered from the Arabic into English by Abdul Hamid Siddiqi), Lahore, 1975, Vol. IV, p. 1259.
6. Hitti, Philip K., *History of the Arabs*, New York, 1973, p. 111.
7. Reade, Winwood, *The Martyrdom of Man*, London, 1932, p. 219.
8. Ibn Khaldun, *The Muqaddimah* (translated from the Arabic into English by Franz Rosenthal), New York, 1967, Vol. 1, pp. 6–7.
9. Muir, Sir William, *Life of Mahomet*, London, 1877, pp. 88–9.
10. Rodinson, Maxime, *Mohammed* (translated into English from the French by Anne Carter), London, 1971, p. 106.
11. Watt, W. Montgomery, *Bell's Introduction to the Qur'an*, Edinburgh, 1970, p. 56.
12. Maududi, Maulana Abul 'ala, *Tafheemul Quran* (Arabic text with Urdu translation), New Delhi, 1978, Vol. III, p. 241.
13. *Ibid.* p. 242.
14. *Ibid.* pp. 243–4.
15. *Ibid.* p. 244.
16. Cragg, Kenneth, *The Event of the Qur'an*, London, 1971, p. 144.
17. Andrae, Tor, *Mohammed: The Man and His Faith*, London, 1956, pp. 19–20.
18. Djait, Hichem, *Europe and Islam*, Berkeley, 1985, p. 13.

19. Gabrieli, Francesco, *Muhammad and the Conquests of Islam*, Italy, 1977, pp. 12–13.
20. *Ibid.* pp. 14–15.
21. Carlyle, Thomas, *On Heroes, Hero-Worship and the Heroic in History*, Oxford, 1935, p. 57.
22. *Ibid.* p. 58.
23. *Ibid.* p. 74.

Wars and Encounters

1. Shaw, George Bernard, *The Prefaces*, London, 1938, p. 540.
2. Lewis, Bernard, *Islam in History*, London, 1973, p. 18.
3. Sale, George, *The Koran* (English translation with notes and an introduction by Sir Edward Denison Ross), London, n.d., p. vii.
4. Iqbal, Muhammad, *Poems from Iqbal* (translated from the Urdu into English by V. G. Kiernan), London, 1955, pp. 52–3.
5. Arnold, T. W., *The Preaching of Islam*, London, 1913, p. 5.
6. Ali, Syed Ameer, *The Spirit of Islam*, London, 1952, p. 59.
7. *Ibid.* p. 273.
8. Watt, W. Montgomery, *Muhammed: Prophet and Statesman*, Oxford 1961, p. 114.
9. Quoted by Barakat Ahmad in his book *Muhammad and the Jews*, New Delhi, 1979, p. 62.
10. Guillaume, A., *The Life of Muhammad* (translation of Ishaq's *Sirat Rasul Allah*), London, 1955, pp. 231–2.
11. *Ibid.* p. 233.
12. Ahmad, Barakat, *Muhammad and the Jews*, op. cit. p. 24.
13. Quoted from Israel Welphenson's *Tarikh al-Yahud fi Bilad* by S. Abul Hasan Ali Nadvi, in his book *Muhammad Rasulullah*, Lucknow, 1982, p. 301.
14. *Encyclopaedia Britannica: Macropaedia*, Chicago, 1974, Vol. 15, p. 600.
15. Lammens, H., *Islam: Beliefs and Institutions*, London, 1968, p. 31.
16. Irving, Washington, *Life of Mahomet*, London, 1915, p. 238.

Muhammad's Wives

1. Muir, Sir William, *Life of Mahomet*, London, 1877, p. 300.
2. Watt, W. Montgomery, *Muhammad at Medina*, Oxford, 1956, p. 329.
3. Carlyle, Thomas, *On Heroes, Hero-Worship and the Heroic in History*, Oxford, 1935, p. 93.

4. Quoted by Fida Hussain Malik in his book, *Wives of the Prophet*, Bombay, 1989, p. 124.

5. Quoted from *Sahi al-Bukhari* by Shibli Nu'mani in his work *Seeratun Nabi* (Urdu text), Vol. II, Azamgarh, 1963, p. 410.

6. Muir, Sir William, op. cit. p. 440.

7. Haykal, Muhammad Husayn, *The Life of Muhammad*, USA, 1976, p. 376.

8. Hitti, Philip K., *History of the Arabs*, New York, 1973, p. 120.

9. Watt, W. Montgomery, op. cit., p. 332.

10. Khalifa, Rashad, *Quran, Hadith and Islam*, Tucson, 1982, Preface.

11. Bodley, R. V. C., *The Messenger: The Life of Muhammad*, London, 1946, p. 203.

12. Quoted by Emile Dermenghem in his book *Muhammad and the Islamic Tradition* (translated from the French into English by Jean M. Watt), New York, 1981, p. 129.

PART II

The Quran: An Explanatory Statement

1. Farah, Caesar E., *Islam: Beliefs and Observances*, New York, 1970, pp. 6–7.

2. Maududi, Maulana Abul 'ala, *Tafheemul Quran* (Arabic text with Urdu translation), Delhi, 1978, Vol. I, p. 234.

3. Quoted by Kenneth W. Morgan in his book *Islam: The Straight Path*, Delhi, 1987, p. 88.

4. Azad, Abul Kalam, *Tarjumanul Quran* (text with Urdu translation and commentary), Delhi, 1966, Vol. II, p. 276.

5. Rumi, Jalaluddin, *Gazliyat-e-Shor Angez-e-Shams Tabrizi* (Persian text); Selections by Fereidookar, Tehran, n.d., p. 333. Also see Rumi's *Diwan-e-Shams Tabriz*, Lahore, n.d., p. 546.

6. Ghazzali, Abu Hamid, *Mishkat al-Anwar* (translated from the Arabic into English by W. H. T. Gairdner), London, 1924, p. 52.

7. Grunebaum, G. E. von, *Islam*, London, 1955, pp. 91–2.

8. Coulson, N. J., *A History of Islamic Law*, Edinburgh, 1971, p. 12.

9. Palmer, E. H., *The Quran* (translated into English and published in the series, *The Sacred Books of the East*), Oxford, 1900, Part I, p. x.

10. *Shorter Encyclopedia of Islam*, Leiden (Holland), 1965, p. 413.

11. Ali, Abdullah Yusuf, *The Holy Quran* (Arabic text with English translation and commentary), Beirut, 1968, p. iii.

12. Rahman, Fazlur, *Islam and Modernity*, Chicago, 1984, p. 19.

13. Hakim, Khalifa Abdul, *Islamic Ideology*, Lahore, 1961, pp. 132–3.

14. *Ibid*. p. 133, quoted from *Sahi Bukhari*.

15. Danner, Victor, *The Islamic Tradition: An Introduction*, New York, 1988, pp. 76–7.

16. Singh, Khushwant, *Complaint and Answer* (English translation of Urdu poem: Iqbal's *Jawab-i-Shikwa*), Delhi, 1981, p. 96.

17. Bell, Richard, *Introduction to the Qur'an*, Edinburgh, 1953, p. 1.

Summaries of Chapters and Selected Verses

1. Qutb, Sayyid, *In the Shade of the Quran* (translated from the Arabic into English), London, 1979, p. 33.

PART III

The Arrangement of the Quran

1. Maududi, Maulana Abul 'ala, *The Meaning of the Quran* (translated from the Urdu into English), Delhi, 1973, Vol. I, p. 18.

2. *Ibid*. pp. 16–17.

3. Sale, George, *The Koran* (translated into English from the original Arabic), London, n.d., p. 48.

BIBLIOGRAPHY

(A) THE QURAN

Adil, Hafiz M., *Introduction to Qur'an*, New Delhi, 1983.

Ahmad, Barakat, *Introduction to Quranic Script*, London, 1985.

Ahmad, Nisar, *The Fundamental Teachings of Quran and Hadith*, Bombay, 1984.

Ali, Abdullah Yusuf, *The Holy Qur'an* (translated into English with notes and commentary), Beirut, 1968.

Ali, Ahmed, *Al-Qur'an* (Arabic text with translation into contemporary English), Bombay, 1987.

Amir-Ali, Hashim, *The Message of the Quran* (Arabic text with English translation and notes), Tokyo, 1974.

Arberry, A. J., *The Koran Interpreted* (English translation), London, 1980.

Ayoub, Mahmoud M., *The Qur'an and its Interpreters: Vol. 1*, New York, 1984.

Azad, Abul Kalam, *Tarjumanul Quran* (Arabic text with Urdu translation and commentary), 4 Vols., Delhi, 1964–70.

Bell, Richard, *Introduction to the Qur'an*, Edinburgh, 1953.

Bhave, Vinoba, *The Essence of Quran* (English translation of selected verses, arranged according to subject), Varanasi, 1963.

Clair-Tisdall, *The Sources of Islam* (translated and abridged by Sir William Muir), New Delhi, 1973.

Cragg, Kenneth, *Readings in the Quran* (selected and translated into English with an introductory essay), London, 1988.
  The Event of the Qur'an, London, 1971.

Daryabadi, Abdul Majid, *Tafsir Ul-Qur'an* (English translation with notes and commentary), 4 Vols., Lucknow, 1981–5.

Dawood, N. J., *The Koran* (English translation), London, 5th edn, 1990.

El-Fandy, Muhammad Jamaluddin, *On Cosmic Verses in the Qur'an* (English translation by Ismail Cashmiry), Cairo, 1961.

Haeri, Shaykh Fadhlalla, *Beams of Illumination from the Divine Revelation* (English translation of the last section, *Juz 'Amma*, of the Quran), London, 1985.

Man in the Qur'an and the Meaning of Furqan, USA, n.d.

Husain, Athar S., *The Message of Quran*, Lucknow, 1975.

Irving, T. B. et al., *The Qur'an: Basic Teachings* (an anthology of selected verses translated into English and arranged according to subject), Leicester, 1979.

Jung, Nizamat, *An Approach to the Study of the Quran*, Lahore, 1973.

Khalifa, Rashad, *Quran, Hadith and Islam*, Tucson, 1982.

Khan, Ghulam Mustafa, *Matalibul Quran* (summaries of the 114 surahs of the Quran in Urdu), Bombay, n.d.

Khan, Muhammad Zafrullah, *The Quran* (Arabic text with English translation), Bombay, n.d.

Khan, Syed Ahmad, *Khutbaat-ul-Ahmadiya* (Urdu text), Karachi, 1964.

Latif, Sayed Abdul, *Al-Quran* (English translation), Hyderabad, 1969.

Maududi, Maulana Abul 'ala, *Tafheemul Quran* (Arabic text with Urdu translation, notes and commentary), 6 Vols., New Delhi, 1978–89.

Merchant, M. M., *Quranic Laws* (a treatise with Quranic text and English translation of laws as expounded in the Quran), New Delhi, 1981.

Mercier, Henry, *The Koran* (English translation from the French of selected verses by Lucien Tremlett), London, 1975.

Mirza, Abu'l-Fazl, *The Koran* (English translation), Bombay, 1955.

Muhammad, Munawwar, *Iqbal and Quranic Wisdom*, New Delhi, 1987.

Muir, William, *Extracts from the Coran* (English translation of selected verses), London, 1885.

The Beacon of Truth (English translation of selected verses with commentary), London, 1894.

Niazi, Kausar, *Towards Understanding the Quran*, Lahore, 1975.

Palmer, E. H., *The Quran* (English translation), 2 Vols., Oxford, 1900.

Penrice, John, *A Dictionary and Glossary of the Koran*, London, 1971.

Pickthall, Marmaduke, *The Meaning of the Glorious Qur'an* (Arabic text with English translation), Delhi, 1983.

Quranic Advices (Urdu text by Jallendhri Fateh Mohammed), New Delhi, 1984.

Qutb, Sayyid, *Fi Zilal ul Quran* (Arabic text and commentary with Urdu translation by Sayyid Hamid Ali), 3 Vols., Delhi, 1989.

In the Shade of the Quran (English translation from the Arabic with commentary of surahs 78–114 by M. A. Salahi and A. A. Shamis), Part 30, London, 1979.

Rippin, Andrew, *Approaches to the History of the Interpretation of the Qur'an*, Oxford, 1988.

Roberts, Robert, *The Social Laws of the Qoran*, London, 1971.

Rodwell, J. M., *The Koran* (English translation with an introduction by G. Margoliouth), London, 1977.

Sale, George, *The Koran* (English translation with notes and also an introduction by Sir Edward Denison Ross), London, n.d.

Shah, Sirdar Ikbal Ali, *Extracts from the Koran*, London, n.d.

Shakir, M. H., *Holy Quran* (Arabic text with English translation), New York, 1987.

Sher'Ali, *The Holy Quran* (Arabic text with English translation) Rabwah, 1955.

Thanvi, Ashraf Ali, *The Quran Majid* (Arabic text with Urdu translation), Bombay, n.d.

Wahiullah, Mir, *Muslim Jurisprudence and the Quranic Law of Crimes*, New Delhi, 1986.

Watt, W. Montgomery, *Companion to the Qur'an* (explanatory notes on Arabic words used in the Quran and translated into English based on the Arberry translation), London, 1967.

Bell's Introduction to the Quran, Edinburgh, 1970.

Wherry, E. M., *A Comprehensive Commentary on the Quran* (with preliminary discourse and notes and emendations), 4 Vols., London, 1896.

Zayid, Muhammad Y., *The Quran* (English translation), Beirut, 1980.

(B) HADITH

Ali, Muhammad, *A Manual of Hadith* (a compendium of selected Hadith from *Sahi Bukhari* with Arabic text and English translation arranged according to subject), Lahore, n.d.

An-Nawawi, Muhyiuddin Abu Zakariyya, *Riyadh as-Salihin* (translated from the Arabic into English by Muhammad Zafrullah Khan with a foreword by C. E. Bosworth), London, 1989.

Asad, Muhammad, *Sahi Al-Bukhari* (translated from the French into English with explanatory notes), Vol. 5, New Delhi, 1978.

Bukhari, Muhammad bin Ismail, *Sahi Al-Bukhari* (translated from the Arabic into English by Muhammad Muhsin Khan with Arabic text), 9 Vols., Medina, 1973.

Malik, ibn Anas, *Muawatta* (translated from the Arabic into English by Muhammad Rahimuddin), New Delhi, 1981.

Muslim, Abul Husain, *Sahi Muslim* (translated from the Arabic into English by Abdul Hamid Siddiqi), 4 Vols., Lahore, 1973–5.

Shafi'i, Muhammad bin Idris, *Risala* (translated from the Arabic into English with an introduction, notes and appendices by Majid Khadduri), Cambridge, 1987.

Tabrizi, Shaikh Waliuddin Abdullah, *Mishkat al-Masabih* (translated from the Arabic into English by James Robson), 4 Vols., Lahore, 1973.

(C) THE PROPHET MUHAMMAD

Ahmad, Barakat, *Muhammad and the Jews*, New Delhi, 1979.

Ahmad, Fazl, *Aisha the Truthful* (Urdu text), Delhi, 1983.

Ahmad, Gulzar, *The Prophet's Concept of War*, Bombay, 1989.

Andrae, Tor, *Mohammed: The Man and His Faith* (translated from the German into English by Theophil Menzel), London, 1956.

Azzam, Abd-al Rahman, *The Eternal Message of Muhammad* (translated from the Arabic into English by Caesar E. Farah), London, 1979.

Balyuzi, H. M., *Muhammad and the Course of Islam*, Oxford, 1976.

Cragg, Kenneth, *Muhammad and the Christian*, London, 1984.

Dermenghem, Emile, *Muhammad and the Islamic Tradition* (translated from the French into English by Jean M. Watt), New York, 1981.

Dinet, E., and Sliman, Ben Ibrahim, *The Life of Mohammad*, Karachi, n.d.

Friedlander, Shems, *Submission: Sayings of the Prophet Muhammad* (Arabic text by Tevfik Topuzoglu), London, 1978.

Gabrieli, Francesco, *Muhammad and the Conquests of Islam*, Italy, 1977.

Hai, Muhammad Abdul, *Uswai Rasool-e-Akram* (English translation from the Urdu by Muhammad Muqtadir), Delhi, 1988.

Haykal, Muhammad Husayn, *The Life of Muhammad* (translated from the Arabic into English by Ismail Ragi A al Faruqi), USA, 1976.

Hussain, Athar S., *Prophet Muhammad and His Mission*, Lucknow, 1978.

Irving, Washington, *Life of Mahomet*, London, 1915.

Johnstone, P. De Lacy, *Muhammad and His Power*, Delhi, 1984.

Khan, Majid Ali, *Muhammad: The Final Messenger*, Delhi, 1980.

Khan, Wahiduddin, *Muhammad: The Prophet of Revolution*, New Delhi, 1986.

Lane-Poole, S., *The Table Talk of Prophet Muhammad* (selected and translated from the Arabic into English with introduction and notes), Lahore, 1971.

Madani, S. M., *The Family of the Holy Prophet*, Bombay, 1989.

Majeed, Abdul, *The Prophet and His Preachings*, Bombay, 1988.

Malik, Fida Hussain, *Wives of the Prophet*, Bombay, 1989.

Malik, S. K., *The Quranic Concept of War*, New Delhi, 1986.

Muhamed, V. B., *The Prophet of Universal Brotherhood*, Cochin, 1973.

Muir, William, *The Life of Mahomet*, London, 1877.

Nadvi, Abul Hasan Ali, *Muhammad Rasulullah* (translated from the Urdu into English by Mohiuddin Ahmad), Lucknow, 1979.

Nadvi, Sayed Sulaiman, *Seeratun Nabi* (Urdu text), Vols. III–VI, Azamgad, 1969.

   Muhammad: The Ideal Prophet (translated from the Urdu into English by Mohiuddin Ahmad), Lucknow, 1977.

   Sirat-i-Aisha (Urdu text), Azamgad, n.d.

Nu'mani, Shibli, *Seeratun Nabi* (Urdu text), Vols. I–II, Azamgadh, 1918–20.

Omer, Mutaharunnisa, *The Holy Prophet and the Satanic Slander*, Madras, 1989.

Pirenne, Henri, *Mohammed and Charlemagne*, London, 1974.

Qureshi, Sultan Ahmed, *Letters from the Holy Prophet* (English translation), Delhi, 1986.

Rida, Muhammad Rashid, *The Revelation to Muhammad* (translated from the Arabic into English by Abdus-Samad Sharafuddin), Bombay, 1960.

Rodinson, Maxime, *Mohammed* (translated from the French into English by Anne Carter), London, 1971.

Schimmel, Annemarie, *And Muhammad is His Messenger*, London, 1985.

Siddiqi, Muhammad Saeed, *The Blessed Women of Islam*, Bombay, 1983.

Siddiqui, Naeem, *Mohammad: The Benefactor of Humanity* (an English condensation by Rahm Ali Hashmi of the Urdu book *Mohsin-e-Insaniyat*), New Delhi, 1971.

Syed, Ameer Ali, *The Spirit of Islam*, London, 1952.

Tabataba'-i-Sayyid, M. H., *The Qur'an in Islam*, London, 1987.

Watt, W. Montgomery, *Muhammad at Mecca*, Oxford, 1953.

   Muhammad at Medina, Oxford, 1956.

   Muhammad: Prophet and Statesman, Oxford, 1961.

Wollaston, Arthur N., *Half Hours with Muhammad*, London, 1886.

(D) ISLAM

Ali, Hadrat, *Nahjul Balagha* (English translation from the Arabic under the title *Peak of Eloquence* by Askari Jafery), Bombay, 1979.

Ali, Muhammad, *The Religion of Islam*, Lahore, 1936.

Arberry, A. J., *Discourses of Rumi*, New York, 1972.

Revelation and Reason in Islam, 2 Vols., London, 1971.

Religion in the Middle East, 2 Vols., London, 1969.

Arnold, T. W., *The Preaching of Islam*, London, 1913.

Asad, Muhammad, *Islam at the Crossroads*, Lahore, 1955.

Coulson, N. J., *A History of Islamic Law*, Edinburgh, 1971.

Cragg, Kenneth, and Speight, Marston, *Islam from Within: Anthology of a Religion*, Belmont, 1980.

Daniel, Norman, *Islam and the West*, Edinburgh, 1960.

Danner, Victor, *The Islamic Tradition: An Introduction*, New York, 1988.

De Boer, T. J., *The History of Philosophy in Islam* (English translation by Edward R. Jones), New Delhi, 1983.

Djait, Hichem, *Europe and Islam*, Berkeley, 1985.

Doi, I Abdur Rahman, *Shari'ah: The Islamic Law*, London, 1984.

Farah, Caesar E., *Islam: Beliefs and Observances*, New York, 1970.

Galwash, Ahmad A., *The Religion of Islam*, Cairo, 1961.

Ghazzali, Abu Hamid, *Ihya Ulum-id-Din* (translated from the Arabic into English by Fazlul Karim), 4 Vols., New Delhi, 1982.

Gibb, H. A. R., *Islam: A Historical Survey*, London, 1975.

Gibb, H. A. R. et al. (eds.), *The Encyclopedia of Islam*, 4 Vols., Leiden, 1960–78.

Gibb, H. A. R., and Kramers, J. H. (eds.), *Shorter Encyclopedia of Islam*, New York, 1965.

Glasse, Cyril, *The Concise Encyclopedia of Islam*, London, 1989.

Grunebaum, G. E. von, *Islam*, London, 1955.

Goldziher, Ignaz, *Introduction to Islamic Theology and Law* (English translation by Andras and Ruth Hamori with an introduction and additional notes by Bernard Lewis), Princeton, 1981.

Hakim, Khalifa Abdul, *Islamic Ideology*, Lahore, 1974.

Hamidullah, Muhammad, *Introduction to Islam*, Kuwait, 1970.

Hitti, Philip K., *History of the Arabs*, New York, 1973.

Hodgson, Marshall G. S., *The Venture of Islam*, 3 Vols., Chicago, 1974.

Holt, P. M. et al. (eds.), *The Cambridge History of Islam*, 2 Vols., London, 1970.

Hughes, T. D., *Notes on Muhammadanism*, Delhi, 1975.

A Dictionary of Islam, Delhi, 1973.

Hurgronje, C. Snouck, *Islam*, New Delhi, 1989.

Iqbal, Muhammad, *The Reconstruction of Religious Thought in Islam*, Lahore, 1971.

Jeffery, Arthur (ed.), *A Reader on Islam*, The Hague, 1962.

Jones, L. Bevan, *The People of the Mosque*, Calcutta, 1939.

Kabbani, Rana, *Letters to Christendom*, London, 1989.

Khaldun, Ibn, *The Muqaddimah* (translated from the Arabic into English by Franz Rosenthal), 3 Vols., New York, 1958.

Khan, Muhammad Zafrulla, *Islam: Its Meaning for Modern Man*, London, 1962.

Klein, F. A., *The Religion of Islam*, London, 1979.

Kritzeck, James, *Anthology of Islamic Literature*, New York, 1964.

Kuraishi, Fazl-I-Ahmad, *Islam: The Religion of Humanity*; Lahore, 1956.

Laffin, John, *The Dagger of Islam*, New York, 1981.

Lammens, H., *Islam: Beliefs and Institutions* (translated from the French by Sir E. Denison Ross), London, 1968.

Latif, Syed Abdul, *The Mind Al-Quran Builds*, Hyderabad, 1952.
   Basic Concepts of the Quran, Hyderabad, 1958.

Levy, Reuben, *The Social Structure of Islam*, Cambridge, 1971.

Lewis, Bernard, *Islam from the Prophet Muhammad to the Capture of Constantinople*, 2 Vols., New York, 1974.
   Islam in History, London, 1973.
   The Muslim Discovery of Europe, London, 1982.

Lewis, Bernard, and Hott, P. M. (eds.), *Historians of Middle East*, London, 1964.

Lisa, Appignanesi, and Maitland, Sara, *The Rushdie File*, New York, 1990.

Macdonald, Duncan B., *Development of Muslim Theology, Jurisprudence and Constitutional Theory*, New Delhi, 1973.

Margoliouth, D. S., *Lectures on Arabic Historians*, Delhi, 1977.

Maududi, Maulana Abul 'ala, *The Islamic Law and Constitution* (English translation by Khurshid Ahmad), Bombay, 1986.
   Fundamentals of Islam (anonymous English translation), Delhi, 1985.
   Towards Understanding Islam (translation by Khurshid Ahmad), Delhi, 1972.

Morgan, Kenneth W. (ed.), *Islam: The Straight Path*, Delhi, 1987.

Nendress, Gerhard, *An Introduction to Islam* (translated from the German into English by Carole Hillenbrand), New York, 1988.

Nicholson, R. A., *A Literary History of the Arabs*, Cambridge, 1969.

Peters, F. E., *Judaism, Christianity and Islam*, 3 Vols., Princeton, 1990.

Qutb, Muhammad, *Islam: The Misunderstood Religion*, Kuwait, 1964.

Rahman, Fazlur, *Islam*, London, 1966.
   Prophecy in Islam, London, 1958.
   Islam and Modernity, Chicago, 1984.

Raschid, M. S., *Iqbal's Concept of God*, London, 1981.

Roy, M. N., *The Historical Role of Islam*, New Delhi, 1981.

Rumi, Jalaluddin, *Masnavi-i-Manavi* (English translation by E. H. Whinfield), London, 1898.

Rushdie, Salman, *The Satanic Verses*, London, 1988.

Ruthven, Malise, *A Satanic Affair: Salman Rushdie and the Rage of Islam*, London, 1990.

Saiyidain, K. G., *Islam: The Religion of Peace*, New Delhi, 1976.

Schacht, Joseph, *An Introduction to Islamic Law*, London, 1964.

Schuon, Frithjof, *Understanding Islam* (English translation by D. M. Matheson), London, 1976.

  Dimensions of Islam (English translation by P. N. Townsend), London, 1969.

Shafi, Mohammad et al. (eds.), *Daura-i-Maarifi-Islamia* (Urdu text), 30 Vols., Lahore, 1980.

Singh, Khushwant, *Complaint and Answer* (English translation of Iqbal's Urdu poem *Shikwa aur Jawab-i-Shikwa*), Delhi, 1981.

Smith, Wilfred Cantwell, *Islam in Modern History*, New York, 1959.

  Modern Islam in India, Lahore, 1947.

Syed, Qasim Mahmud, *Islam: Encyclopaedia* (Urdu text), Karachi, 1984.

Tabataba'i, Allamah, *Shi'ite Islam* (translated from the Persian into English by Seyyed Hossein Nasr), London, 1975.

Tritton, A. S., *Islam*, London, 1968.

Watt, W. Montgomery, *What is Islam?*, London, 1979.

  The Faith and Practice of al-Ghazali, London, 1953.

  Islamic Revelation in the Modern World. Edinburgh, 1969.

Wensinck, A. J., *The Muslim Creed*, New Delhi, 1979.

Williams, John Alden, *Islam*, New York, 1967.

Ye'or, Bat, *The Dhimmi: Jews and Christians Under Islam* (translated from the French into English by David Maisel, Paul Fenton and David Littman), London, 1985.

Zakaria, Rafiq, *The Struggle Within Islam*, London, 1989.

Zwemer, Samuel M., *Islam: A Challenge to Faith*, London, 1909.

(E) GENERAL

Carlyle, Thomas, *On Heroes, Hero-worship and the Heroic in History*, London, 1935.

Gibbon, Edward, *The Decline and Fall of the Roman Empire*, 3 Vols., New York, n.d.

Green, Ronald M., *Religious Reason*, New York, 1978.

Reade, Winwood, *The Martyrdom of Man*, London, 1932.

Shaw, George Bernard, *The Prefaces*, London, 1938.

Toynbee, Arnold, *An Historian's Approach to Religion*, Oxford, 1956.

Wells, H. G., *An Outline of History*, London, 1956.

INDEX

MORE ABOUT PENGUINS

For further information about books available from Penguins in India write to Penguin Books (India) Ltd, B4/246, Safdarjung Enclave, New Delhi 110 029.

In the UK: For a complete list of books available from Penguins in the United Kingdom write to Dept. EP, Penguin Books Ltd, Harmondsworth, Middlesex UB7 0DA.

In the U.S.A.: For a complete list of books available from Penguins in the United States write to Dept. DG, Penguin Books, 299 Murray Hill Parkway, East Rutherford, New Jersey 07073.

In Canada: For a complete list of books available from Penguins in Canada write to Penguin Books Canada Ltd, 2801 John Street, Markham, Ontario L3R 1B4.

In Australia: For a complete list of books available from Penguins in Australia write to the Marketing Department, Penguin Books Australia Ltd, P.O. Box 257, Ringwood, Victoria 3134.

In New Zealand: For a complete list of books available from Penguins in New Zealand write to the Marketing Department, Penguin Books (N.Z.) Ltd, Private Bag, Takapuna, Auckland 9.

THE STRUGGLE WITHIN
ISLAM
Rafiq Zakaria

For centuries now, religious institutions and the State have been opposed, and this has been especially true of the world of Islam. In this exceptionally detailed study, Rafiq Zakaria, an eminent Islamic scholar, examines the historical roots and other aspects of the conflict and suggests possible ways in which it might be resolved.

"Dr Zakaria has displayed considerable erudition and analytical ability in describing the fundamentalist-secularist tension in all its manifestations, from the early history of Islam to today's situation."

—*Deccan Chronicle*

UNDERSTANDING THE
MUSLIM MIND
Rajmohan Gandhi

Through the lives and philosophies of eight
prominent Muslim personalities—Sayyid
Ahmed Khan, Fazlul Haq, Muhammad Ali
Jinnah, Muhammad Iqbal, Muhammad Ali,
Abul Kalam Azad, Liaqat Ali Khan and
Zakir Hussain—the author sketches a fasci-
nating and insightful picture of the Islamic
community in the subcontinent today.

'Rajmohan Gandhi's excellent book should
waken us to the many why's of Hindu-
Muslim relationships that remain un-
answered to this day'. —M.V. Kamath in
the *Telegraph*

'At long last we have a dispassionate analysis of the making of Indian Muslims psyche'.
—*The Hindustan Times*

INDIA'S STRUGGLE FOR INDEPENDENCE

Bipan Chandra
Mridula Mukherjee • Aditya Mukherjee
K.N. Panikkar • Sucheta Mahajan

India's struggle for independence has been studied before by historians, but this is the first major study from the nationalist point of view. Basing their arguments on several hundred interviews with freedom fighters and others who participated in the freedom struggle, and years of research, Bipan Chandra and his associates take the reader through every step of the independence struggle—from the abortive Revolt of 1857 to the time India became independent in 1947—explaining and analysing events that have either been distorted or misinterpreted in most of the other histories of the period.

"Indispensable for students and for all those who want to know our past in order to understand our present."
—*Indian Express*

BHOPAL:

The Lessons of a Tragedy
Sanjoy Hazarika

The chilling story of the world's worst industrial accident that occurred at the Union Carbide factory in Bhopal, the capital of the central Indian state of Madhya Pradesh. Years after thousands of people died when a deadly gas leaked from a storage tank at the Carbide pesticides factory, no one knows what really happened. Who was really responsible for the disaster? Was it an accident or was it sabotage? Will the billions of dollars being fought over in the courts ever get to the victims of the tragedy? The book seeks to answer these and the larger questions Bhopal raised—the degradation of the environment by big industry, the irresponsible business methods of large multinational corporations, the problems of development in the Third World—by thoroughly examining every aspect of the tragedy, its aftermath and similar tragedies that have happened before.

GHALIB: THE MAN, THE TIMES
by Pavan K. Varma

Mirza Mohammed Asadullah Khan Ghalib, arguably nineteenth century India's greatest poet, lived in Delhi and was the chronicler of one of the most turbulent periods in modern Indian history. A precocious genius, Ghalib, who began writing poetry at the age of nine, was ideally placed to record the downfall of the last Mughal Emperor, Bahadur Shah Zafar, the Revolt of 1857 and the rise of British power after 1857. In the book, Pavan K. Varma captures the essential greatness of the man and his literary achievements and the spirit of the times he lived in.

"Pavan K. Varma's book deserves to be widely read." —*The Telegraph*